Liberated from Religion
The Inestimable Pleasure of Being a Freethinker

Paulo Bitencourt

FREE THOUGHT

Universe, Pisces-Cetus Supercluster Complex,
Laniakea Supercluster, Virgo Supercluster, Local Group,
Milky Way, Orion Arm, Radcliffe Wave, Local Bubble,
Local Interstellar Cloud, Solar System, Earth

Challenge

If you are one of those Christians who read the Bible, I imagine that you are an Evangelical, and if you are an Evangelical I consider it a miracle that you are reading this book. No offense, but Evangelicals do not read anything that has not been published by a Christian publishing house, let alone books that stimulate critical thinking. I know what I am talking about, because I too was an Evangelical and my entire family is. That said, it is likely that this book came into your hands by recommendation, and even more likely that already the first paragraphs of the first chapter will make you stop reading.

The reason why devout believers, especially Evangelicals, do not read anything that induces free thinking is very simple: fear of losing faith. Well, if you are afraid of losing your faith, it is not firm, and if it is not firm, you are, besides being deceived, deceiving yourself. On the other hand, if your faith is firm, how can you be sure of that, if you do not put it to the test?

I challenge you, therefore, to read this book to the end, thus proving to yourself that you do not belong to the gigantic group of believers who are afraid of losing faith. If *Liberated from Religion* does not make you doubt even a single one of the things you believe, you will be able to say that your faith really is unshakable.

Paulo Biten who?

I was born in the state of Paraná, Brazil, in 1966, but spent my childhood in the city of Rio de Janeiro. My mother took me and my three brothers to the Evangelical church to which her father had taken her and her eight siblings. When I became an adult, my father, who was a lapsed Catholic, converted to that church.

I dreamed of being a comic book artist, but a voice in my head, of an invisible being who lives in an invisible place, commanded me to attend a Theology college and work for him. Instead of turning me into a man of God, studying Theology made me have doubts. At the end of the fifth semester, I abandoned studies and moved to Europe. I only did not get swallowed by a whale because I went by plane. After a short stay in several countries, in 1990 I settled in Austria, where I graduated in Opera Singing from the Conservatory of the City of Vienna. I have Austrian citizenship.

I am the author also of the books *Wasting Time on God: Why I Am an Atheist* and *Com Zeus Não Se Brinca: Loucuras da Crença em Deus (Zeus Is Not to Be Played With: Madnesses of the Belief in God)*.

To my son Evgeny

May you live in a world ever more free of superstitions and irrationalities.

Table of Contents

Preface

Imagine, dear reader, someone telling you a fantastic story, saying that, if you believe it, you will be criticized for believing what the world considers madness, but that this should make you happy, because you will be victim of persecution, which proves that that story is true and that you are part of a select group of privileged people. As soon as you believe that story and feel chosen, you are warned that, just like those who consider it madness, you will suffer severe consequences, in case you doubt it.

Quite a cunning way to make you block out all critical thinking and reject whatever might induce you to subject that story to rational scrutiny, is it not?

That, dear reader, is called religion. In countries where for centuries that story has been passed down from generation to generation as sacred, it is so deeply rooted that it is part of their tradition and culture. Thus, it is not surprising that, from the cradle up, millions of people are taught to see it as incontestable universal truth, which causes conditioning of the mind and results in a religious automatism that prevents the majority of them from stopping to ask themselves whether that story makes sense and believing it is sensible and necessary.

Paradoxically, at the same time they take criticism of their beliefs as offense, these believers find it natural to criticize other people's beliefs. All religious people reject tens of thousands of religions as absurd, over which they do not lose a single minute of sleep. The difference between believers and me is, then, tiny: I reject only one religion more than they do.

If Christianity is the belief I most dissect, this is due to the simple fact that I was a Christian and that it is not only the largest religion in the world but also the most followed by Occidentals. It does not make much sense to write books about the irrationalities, for example, of Islam where this religion is practiced by a tiny minority. Actually, it is not even necessary, because all religions boil down to this: believing in the existence of things of which one has no evidence. By the way, since they are related religions, an analysis of Christianity is almost an analysis of Islam.

Where there is no reflection, there is manipulation. It is evident that religions make use of fear as an instrument of domination, first to deceive, then to prevent reflection and consequent deconversion of their adherents. In fact, any ideology that threatens with punishment those who reject it is perverse and deserves to be rejected. Those who are afraid of Hell are on the same intellectual level as those who are afraid of the Bogeyman.

One of the principal objectives of this book is to show that there are no reasons whatsoever to follow religions and that there are plenty of reasons to be a freethinker.

Paulo Bitencourt

PS: The quotations at the beginning of the chapters are taken from Brazilian songs.

"There is no greater pleasure than to be a freethinker."

— Paulo Bitencourt

1

Fear

"My mother told me, some time ago:
'Wherever you go, God follows you.
God always sees everything you do'.
I was so afraid to get out of bed at night to go to the bathroom,
afraid to know I wasn't there alone,
because I always, always, always was with God."

— Raul Seixas
(*Paranoia*)

GEORGE CARLIN, A famous American comedian, performed, in 1972, a monologue entitled *Seven Words You Can Never Say on Television*. Since I sense that the dear reader is dying to know these words, here they are: [censored], [censored], [censored], [censored], [censored], [censored] and [censored]. The joke consisted in Carlin dissecting these seven swear words in such a way that in the end they lost all obscenity, becoming ordinary words.

In the medium-sized city where I was born, there were two movie theaters: the Maharaja and the Plaza. While the Maharaja specialized in kung fu and Spaghetti Western, the more sophisti-cated Plaza projected, many months late, the latest Hollywood hits, but without leaving aside the popular sex comedies of the 1970s. Boys in full hormonal explosion, like me, were delighted with the "obscenity" of the posters of these films, which at that time were considered pornographic, but less than a decade later came to be shown on TV and today do not scandalize even cente-nary grannies.

Although not uniformly, around the globe the expansion of knowledge, advancement of Science, general increase in the level of education and popularization of the internet tend to make peo-ple ever less ingenuous. Much of what in the previous generation was reproachable is today acceptable or tolerable. As ingenuous-ness decreases, taboos lose their force or disappear.

Since 1826, the year in which teacher Cayetano Ripoll was hanged by Catholic tribunal Junta de Fé, in Valencia, Spain, no one in the Occident has to be afraid anymore of being sentenced to death for blasphemy or heresy. Even so, for many people deities and religions remain sacrosanct and frightening taboos. If we take Christianity and Islam, we have a total of 4.2 billion people, more than half the world's population, who dare not doubt, let alone question the dogmas of the two largest religions, despite knowing they are not based on evidence. While in much of the Islamic world criticism of religion and disbelief are subject to the death penalty, in the Christian world people can still be imprisoned for publicly opposing religious convictions. If the dear reader is an atheist and planning to spend some time in Russia, when you are there do not say in a virtual chat "God doesn't exist", unless you are in the mood to watch the Sun rise square (Brazilian expression that means to go to prison).

Not a few believers demand for Christianity to be uncriticizable. Despite all enlightenment and liberty, in Brazil it is common for administrators of YouTube channels and Facebook pages to be threatened with death or sued for criticizing or parodying the Christian faith. Around the world, anyone who states not to believe in invisible beings will be seen as normal. In the Occident, anyone who states not to believe in the invisible beings of the indigenous, African and Asian religions will also be seen as normal. In contrast, in the Americas anyone who states not to believe in the invisible beings of the Judeo-Christian religion will be seen with suspicion and may suffer hostilities.

One of the principal attributes of the Christian god is to be holy. What is holy is sacred; what is sacred, inviolable; what is inviolable, unquestionable; what is unquestionable, indisputable. Thus, it is not surprising that in a country where, according to the 2010 Census of the Brazilian Institute of Geography and Statistics, only 8% of people have no religion, 86.8% practice Christianity and Christian fundamentalism is growing at a vertiginous rate, critically reflecting on God and religion is neither common nor acceptable.

The essence of many religions is the same: however simple and unknown they may be, they preach the existence of at least one god who rewards those who please him and punishes those who displease him. One characteristic common to all religions is that gods are not in the least interested in ending the doubts and heated discussions about their existence. If the Christian god exists, it would be so easy for him to put an end to the affliction of those who yearn to discover the meaning of life, to the anguish of those who think they need to be sure that death is not the end and to the enmity between different religions and their sects, which throughout History has killed millions of people and still generates arrogance, intolerance, discord and division: it would suffice that he appeared to Humanity. As an omniscient and all-powerful god, he knows how he could do it in an unequivocal way, dispelling any and all doubts. Why, then, does he not do it?

The biblical god supposedly inspired some men from the Iron Age to write a handbook with accounts also from the Bronze Age, made some of them have enigmatic dreams, revealing to them future events by means of obscure symbolisms, and called people to found churches. Since then, he keeps watching his creatures struggle with the interpretation of his literary inspirations, curious to see who of them decipher them correctly and how many accept them without question. It is said that all that is good must be achieved through hard effort. That being so, it is as if God took pleasure in putting to the test man's capacity to believe, execute and hope. Only those who pass this test qualify to receive the prize: to live in a mansion of gold for infinite centillions of years.

Christianity's greatest figure, apostle Paul compares faith in God to a fight, but principally to a race. For me, and I think for many people, a not very motivating comparison. In school, we had a terrible Physical Education teacher. Instead of teaching us different sport modalities, he would make the class run under the burning sun, reason why we nicknamed him track teacher. In the bimonthly tests, he would give us one point for each lap around the soccer field. Since we hated running, the majority of us would do only five laps, just enough to pass. If Paradise is attainable only by means of running and fighting, those who like neither running nor fighting are lost.

Religious people see life as a test administered by God. However, the conception that he tests us is an incoherence. First, because it is not just any test, like the school ones, which the student, if he fails, has the chance to retake. The divine test lasts a lifetime and its objective is not to qualify a person for professional life, but to determine where he will spend eternity: whether playing the harp and singing praises in high and glowing clouds or being fried and howling in pain in the dark depths of the Tartarus. And second, because human beings are not equal in a number of aspects, such as intellect, health status, socio-economic status, education, inclinations and opportunities. Therefore, given the terrible consequences of a failure, if life were a divine test it would not be fair. At the same time race and trial, the life of some has more obstacles and is harder than that of others.

Nor is equal in all people the predisposition to believe in the existence of gods and follow religions. Some find it very easy to believe, as well as to submit to ecclesiastical authorities. In contrast, the more free-spirited, who believers like to classify as rebels, are less or not at all inclined to religiosity. Similarly, the propensity to do good and do evil is not the same in everyone. On the other hand, if we were the same the result of everyone's test would be the same, making it meaningless, which it, in fact, is, because God, being omniscient, knows the future and the result of the test before applying it. That's right. In this exact moment, God already knows who will pass the test who will not, who will go to Heaven who will go to Hell. What Christian would dare to claim that God did not know the result of the macabre and sadistic test he gave Abraham, when he commanded him to sacrifice his son Isaac?

Flashing like the neon sign of a Las Vegas casino, two words leap to the eye of those who, free from religious bias, reflect on the conception of God taught by many religions: infantility and sadism. God creates human beings different from each other, yet he ignores their differences and expects from all of them unconditional submission, punishing those who do not agree with what is taught about him. In what way does such a god differ from dictators and tyrants?

By all appearances, God seems to be a bit tired of his millenary public image of a grumpy old man with a white beard. Because of this, to improve it, he hired the professional help of public-relations specialists: neo-Pentecostal pastors. The strategy consists in making the faithful forget that Yahweh, the bad-tempered and implacable god, who killed and commanded the killing even of children, and Jesus, the god who liked children, are the same deity. Grumpy Yahweh is the god only of the Jews. The god of the Christians is another one, completely different: Jesus, the comradely deity, bringer of cure and fortune.

And speaking of implacable, there are those who claim that they became atheists after reading the Bible carefully. At a press conference on the occasion of the release of Ridley Scott's film *Exodus: Gods and Kings*, actor Christian Bale referred to his character Moses thus: "I think the man was likely schizophrenic and was one of the most barbaric individuals that I ever read about in my life". God spoke to Moses directly and almost everything the most important figure in the Bible said, especially the orders to destroy entire cities, exterminating all their inhabitants, which included children, began with a frightening "Thus says the Lord".

If we give someone who has never heard of the Bible Deuteronomy chapter 28 to read, he will certainly think it is the script of a horror movie. Under divine inspiration, Moses lists the curses with which Yahweh promises to punish his people, in case they dare "not to carefully follow all his commands":

The Lord will plague you with diseases until he has destroyed you from the land [...]. The Lord will strike you with wasting disease, with fever and inflammation, with scorching heat and drought, with blight and mildew, which will plague you until you perish [...]. The Lord will afflict you with the boils of Egypt and with tumors, festering sores and the itch, from which you cannot be cured. The Lord will afflict you with madness, blindness and confusion of mind [...]. The Lord will afflict your knees and legs with painful boils that cannot be cured, spreading from the soles of your feet to the top of your head [...]. All these curses will come on you. They will pursue you and overtake you until you are destroyed [...]. You will eat the fruit of the womb, the flesh of the sons and daughters [...]. It will please him to ruin and destroy you.

Apropos of that, why does the Bible make such a point of stressing God's goodness? If it did not contain passages like "Give thanks to the Lord, for he is good" (Psalms 107:1), would we at the end of reading it conclude that the biblical deity is kind? At least 60 verses of the Word of God are dedicated to convincing the reader that the god who punishes those who do not worship him is good, a clear sign that this does not become evident.

How could the extra-biblical prohibitions imposed by many Evangelical denominations, which can range from smoking, drinking alcoholic beverages and coffee, eating pork and seafood, watching television, going to the movies and the theater, reading novels and scientific books, listening to nonreligious music, dancing, playing sports and wearing long pants, short hair, jewelry and makeup to painting one's nails, not be reflexes of the severity of the god of the Bible?

If there is anything that really bothers the biblical deity, it is the sexual pleasure of his creatures. While masturbation, which filmmaker Woody Allen calls sex with someone he loves, and extramarital sex are sin, homosexuality is much more than that: aberration. Officially, Catholicism sees sex as an act reserved uniquely for procreation. On the other side of the coin, is it a coincidence that the largest Protestant country, the United States, is also the one that has the most bizarre sexual laws? Believe it or not, in several American states all sexual positions are forbidden, with the exception of that one in which the man lies on top of the woman, known precisely as the missionary position. In the state of Alabama, no one needs a permit to buy a gun or is required to register it. Like in western movies, one can carry it almost anywhere. However, selling and gifting erotic toys, such as vibrators, incur a US$ 10,000 fine and one year detention. Recidivism can result in up to ten years of "watching the Sun rise square". Is it because vibrators are lethal, while firearms are harmless?

The fury of the *Old Testament* god is embarrassing for many Christians, yet they have no way to extricate themselves from it, because, in addition to Jesus having neither disapproved nor revoked a single letter of what is written in the *Hebrew Bible*, Yahweh and his son are the very same deity. As a result, however much his followers squirm to see him as such, there is no way that Jesus can be different from Yahweh, that is, be his good version. Those who think that the *New Testament* god is all about peace and love need to read, for example, John 3:36: "Whoever believes in the Son has eternal life, but whoever rejects the Son will not see life, for God's wrath remains on them".

The dear reader has certainly heard of a lake of fire and brimstone in which people are tortured for infinite centillions of years, have you not? Incredible as it may seem, that place of unspeakable terror is a doctrine far more of the *New* than of the *Old Testament*. Destruction, perdition and Hell were among the favorite themes of Jesus, who referred to them more than 40 times, as on this occasion: "You have heard that it was said to the people long ago, 'You shall not murder, and anyone who murders will be subject to judgment.' But I tell you that anyone who [...] says to a brother or sister [...], 'You fool!' will be in danger of the fire of hell" (Matthew 5:21-22). Like a neo-Pentecostal pastor, Jesus could not go too long without citing Devil, demons and divine punishment. It even was he who pronounced the sentence that most gives Christians the creeps: "Anyone who speaks against the Holy Spirit will not be forgiven" (Matthew 12:32).

Could there be anything more distressing for a believer than being repentant and not forgiven by God? If speaking against the Holy Spirit is the only unforgivable sin, that is not trivial information, but crucial. Even so, the Nazarene did not take the trouble to convey it clearly, reason why among Christians there is no consensus on what "speaking against the Holy Spirit" means. This makes many believers panic. In online articles on the subject, terrified believers leave desperate comments, begging for someone to assure them that they have not committed the gravest of all sins.

All churches preach that the human being is lost, but that to be saved it suffices to believe in Jesus. Curiously, I have never heard of a president of a Christian denomination who opened a conference with the following words: "Sisters and brothers, Jesus said: 'He who believes in me has eternal life'. Reflecting deeply on this, it became to me as clear as the Sun that the church is a superfluous institution, because, as the Bible says, believing in Christ is sufficient. So, I hereby submit my letter of resignation and propose the dissolution of our organizations. Oh, and to those who are sad because they don't know what to do with the tithe money, I recommend that, from now on, they donate it to charities".

Why will we never hear a speech like that? Because, besides churches being fantastic businesses, what could be more fascinating than being the representative of the authority of none other than the Creator of the Universe himself? In Hebrews 13:17, God orders: "Have confidence in your leaders and submit to their authority". Well, if the church represents God on Earth and the Holy Spirit makes use of "men of God" to instruct people, the voice of the church is the voice of God himself. Consequently, to diverge from church directives is to oppose divine authority and to close one's ears to the voice of the Holy Spirit, a sin for which, as Jesus said, there is no forgiveness.

What instrument of manipulation could be better than this? It does not take a very smart person to realize that there is a relation between God, religion, church, authority, fear and submission. Add business to this relation and it becomes even easier to understand why leading a church is so tempting.

They say that if you wring a crime tabloid, blood comes out. With the Bible, it would be no different. It is simply replete with violence, almost always extreme. There would be no problem with that, if the Bible were by all considered what it really is: a historical-mythological work. Yet, for 2.4 billion people it is the book by means of which the Creator of the Universe teaches his creatures to be compassionate, forgiving and moral. The truth is that the Bible would only come close to being a moral book if we cut out all the accounts in which the biblical god himself does not set a good example, such as the stoning of a man for gathering firewood on the Sabbath and the tearing to pieces of 42 boys for mocking the bald head of a prophet.

When some Israelites turned to other gods, which happened frequently, the deity inventor of free will charged someone with putting them "to the sword". If the number of infidels was significant, Yahweh sent droughts that lasted for years and made all the people go hungry, which includes pregnant women, children, the elderly and the sick. Despite the efforts of some writers of the Book of Books to convince its readers that its god is good and a moral example, many of its accounts clearly show that Yahweh felt no restraint in killing innocents or making them suffer.

By the way, sometimes God poured out his wrath entirely on the innocent. After impregnating the wife of one of his soldiers, David gave instructions for the cuckold to be positioned in the battlefront's most dangerous segment, where kicking the bucket was practically inevitable. Instead of punishing the king for both adultery and murder, God struck the baby who was born of that illicit union, making him suffer from a lethal disease and killing him after seven days of agony. On another occasion, David ordered a census to be taken, which displeased the biblical god, who once again did not punish the culprit. Instead, Yahweh sent a plague that killed 70,000 men who had nothing to do with it.

What function do the many biblical accounts of the more than excessive divine punishments have if not of inculcating fear? Afraid of losing his salvation, a member of the Orthodox Church in America wrote to the parish priest, saying he was confused about what "mortal sins" were and asking for a list of them. It would help him not to commit them. In his reply, published on the church's website, the clergyman clarifies that God makes no distinction between sins. All are mortal. According to the priest, *hamartía*, the Greek word for sin, means "missing the mark", which consists in living as Christ lived, that is, without sin. Every time we miss the mark, we sin, no matter if we miss it by an inch or a meter. Citing an example, he says that not going to Mass is as mortal a sin as murdering someone.

In view of so many examples, both in the *Old* and in the *New Testament*, of how God makes a point of being feared, it is impossible for his relationship with his followers not to be permeated by fear, especially when one of Christianity's principal dogmas is eternal torment. As the famous hymn *Onward, Christian Soldiers!*, by Anglican Reverend Sabine Baring-Gould, says, Christians are at war with the forces of evil, reason why they have to incessantly watch and pray lest they fall into temptation, because "the flesh is weak" and "wide is the gate and broad is the road that leads to destruction". The fear of losing salvation is, therefore, a defining characteristic of the Christian religion. However, could it be psychologically healthy to live with a constant fear of displeasing the Big Father, who day and night watches his children, writing down in a gigantic book not only all their actions but even all their thoughts?

Notwithstanding Yahweh's implacable wrath and Jesus' emphasis on Final Judgment and Hell, Christians do not consider Christianity a religion of fear. Because it is their religion, Christians obviously see Christianity through the lens of idealization, just as Catholics idealize Catholicism and Protestants Protestantism.

There is a lot of talk about the ugly side of the Catholic Church, but never about the ugly side of the Protestant Reformation. I too was part of the overwhelming majority of Evangelicals who ignore that Protestantism was as intolerant and cruel as the church from which it had separated with the purpose of being a better Christianity, that is, the true Christianity. In fact, the dark past of Protestantism is not mentioned even in Evangelical faculties of Theology. In the most important book published by the denomination to which I belonged, reformer Martin Luther is portrayed as an exemplary Christian, a true hero of the faith with a guaranteed place in Heaven. There is just one little problem with the quasi-saint image that Evangelicals like to diffuse of the greatest of their icons: the Father of the Reformation was anything but an exemplary Christian.

As everyone knows, the man-god followed by Protestants was Jewish. However, like the Catholic Church, the Protestant Church does not have and has never had any problem with anti-Semitism. Quite the contrary. Thomas Mann, a German novelist, winner of the Nobel Prize in Literature, defined the monk Martin Luther thus: "He is eager to rant, quarrelsome, a powerful hater, with all his heart ready to shed blood". Luther hated Jews with such ferocity that, in 1543, he even published a book entitled *Von den Juden und Ihren Lügen (On the Jews and Their Lies)*, in which he incites to the burning of their synagogues and houses. It was the will of the Father of the Reformation that Jews be treated like gypsies (another people towards whom he felt disgust), dwell in stables, have their books confiscated and, under threat of death, rabbis be forbidden to teach. Luther's anti-Semitism was so inflamed that in the book *Mein Kampf (My Struggle)* Adolf Hitler exalts the monk as one of his greatest idols.

In view of the Lutheran hatred for Jews, it is not surprising that the Protestant Church not only did not oppose Nazism but even welcomed it with open arms. Following Hitler's seizure of power, respected Protestant theologian Emanuel Hirsch, a specialist in Kierkegaard and author of several books, wrote: "Not a single nation possesses such a statesman as ours, who takes Christianity so seriously. When, on May 1st, Adolf Hitler closed his great speech with a prayer, everyone felt his wonderful sincerity".

In 1933, Friedrich Otto Dibelius, general superintendent of the Prussian Union of Churches and, therefore, one of the most important personalities of Protestantism, preached in the Sankt Nikolai church, in Potsdam, to Protestant members of Parliament, extolling the Nazi policy of persecution of Jews and other groups: "We learned from Doctor Martin Luther that the Church must not prevent the legal authorities from doing what they have been called upon to do, even if it is harsh and merciless". Days later, Dibelius wrote a letter saying: "I have always seen myself as an anti-Semite. There is no denying that in all occurrences of corrosion of modern civilization Judaism plays a principal role".

In the relations between the Protestant Church and Nazism, one of the most disturbing and embarrassing cases is that of Walter Hoff, pastor of the Lutheran Church and member of the Deutsche Christen (German Christians) movement, a racist arm of Protestantism, founded by Pastor Joachim Hossenfelder. The German Christians' flag emblazoned a fusion of the cross of Christ and the Nazi swastika. In 1940, Hoff enlisted in the Wehrmacht, Hitler's armed forces, going to fight on the Eastern Front, where he was decorated with the War Merit Cross. From there, the pastor wrote a letter in which he boasted of his devotion to Nazism: "In Soviet Russia, I helped liquidate a considerable number, that is, many hundreds of Jews". Even so, when the war was over the Lutheran Church appointed Hoff to the post of spiritual advisor in a hospital near Hamburg.

In case the dear reader is Evangelical, what do you expect from a man of God like the American pastor Billy Graham, considered the greatest evangelist in the world, who spent decades preaching on TV and in soccer stadiums to millions of people? Surely that he be an exemplary Christian, a person who exudes from every pore the virtues attributed to Jesus, such as humility, compassion and love, right? Graham, who had a fortune that would make any Evangelical envious, estimated in 25 million dollars, was a friend and advisor of several American presidents, among them Richard Nixon, the one who, in the Vietnam War, expanded the combat to the neighboring countries, covering Cambodia with a carpet of bombs. In 1989, a memo that Pastor Graham had written to Nixon came to light. In it, the same man of God who moved the masses by preaching the love of Jesus encourages Nixon to bomb the North Vietnamese dams. Graham suggests that such attacks "could overnight destroy the economy of North Vietnam". According to estimates, this onslaught would have resulted in the deaths of one million people. In 2002, it was the turn of the transcript of recorded conversations between Graham and Nixon to become public. In one of them, the pastor congratulates Nixon "on everything" and says: "I believe the Lord is with you". The president complains about the Jewish influence on Hollywood and the media, which are "totally dominated by the Jews". Graham adds: "They're the ones putting out the pornographic stuff. [...] This stranglehold has got to be broken or this country's going down the drain". "You believe that?", asks the president. "Yes, sir", replies the pastor. Nixon: "So do I. I can't ever say that, but I believe it". Graham: "But if you get elected a second time, then we might be able to do something".

Despite Luther's insistence, and although agreeing with some of his theological views, Erasmus of Rotterdam, the most respected intellectual of the time, never wanted to join the Father of the Reformation. The humanist too was critical of the decadence in the Catholic Church, but the aggressiveness of the Lutheran radicalism repelled him. Averse to extremes, Erasmus opposed the division of the Church, longing for a reform within it. His distancing himself from Luther so infuriated the reformer that he vociferated: "He who crushes Erasmus cracks a bug which stinks even worse when dead than when alive". Commenting on Luther's extremism, Stefan Zweig, an Austrian author who lived in Brazil, wrote: "This combative man tolerates no other end to a conflict than the absolute and unconditional annihilation of his adversary".

In search of peace, Erasmus of Rotterdam moved to Basel, in Switzerland, not imagining that soon that city too would be taken over by what Zweig classified as "Reformation fever". Before long, the masses invaded the churches, tore images and sculptures from the altars and burned them in three large bonfires in front of the cathedral. Disappointed with these excesses, Erasmus went to live in Catholic Freiburg im Breisgau, a German city not yet reached by the religious turmoil triggered by the Protestant Reformation.

In 1524, influenced by reformist ideals, peasants united to demand an end to their exploitation and oppression by the aristocracy. In a pamphlet entitled *Wider die Räuberischen und Mörderischen Rotten der Bauern (Against the Murderous, Thieving Hordes of Peasants)*, Martin Luther got straight to the point: "Everyone who can, smite, slay and stab them, secretly or openly [...]. It is just as when one must kill a mad dog". An aristocrat wrote to Philipp Melanchthon, Luther's right-hand man and intellectual leader of the Reformation, revered as "The Teacher of Germany", asking for his advice on the peasant rebellion and received the following reply: "Against such a rude, wicked, and bloodthirsty people, God calls for the sword". With the endorsement and moral support of the reformers, the aristocracy suppressed the rural revolt with such rigor that some 100,000 peasants were massacred in what became known as the Peasants' War. None of their demands were implemented.

Through the direct influence of John Calvin, the second greatest great of the Reformation and a kind of high priest of Geneva, in Switzerland, 34 people accused of black magic were burned at the stake. Calvin was responsible also for the capital punishment imposed on Michael Servetus, a Spanish scientist and theologian, who was burned alive for denying the dogma of the Trinity and opposing infant baptism. In a letter to reformer Guillaume Farel,

Calvin wrote: "I hope that upon him [Servetus] will be imposed at least the death penalty". Bizarrely, just months before recommending Servetus' execution, Calvin had interceded for five theology students arrested for heresy in Lyon, in Catholic France. Needless to say, unlike Servetus, these young men followed to the letter the doctrines of their defender. It is important to note that in sentencing the Spaniard to the stake, Calvin had the official endorsement of all the Protestant cantons in Switzerland. A year after Servetus' execution, he still received praises from other reformers, such as Melanchthon, who wrote to him: "Dear brother, the Church thanks you today and will thank you in the future. Your magistrates did well to condemn that blasphemer to death".

Calvin had as much authority over Protestants as the Pope over Catholics. Very few dared to diverge from him, since those who did did not go unpunished. This was the case with Sebastian Castellio, a French theologian whom Calvin had established as pastor of a church and dean of the Latin School of Geneva. Because he did not like the translations that Castellio did of biblical passages for a school textbook, Calvin did not authorize its publication, which created tension between the two. During an epidemic of bubonic plague, Castellio criticized the indifference of the pastors who, instead of helping the sick, hurriedly abandoned the city. Accused of compromising the unity of the clerical body with his criticism, Calvin fired him. Castellio was forced to leave Geneva, moving with his family to Basel, where, however, no church wanted to employ him.

In several of his publications, Castellio condemned Calvin's inflexible and ruthless stance, especially in Michael Servetus' case: "Killing a man does not mean defending a doctrine. It means killing a man" and "If Servetus' weapons were reason and writing, he should have been fought with reason and writing". For him, the Reformed Church was in no way different from the Catholic Inquisition. Banned, his last book, entitled *On the Art of Doubting*, was published only in 1981. Even with the death of the Protestant pope, hostilities against Castellio did not cease. Calvin's successor, reformer Theodore Beza, accused Castellio of various heresies. Luckily, natural death saved him from imminent doom.

Today, Sebastian Castellio is considered a great forerunner of religious tolerance and freedom of conscience.

Does the dear reader know what defenestration is? No? No problem, I will explain. It comes from the Latin word *fenestra* (window) and means "to throw someone out of a window". That is exactly what, on two occasions, the Hussites, the followers of Jan Hus, a precursor of the Protestant Reformation in Bohemia, today's Czech Republic, did. In 1410, the Catholic Church was mired in immorality and divided among three popes. With the sale of indulgences, or forgiveness of sins, one of them financed an armed struggle against one of his rivals. Huss' critical stance against the corruption of the Church brought him great prestige among the Czech population, but aroused the wrath of the rulers. Because of this, in 1415 he was burned at the stake and his followers came to be persecuted. The first defenestration took place in 1419, when revolted Protestants stormed Prague's city hall to demand the release of supporters. However, their demand quickly turned into a thirst for revenge for the reformer's death. Infuriated, the Hussites threw the mayor and nine public servants down the window. Those who did not die on the spot were stabbed by the mob waiting in front of the building. One survivor was taken to a torture chamber and brutalized to death. Three weeks later, Hus' followers raided several churches and monasteries, vandalizing some and burning others. These episodes triggered the Hussite Wars, religious conflicts that lasted about 25 years and made Bohemia forever lose its position as an economic and cultural power.

The second defenestration occurred almost two hundred years later. Although Protestantism was already rooted in Bohemia, the tension between Protestants and the Catholic authorities still caused clashes. One of the first things Ferdinand II of Habsburg did when he, in 1617, became king of Bohemia was to try to re-catholize his kingdom by force, which obviously threw gasoline on the fire of hatred that existed between the two rival Christianities. Furious, about two hundred Protestants stormed Prague Castle and threw three court secretaries out of the window. This defenestration kicked off the Thirty Years' War, a religious conflict that spread through several European countries and, as a consequence of the deaths of millions of people, devastated vast areas. In some regions of Germany, up to 70% of the population was decimated, not only by the combats but also by the epidemics that resulted from them.

According to Gallup International's 2012 *Global Index of Religiosity and Atheism*, today 48% of Czechs consider themselves irreligious and 30% claim to be staunch atheists, placing the Czech Republic third on the list of the world's most atheistic countries. Coincidence, or is its long and violent past of religious wars the cause of the Czechs' deep aversion to religion?

The infant baptism practiced by the Catholic Church was never a principle fought against by the reformers. Even so, many Protestants considered it unbiblical and rebaptized themselves, reason why they were called Anabaptists, from the Greek "rebaptism". Predominantly pacifists, Anabaptists refused to take up arms and were opposed to the union between Church and State, something the Reformation insisted on maintaining. Because of this, these Protestants were harshly and long persecuted throughout Europe also by Protestantism.

What Calvin was to Geneva reformer Huldrych Zwingli was to Zurich. In dogmatic disputes, his opinion was law. Zwingli condemned Anabaptist doctrines and the City Council ordered the banishment of all people who refused to baptize their babies. A little later, it was opted for zero tolerance: those who professed Anabaptism would be punished with death.

Zwingli had a fellow student named Felix Manz. While the former advanced to Protestant pope of Zurich, the latter became one of the founders of Anabaptism. Due to the prohibition of this movement, declared heretical by Zwingli, Manz was imprisoned several times, occasions in which the reformer urged him to deny his faith. For remaining firm in his convictions, in 1527 the Anabaptist leader was sentenced to death by drowning in the Limmat River. Felix Manz was the first Swiss Protestant to be martyred by the hands of other Protestants.

A parenthesis on the dark side of Protestantism to relate the most grotesque case of hatred of Anabaptism, performed by the Catholic Church. The Anabaptist Dirk Willems, from Asperen, in the Netherlands, was arrested for rebaptizing himself. Using a makeshift rope, he managed to escape through the window. However, in addition to having been seen by the sentry, he had to cross a lake covered with a thin layer of ice. Willems made it across, but it could not bear the weight of the watchman, who, sinking, screamed for help. Instead of continuing to save his own skin, the pursued returned and pulled his pursuer out of the water. Despite this incomparable example of altruism, the guard arrested the Anabaptist, who ended up being sentenced to the stake. On May 16, 1569, the wind was very strong and the flames did not reach Willems with sufficient intensity to kill him. His torture was such that, unable to bear that sight, an authority ordered that he be given a coup de grâce, putting an end to the Anabaptist's torment.

Basing himself on texts by Luther, in 1530 Philipp Melanchthon wrote the *Augsburg Confession*. Articles 5, 9, 16 and 17 read: "Damned are the Anabaptists". Article 16 states: "Christians may punish evildoers with the sword and wage wars". Believe it or not, the *Augsburg Confession* still today is the official creed of the Lutheran Church. A year later, Melanchthon was commissioned by the Elector of Saxony to issue an opinion on Anabaptism. With Luther's endorsement, the reformer recommended the death penalty for Anabaptist leaders and the banishment of their followers.

Shortly after Luther died, Melanchthon vented in a letter that enduring the temperamental outbursts of the Father of the Reformation was a "humiliating servitude".

Persecution, torture and sentencing to death occurred in many Protestant cities in Europe. In accordance with Exodus 22:18, which reads: "Do not allow a sorceress to live", both Luther and Calvin were energetic advocates and promoters of witch-hunt, which took the lives of some 70,000 people. On May 6, 1526, Luther preached in a church: "It is an exceedingly just law that the sorceresses be killed". In the regions of Switzerland where Protestantism became the official religion, persecuting witches was common. The last witch to be executed in Europe was Anna Göldi, from Glarus, a Protestant town in Switzerland, 265 long years after Luther's 95 Theses denouncing the errors of the Catholic Church were written.

At least 4,000 people were victims of witch-hunts in Protestant Scotland, between 1563 and 1727, a period that Scottish historian Roy Pugh classifies as "mini-holocaust". According to him, civil and religious leaders nurtured the belief in witches as a way of "controlling the population through religious fanaticism".

The only known case of a Protestant clergyman who opposed this barbarism is that of the court chaplain Anton Praetorius, in the city of Birstein, Germany. When, in 1597, four women were accused of witchcraft, Praetorius was summoned to join the tribunal that would try them. After three of them had perished in the horrifying interrogations, no longer bearing to hear the screams of the unfortunate fourth the pastor pounded the door of the torture chamber with such force and for so long that the poor woman was eventually set free. As a result, Praetorius was fired and forced to move to another city.

At that time, the only Protestant region in Europe where there was a certain degree of religious tolerance was the Netherlands. For this reason, many oppressed and persecuted people emigrated there, among them merchants, philosophers, scientists and artists. This relative freedom catapulted the modest Republic of the Seven United Netherlands to the rank of greatest economic, scientific and cultural power in the world, a period that became known as the Dutch Golden Age. It gave rise to the Enlightenment, or Century of Lights, or even Age of Reason, whose principal precursor is identified by many historians in the person of philosopher Bento de Spinoza, also known as Baruch Spinoza.

As incredible as it may seem, during the centuries in which the Iberian Peninsula was under Islamic domination Judaism and Christianity could be freely practiced. As soon as, in 1492, the Christians expelled the Muslims, the Jews were forbidden to follow their religion and forced to convert to Christianity. Since not following the religion of Christ's love meant certain death, many Jews converted. Risking arrest at any moment, the majority of them continued to practice Judaism on the sly, but those who could went to seek refuge in Holland. That is exactly what Espinosa's family did, which fled from the Portuguese Inquisition.

Idea for a documentary scene. At the door of a Catholic church, ask the faithful coming out of Mass: "What do you think about Catholicism having taken the Inquisition to India?".

Just as the Catholic Church does with the Inquisition, the Protestant Church attempts to relativize the dark side of its history, justifying it. In an article entitled *Hexen bei Zwingli (Zwingli and the Witches)*, from its online lexicon, the Evangelical Reformed Church of Zürich minimizes the atrocities committed by Swiss Protestantism, labeling them as necessary evils, which were blessings in disguise: "Whether the Reformation really attacked this world of the imagination, this, to my knowledge, is a disputed question. If so, the witch-hunts were, so to speak, a work accident in the course of the disenchantment of the world introduced by the Reformation". In other words, Protestantism is the medicine; torturing, strangling, hanging, drowning, beheading and burning people, its side effects.

In Austria and Germany, the genocidal Hitler is still admired by many people, because he supposedly improved people's living conditions and fought Communism. The same happens with the exterminator Stalin, still revered by many as a hero, especially for industrializing Russia and defeating Hitler. In Brazil, many claim the torture and executions committed by the military dictatorship also were "work accidents", necessary evils in the fight against a supposed Communism. In 2016, the whole of Brazil saw and heard on TV Catholic congressman Jair Bolsonaro glorify torture. Despite this and his campaign tainted by racist, misogynistic and authoritarian speeches, he is idolized by millions of Christ's followers, who, in 2018, elected him president of the Republic. If cynicism is common in political ideologies, for obvious reasons it should not exist in religious ones.

And speaking of witches, with what does the dear reader associate the name James I of England? Correct, with the *King James Bible*, better known as the *King James Version*, one of the most respected translations of the Holy Scriptures, sponsored by the King of England, who also ruled Scotland under the name of James VI. In 1590, in Edinburgh, Protestant James established a tribunal to try 70 people accused of witchcraft. The king was present at the torture sessions and personally conducted the interrogations of several of the defendants, such as those of midwife Agnes Sampson, accused of making use of black magic to try to sink the royal ship on its return from a trip to Denmark. Heavy storms had forced it to make a stopover of a few weeks in Norway. Sampson was subjected to horrific torture and chained to the wall of the prison. Her head was locked in an iron mask, from which four spikes penetrated her mouth, two pressing on her tongue, the other two on the inside of her cheeks. After declaring herself guilty of the 53 charges brought against her, the midwife was strangled and burned at a stake.

Jesus said the children of God are the peacemakers, but if Christianity once was peaceful, this was before it became the dominant religion of the Roman Empire, that is, about 1,700 years ago. In 2012, the Public Religion Research Institute, in Washington, found that 58% of white Evangelicals and 32% of all Catholics own firearms. This means that in the United States alone over 120 million Christians own revolvers, shotguns, rifles, etc. Even if a Christian claims to use them solely for self-defense, he still contradicts his religion, since he disregards one of the best-known precepts of Christ:

Do not resist an evil person. If anyone slaps you on the right cheek, turn to them the other cheek also [...]. Love your enemies and pray for those who persecute you, that you may be children of your Father in heaven.

(Matthew 5:39,44-45)

This is one more of the innumerable biblical passages that cause divergence among believers. Those who argue Jesus was not a pacifist need to pay attention to the phrase "Love your enemies" and reflect on it. Well, it is impossible to love your enemies and at the same time use weapons against them. If Jesus was not a pacifist, but favorable to the use of weapons to at least defend oneself,

29

it would not have cost the Creator of the Universe much to formulate the sentence thus: "Love your enemies and pray for those who persecute you, unless they attack you". Furthermore, if Christians "are not of the world" (John 17:14) and are fully convinced those who believe in Christ will be with him in Paradise, they would not even think of defending themselves, because "to die is gain" (Philippians 1:21).

The reason why Christians do not love their enemies is very simple: they know that "Love your enemies" is an irrational commandment. We can abstain from revenge. One may even be able to forgive his daughter's rapist and murderer, but love him? Besides not being necessary, Christians feel that this is not possible. Hence, this is one of those maxims that Christians like to use to advertise the supposed exceptional wisdom of Jesus, but which in reality are unfounded and even contradictory. Yahweh was not violent. He was extremely violent. It would, therefore, be grotesque, if a deity who calls himself "Lord of Hosts" had anything against weapons. Jesus, on the other hand, was a pacifist. This is undeniable. The discrepancy here is obvious: as every Christian knows, Yahweh and Jesus are the same god.

At the peak of its heinous activities, the American racist organization Ku Klux Klan had around six million adherents, almost all of them Protestants. According to historian Brian Farmer, throughout the existence of the Klan two thirds of its leadership have been consisting of Evangelical pastors, as is the case of the current director of its political branch, The Knights Party. Radical Christian groups do not exist because of mere mental insanity, but because the Judeo-Christian religion contains elements that give rise to extremist conceptions. It would be difficult for the KKK to base its supremacist ideology on the Bible, if it did not teach that slavery is legal and God's plan includes setting people apart to be exalted as his chosen people, whom he has empowered to commit ethnic cleansing against other peoples and usurp their land.

When a religious belief becomes the official religion of a country, it starts to oppress the others. Although it was persecuted by the Roman Empire, as soon as it rose to the rank of dominant religion Christianity itself became a persecutor. Where Catholicism ruled, it oppressed Protestantism. Where the dominance was in the hands of Protestantism, Catholicism was oppressed.

After becoming the official religion of England and Scotland, in the 16th century, Protestantism tried to extinguish Catholicism in the United Kingdom, banning it for more than 200 long years. During that period, there was a real anti-Catholic hysteria, especially in Ireland, whose people did not adhere to the Protestantism imposed by the English invaders. On pain of fines, members of the Catholic Church were forced to attend the worship services of the Church of Ireland and were not allowed to own land, houses and horses, which impoverished them to such an extent that thousands of them were forced to leave the country and become soldiers in the armies of Spain and France.

A law of August 1643 forced all Catholic clerics to abjure their belief:

> I do abjure and renounce the Pope's supremacy and authority over the Catholic Church in general, and over my self in particular; and I do believe that there is not any transubstantiation in the sacrament of the Lord's Supper, or in the elements of bread and wine [...]. And I do also believe that there is not any purgatory, or that the consecrated Host, crucifixes or images ought to be worshipped [...]. I do abjure and renounce, without any equivocation, mental reservation or secret evasion whatsoever, taking the words by me spoken, according to the common and usual meaning of them. So help me God.

Catholics who refused to renounce their creed were sentenced to death and cash rewards were offered to anyone who captured priests and bishops.

If the dear reader has been to Geneva, you may have visited the Reformation Wall. Among the personalities immortalized in that monument as Protestant heroes is the statue of warrior Oliver Cromwell, Lord Protector and military and political leader of the Commonwealth of England. The motto on Cromwell's coat of arms was "Peace is sought through war". Well in the style of biblical battles, he was convinced his military strikes were guided by God. In 1641, Catholics revolted against the prohibition of their religion and by the policy of dispossession and occupation of their land by Protestant settlers rose up and killed many English and Scots, instituting an autonomous government and re-establishing Catholicism in Ireland. Eight years later, the troops of Cromwell, who felt a real loathing for Catholics, invaded the Irish nation, massacring thousands of people and confiscating their properties. About this onslaught Protestant Cromwell wrote: "A righteous judgement of God upon these barbarous wretches". Almost 400 years later, the wounds opened by these religious conflicts still have not healed.

If Martin Luther's objective was to purify Christianity from what he considered false doctrines of the Catholic Church, for John Calvin this purification had not been sufficiently deep. Because of this, the Calvinist version of the Reformation is regarded as more rigid, austere, severe. Nevertheless, within Calvinism there were those who wanted it even more fundamentalistic, that is, pure. This ultra-conservative movement became known as Puritanism and reached its peak during the military dictatorship of the Puritan Oliver Cromwell. For the Puritans, going to church was not enough. Their purpose was to achieve absolute moral purity through a life totally centered on religion and regulated by it down to the smallest details. Basing themselves on the biblical principle that man was created for the glory of his Creator, for the Puritans all the time one did not spend with work should be dedicated to communion with God, reason why a good Puritan abstained from all kinds of recreations. American journalist Henry Louis Mencken defined Puritanism thus: "The haunting fear that someone, somewhere, may be happy".

Disgusted with Catholicism, the Puritans wanted Anglican churches to be different from Catholic churches in everything. They would fight even to have the stone altar replaced by a wooden table. In his autobiography, William Weston, who, for being a Jesuit, spent fifteen years in prison, relates:

The Puritans used to come in crowds, flocking from all quarters to be present at their exercises. These they used to begin with three or four sermons, preached one after the other. [...] They all had their Bibles and looked diligently for the texts that were quoted by their preachers, comparing different passages to see if they had been brought forward truly and to the point [...]. All of them, men and women, boys and girls, labourers, workmen and simpletons; and these discussions were often wont, as it was said, to produce quarrels and fights. [...] When the congregation was dismissed, after the long fast that had been imposed upon them all, and after the whole day had been consumed in these exercises, they ended the farce with a plentiful supper.

With the end of the Puritan Cromwell era and the restoration of the monarchy, the radicalism of the Puritans came to be seen as a threat to the unity of the Church and authority of the State. Persecuted, thousands of them emigrated to the United States of America, where they would have full freedom to implement their religious fundamentalism.

In Puritan New England, in 1692, took place the phenomenon of collective religious hysteria known as the Salem Witch Trials, in witch, pardon, in which nineteen women were executed by hanging and one man was pressed to death. Giles Corey was a 71-year-old farmer who had beaten one of his farm workers to death for allegedly stealing apples. For this and other reasons, Corey did not enjoy the best of reputations, being seen as a grumpy and odd man. When he tried to defend his wife against the charge of witchcraft, he himself ended up being accused. Paranoid young women recounted that Corey's spirit had appeared to them and tortured them, forcing them to sign a Devil's book. To extract a confession from the old man, boards were laid on his chest and belly, upon which heavy stones were placed. The more he refused to admit his guilt, the more stones were piled up. On his third day of agony, he was asked once more if he had changed his mind and was willing to confess. Corey shouted: "More weight!", and died. A witness reported: "Giles Corey's tongue was pressed out of his mouth. The Sheriff, with his cane, forced it in again".

Horrifying? Believe it or not, today, the day I write these lines, is Halloween.

Perhaps the most eloquent of all the Puritan preachers was Jonathan Edwards, of Connecticut. Because it is an excellent example of Puritan theology, focused on God's wrath, damnation, Devil and Hell, his sermon *Sinners in the Hands of an Angry God*, from 1741, still today is an object of study for laymen, pastors and theologians. In it, the word hell is mentioned 51 times. Some excerpts:

> There are the black clouds of God's wrath now hanging directly over your heads, full of the dreadful storm, and big with thunder; and were it not for the restraining hand of God, it would immediately burst forth upon you. The sovereign pleasure of God, for the present, stays his rough wind; otherwise it would come with fury, and your destruction would come like a whirlwind, and you would be like the chaff of the summer threshing floor. [...] The bow of God's wrath is bent, and the arrow made ready on the string, and justice bends the arrow at your heart, and strains the bow, and it is nothing but the mere pleasure of God, and that of an angry God, without any promise or obligation at all, that keeps the arrow one moment from being made drunk with your blood. [...] The God that holds you over the pit of hell, much as one holds a spider, or some loathsome insect over the fire, abhors you, and is dreadfully provoked: his wrath towards you burns like fire; he looks upon you as worthy of nothing else, but to be cast into the fire. [...] And it would be a wonder, if some that are now present should not be in hell in a very short time, even before this year is out. And it would be no wonder if some persons, that now sit here, in some seats of this meeting-house, in health, quiet and secure, should be there before tomorrow morning.

In the 19th century, American Puritanism went through a phase of great spiritual revivals that resulted in what became known as Evangelicalism, a biblical-fundamentalist movement that produced several denominations that would expand globally, whose focus is salvation through baptism, the study of the biblical prophecies and missionary work.

With the addition of rules for an even stricter lifestyle and the introduction of the baptism in the Holy Spirit, who supposedly confers believers the power to cure and the capacity to speak in strange tongues and prophesy, Evangelicalism subdivided, creating, in the early 20th century, Pentecostalism.

Decades later, liberal dress and appearance rules, but an even greater focus on curing and casting out demons and the addition of divine reward already in this life created a new subdivision: Neo-Pentecostalism.

In the fashion of what was one of the principal reasons for the rise of Protestantism — the sale of indulgences — Prosperity Theology, a trademark of Neo-Pentecostalism, is nothing but the trade of divine favors. While the Catholic Church sold the remission of the so-called temporal penalties, neo-Pentecostal pastors sell promises of miracles, success and fortune.

The interesting thing about Prosperity Theology is that it actually works — for those who sell it. In 2013, the US magazine *Forbes* published a list of the richest neo-Pentecostal leaders in Brazil:

1) Edir Macedo: US$ 950 million.
2) Valdemiro Santiago: US$ 220 million.
3) Silas Malafaia: US$ 150 million.
4) Romildo Ribeiro Soares: US$ 125 million.
5) Estevam Hernandes: US$ 65 million.

In Europe, Evangelicalism is insignificant. Anyone who wanders the streets, for example, of Vienna will not come across any of the Evangelical churches upon which we stumble in Brazil on almost every corner. Even the best known ones, such as the Baptist Church and the Adventist Church, have very few temples and usually operate in adapted halls of old residential buildings. Quite different from the Third World, which received and still receives American denominations with open arms and copies them. Thanks above all to the less educated segment of the population, Brazil has become the second largest country in number of members of fundamentalistic Evangelical churches. It is around 47 million Brazilians who live according to religion and believe, among other things, that the Universe is 6,000 years old, the woman was made from a man's rib and snakes and donkeys can talk.

In general, the various Evangelical denominations despise each other, but when it comes to demonizing the Catholic Church they curiously unite as if they loved each other. On Google, anyone who types in "Catholic Church whore" or "Catholic Church Babylon" or "pope beast Revelation" will be bestowed with many thousands of links. This is not by chance. The Evangelical conception that the Catholic Church is Babylon and a prostitute and the Pope the Beast of Revelation goes back to the writings of Doctor Martin Luther, the same choleric misogynist who called for the burning of Jewish homes and hunting of witches.

In comparison with Evangelicals, Catholics generally practice their religion in a more relaxed way. While the majority of Catholics were born into Catholicism and just carry on the religious tradition of their parents, many Evangelicals were "born again", that is, converted, an experience that makes them have a closer bond with their church. This results in a dogmatism and fundamentalism that are not very common among Catholics, for whom spirituality through the practice of liturgical rituals is more important than, for example, dissecting biblical prophecies about the end of the world.

By virtue of the fundamentalist character of Evangelicalism, there is normally no difference between the degree of dogmatism of a poorly educated Evangelical and an educated one. An Evangelical with a doctorate takes the Bible as literally and observes the precepts of the church as to the letter as a semi-literate Evangelical. In contrast, an enlightened Catholic will have no difficulty taking a critical stance towards some of the doctrines of his church. Let us take Eve and Adam as an example. Although, because of irrefutable scientific evidence, Catholicism today sees the biblical account of creation as an allegory, the historical existence of the first pair of humans continues to be an irrevocable part of its dogmas. Even so, a Catholic who considers Eve and Adam mythological figures does not suffer from a crisis of conscience. Another example is the use of contraceptives, officially forbidden by the Catholic Church. A survey by the Guttmacher Institute, in New York, conducted in 2012, shows that 98% of Catholic women between the ages of 15 and 45 made or make use of some type of contraceptive. Taking liberties with doctrines is unthinkable in Evangelicalism, which demands uniformity of thought and total obedience, even far beyond what the Bible demands. As absurd as it may seem, an Evangelical who is caught, for example, dancing will be frowned upon by his coreligionists and have serious problems with the leadership of his church.

One of the distinguishing features of which Evangelicals are most proud is their less formal style of congregating. They like to imagine and advertise their churches as an extension of their own families. From a distance, that seems to be a good thing, but a closer look reveals otherwise. It is true that in the family we can feel supported, but often it also is an environment of frequent tensions and collisions and can bind and control us. Intrigues, psychological pressure and control are frequent elements in Evangelical churches precisely because they are run like families.

The long past of religious and ideological wars left deep marks in Europeans and made most of them people who value autonomy of thought and are averse to exaggerations and manipulations, especially of an ecclesiastical nature, reason why in Europe Evangelicalism has enormous difficulty growing. After many years of abstinence, one beautiful day I got curious to know how I would feel going, in Vienna, to the worship service of the denomination of which I had been part until I was 25 years old. A native of St. Petersburg and baptized in the Russian Orthodox Church, my then girlfriend knew little about Protestantism and had never set foot in an Evangelical church. At the entrance, a man greeted us with a handshake. Other people, equally unknown to us, also shook our hands. The receptionist led us into the church and pointed to the free seats. As soon as we sat down, our seat neighbors shook our hands. At some point, the visitors were asked to stand up and introduce themselves. Following that, the entire congregation rose to their feet for a greeting ritual. From all sides came handshakes. On the way out, between handshakes, the pastor wanted to have our telephone numbers. In the hall next to the church, while eating and drinking, more handshakes. Believing that my girlfriend, a sociable and communicative woman, had loved all that human warmth, on the way back home I asked her what she thought. She answered: "I just didn't like that bunch of handshakes".

Accustomed to the total anonymity of the Masses in the Russian churches, in which there is no social appeal, it transpired to my girlfriend that behind all that Evangelical fraternity hides the intention to impress, involve, hold. When church and social club get mixed up, it is easier to be influenced, manipulated and dominated by religion. The more involved, the more assimilated; the more assimilated, the more uniformed; the more uniformed, the more adjusted; the more adjusted, the more submissive. Unlike in other social circles, in a religious congregation the participants are united by an ideology that deals with what they think is the absolute truth, which, being indisputable, has deeper psychological implications than other ideologies.

Many Christians like to see in the fact that Christianity is the largest religion the proof that what it preaches is true. They ignore that it spread principally by means of wars and conquests. Would Christianity today be so large, if the Portuguese, Spanish, English, French and Dutch conquerors had not imposed it on the people of the nations they subjugated? And what paths would Christianity have taken, if Saint Constantine, "The Great, Equal to the Apostles", as Emperor Constantine I is revered in Orthodox churches, had not privileged it in the Roman Empire? Hard to say, but it might well have had the same fate as religions now extinct.

Be that as it may, if today it is no longer possible for Christians to impose Christianity their only way out is to spread it through missionary work. Yet, in a country that, like Brazil, already has a Christian majority, missionaries are left only with stealing, that is, converting believers from one denomination to another. If, however, the level of education of Brazilians were high, that would not be so easy. Furthermore, Pentecostal churches would not have had the success they had and continue to have.

The more educated a nonreligious person is, the more self-confident and the less willing he is to allow being dictated how to think. The likelihood of a person versed in natural sciences converting to a biblical-fundamentalist religion is almost zero, reason why of the minority of theistic scientists the great majority does not believe in the biblical account of creation, because they acknowledge the incontestability of the scientific evidence of Evolution.

For someone who grew up or spent decades in the parallel world of religion, leaving it behind is not as simple as turning the page of a book. Based on the biblical notion that the followers of Christ "are not of the world", which results in almost everything being worldly and, therefore, despicable, much of his life revolves around church-related things. His recreational activities, music, books and magazines, movies and TV shows, clothes, the school of the children, practically everything is under the influence of the religious organization to which he belongs. His social circle is composed almost exclusively of brothers in the faith and it is very likely that also his relatives are members of the church. In view of this, there is no way that the psychological pressure is not great and it is almost impossible that the process of separation from the church is not painful, even traumatic.

Most of the time, those who break free from the ties of Evangelicalism start to live under the social stigma of the black sheep. People close to an ex-Evangelical will always see him as a rebel who is under the influence of evil forces that want to lead him to perdition, a deviant who needs many prayers, so that he, like the Prodigal Son, recognizes his mistake and returns to the bosom of the church, without which it makes no sense to live.

Add to that the believers who start to speak ill of the rebel, with judgments like "He never was a real Christian" or "He wants to be free to sin". What should be the most natural thing in the world — living without religion — is seen as something vile. As incredible as it seems, videos of people sharing on the internet their deconversion experience receive innumerable negative comments from believers, ranging from threats of eternal punishment to curses.

Needless to say, religious people regard their religions as indispensable. It is impossible for them to conceive that anyone could have legitimate reasons for not wanting to belong to them, let alone leave them. Would, therefore, parents who see their church as something essential to themselves not want it to be seen in the same way by their children? And how could this mentality not exert psychological pressure on the latter? Those who think that children of Evangelical parents are free to leave the church without any embarrassment are ignorant of reality. The internet is full of testimonies from teenagers and young people who want to break with religion, but suffer with the inevitable disappointment of their parents and family members and the possibility of coming into conflict with them, which makes the majority choose to continue pretending.

Long decades of intense religious indoctrination lead many believers to see church and God as an amalgam, from which it follows that turning one's back on the church is seen as turning one's back on God himself. The roots of catechism are so deep that in the minds of many of those who liberate themselves from the church something survives of the biblical conception of a zealous God who does not tolerate dissent, and this eventually leads some strays to return to the fold, especially when their families never tire of making them feel that to live without religion is to walk the path that leads to perdition.

When, in Austria, the pastor of the church I attended noticed that I was no longer coming to the worship services, he called me in an attempt to persuade me not to stray from his corral. Realizing that nothing he said was having any effect, the pastor played his last card, the one every clergyman has in his suit jacket sleeve: the imposition of fear, through a "Don't you want to go to Heaven?". Indignant, I replied: "*Nein!*", when in fact what I wanted was for him to leave me alone.

What would become of religions, if everyone accepted the obvious, that is, the fact that no one knows if Heaven exists? Similar to the famous phrase "Every accused person is considered innocent, until proven guilty", Heaven does not exist until proven otherwise. Should that not be the natural way of thinking? Is it possible that Heaven exists? Yes. Theoretically, many things are possible, including parallel universes. The dear reader believes in parallel universes, correct? No? Strange, because not a few cosmologists claim it is possible that other universes exist. Even so, no physicist would be crazy to claim parallel universes really exist. Like life after death, Heaven and Hell, the Multiverse is nothing but speculation, since we have no evidence of it.

There are things we cannot see, but whose effects can be observed or measured. Electricity is one of the simplest. Likewise, no one is able to see black holes or dark matter, but what they cause can be observed and measured. By the way, the biblical fundamentalist who thinks that black holes are mad scientists stuff needs only to get his head out of the hole and research Sagittarius A*, with an asterisk, to convince himself that these devourers of suns really exist.

Has the dear reader ever seen an intellectually honest priest or pastor? Neither have I, because to be intellectually honest priests and pastors would have to start a sermon thus: "Sisters and brothers, if he exists, I imagine that God repudiates dishonest people. Because of this, from now on I will talk only about things I know exist. Obviously, I wish that eternal life and Heaven are real, but I don't know if they exist, because there is no evidence of them. This book here says they exist. However, if they exist because this book says so, then the planet Krypton and Superman also exist, because that's what this magazine here says".

How many members would churches have whose priests and pastors were intellectually honest? Exactly. Religious people are not interested in the truth, because the truth is that, until proven otherwise, God, gods, angels, Devil, demons, eternal life, Heaven and Hell do not exist. Setbacks, suffering and indignation about death lead people to flee from reality, that is, from the truth, and seek consolation and hope in religions. That would not be entirely reprehensible, were it not for the fact that religions induce their followers to be afraid of rejecting someone no one knows exists — God —, be afraid of not receiving something no one knows exists — eternal life —, be afraid of not going to a place no one knows exists — Heaven — and be afraid of going to a place no one knows exists — Hell. Eternal life and Paradise would be harmless hopes, if they were not intrinsically linked to the nefarious notion of chosen people, which leads members of a club to find it natural that people be punished for being members of other clubs, or of none.

In one of the innumerable Evangelical programs with which Brazilian television is infested, a pastor said that believing in God is a matter of mathematical logic. According to him, it is fifty-fifty: there is a 50% chance that God exists and a 50% chance that he does not exist. If God exists and I believed in him, I will go to

Heaven. If God does not exist and I believed in him, I will have believed in vain, but lost nothing (except time and, every month, at least 10% of my salary). On the other hand, if God exists but I did not believe in him, he will cast me into Hell, where "there will be weeping and gnashing of teeth". In short: just in case, it is better to believe in God. There are several flaws in this argumentative proposal, known as Pascal's Wager. The principal one is that it applies to any deity of any religion. What face will Christians make, when they, beaming with happiness, approach the gates of Heaven and are greeted by a celestial being saying: "Let me see… Christians, am I right? You guys are so screwed! The real god is Nhanderuvuçu [creator god of the Tupi-Guarani people]. Yeah, who told the Portuguese and Spanish not to listen to the natives? Ha, ha, ha… Well, you see that sign behind you with the word Anhangaratá [Hell]? So, that's where you're going. Don't worry, Jurupari [the Devil] will take care of you. With pleasure! Ha, ha, ha…".

Pascal's Wager is excellent to demonstrate how fear is the essence of most religions, but especially the monotheistic ones. According to Christianity, it is better to believe in God than to risk being tortured in a lake of fire and brimstone. In other words, be, dear reader, afraid not to believe in God. If you decided not to risk it and already believe in God, be afraid of not being believing in the true god. If you are convinced you believe in the true god, be afraid of not being doing it the right way. Do you want to be sure you are believing in the true god the right way? Nothing simpler: it suffices to become a member of the true church. Oh, you do not know which of the 40,000 Christian denominations is the true one? Do not despair. No one knows. So, take any one. The one nearest your home, for example, or the one whose music style you like the most. Then just hope it is the one that represents the true god the right way. Or do as I do: acknowledge the irrationality of it all and relax.

If it is true that God gave us free will (something on which scholars differ and the majority of them reject), not wanting anyone to believe in him by force, then the notion that he will punish those who do not believe in him is mistaken, because disbelieving is not evil. Otherwise, Christians are evil for not believing in Odin, the Norse god, father of Thor. The disbeliever in God is as sincere in his disbelief as the believer in his belief. By Christianity's own logic, God would be a tyrant if he sent someone to Hell just for not believing.

If God exists, those who do not see evidence of his existence and do not believe in him at least do not do anything that represents him in an erroneous, distorted way. In contrast, the mere fact that there are thousands of religions means that God is at all times misrepresented by believers around the world. Despite his unshakable belief in the existence of God, a religious person may be constantly teaching falsehoods about him and in his name committing absurdities. Because of this, as the French author Edmond de Goncourt said, "If there is a God, Atheism must seem to him a lesser insult than religion".

I echo the words of Thomas Jefferson, author of the United States Declaration of Independence: "Question with boldness even the existence of a god; because, if there be one, he must more approve the homage of reason, than that of blindfolded fear".

2

Logic

"Sometimes, I want to believe, but am unable to.
It's all a total nonsense.
Then I ask God: 'Listen, my friend,
if it was to unmake it, why did you make it?'"

— Vinicius de Moraes
(*Cotidiano Nº 2*)

IN AN EPISODE of the *Even Stevphen* segment of the American television program *The Daily Show*, comedians Steve Carell and Stephen Colbert play a Muslim and a Christian who squabble over which religion is the most logical and, therefore, the true one. The Muslim: "Stephen, what part of 'There is no God but Allah, and Muhammad is His prophet' don't you understand? Let's assume for the sake of argument that your God is the one true God. That would mean Allah is not the one true God, which we know he is. Don't you see? Your logic eats itself". The Christian: "First off, it's not my logic, Steve. It's God's logic, as written in the Bible, every word of which is true. And we know every word is true because the Bible says that the Bible is true, and if you remember from earlier in this sentence, every word of the Bible is true. Now, are you following me here or are you some kind of mindless zealot?".

If the dear reader is religious and was born in Japan, the probability is enormous that you are a Shintoist. In Indonesia, you would be a Muslim; in Cambodia, a Buddhist; in India, a Hindu. If you are a Christian, it is because you very likely were born somewhere in Europe or the Americas. For those who are natives of the Occident, it is natural that Christianity should be the most natural thing in the world. And even if the dear reader is not religious, the mere fact that you grew up in a predominantly Christian country makes the ingredients of Christianity not seem absurd to you. It is no wonder, then, that Christians consider illogical the religions with which they, for merely geographical reasons, are not culturally related. If this is so with the large religions, even more so with the small and little-known ones.

I have heard people claim with visible self-confidence they are Christians because Christianity is the most logical religion. Evidently, they would never say that if they were Buddhists. There are Buddhists who convert to Christianity, but that in no way points to a logical superiority of the Christian belief, because there are also Christians who convert to Buddhism, which frequently happens especially in developed countries.

The supposed logical superiority of Christianity could only be attested if it were possible to find people who had never heard of any religion. After being initiated into the basic teachings of the major religions, we would ask them to vote for the one that to them made the most sense. Since finding such people is impossible, the way out is to try to simulate the impression Christianity would make on someone who had never heard of it.

Imagine, dear reader, you are that someone. You have no knowledge whatsoever of the Christian doctrine. Zero. *Niente*, really nothing at all. Now, visualize in your mind that a missionary approaches you and says: "My friend, I have a religion for you. It's not like the others, which are weird. No, no. In my religion, everything makes sense. Because of that, it's very easy to understand and practice. I'll try to summarize it as much as possible for you, OK? So, let's go. Before there was anything, anything at all, there was a being called God. He has neither beginning nor end and is sitting on a throne. On God's right hand, there's another throne, where his son is sitting. On the left hand, there's no throne, only on the right hand, OK? So, father and son have a spirit, and his name is Holy. Holy Spirit. He's wandering around everywhere, although father and son, despite sitting on thrones, also are everywhere… uh… at the same time. Remember that 3-in-1 music system? Well, it's more or less like that. Father, son and their spirit are one and the same being. They are three… persons in one, OK? It's like… Well, never mind. It sounds complicated, but it's not. One beautiful day, tired of staring into the nothingness, God decided to create the Universe. Instead of simply snapping his fingers and making everything appear at once, God wanted to create Earth in six days. After all, haste makes waste, right? So, in some corner of the Universe there's a place called Heaven, which is invisible, OK? There, God created the angels. Like God, angels also are invisible beings, only with wings on their backs. Apart from that, they have no sex and wield swords of fire. Have you served in the army? So, just like in the army, among the angels there's a hierarchy: archangels, cherubim and seraphim. Each of these types of angels performs specific tasks, which I'm not sure what they are, but that doesn't matter now either. The most important thing is that we all have a guardian angel. He's always by our side, guarding us from all dangers. Except when God wants to teach us a lesson. So, the general of that army of angels was called Lucifer, the most intelligent and beautiful angel. In Heaven, everything was peace and love until, one beautiful day, Lucifer's intelligence and beauty began to go to his head, to the point where he wanted to be like God. That's how Lucifer invented the sin thing. Angry with God, he started to speak ill of him to the other angels, causing a revolt. God then, in his infinite mercy, had no choice but to expel Lucifer from that invisible place. A third of the angels, which nobody knows how many they are, were banished along with him. On that day, Lucifer began to be called Satan, better known as Devil, but who some also call Beelzebub, besides other funny names. Lucifer's henchmen received the name demons. Sometimes they get inside people and it's a real pain to get them out. Well, they all came here to Earth, where God had planted a garden and made a mud doll, into whose nostrils he breathed and the doll walked. That doll was neither an archangel, nor a cherub, nor a seraph, nor a guardian angel. It was a man, and his name was Adam. Adam was sad because he had no wife. So, God made him sleep, opened his chest, took out a rib and made another doll: the woman. Her name was Eve. To fill Earth with people, Adam and Eve's sons had to… uh… marry their own sisters. You and me are descendants of these two dolls, I mean, of these two people, OK? So, in that garden everything was peace and love. So much so that Eve and Adam walked around naked and didn't care. They could eat the fruits of all the trees, except one. It was a tree that God had planted to serve as a test of obedience. If they ate the fruit of that tree, they would die. The man was naive, but the woman… Well, you know how women are, don't you? One beautiful day, the Devil dressed up as a snake and told Eve it was a lie that she and her husband would die, if they ate the fruit of the magic tree. Eve, the naive poor thing, believed the talking snake and took a bite. The rest of the fruit she took to her husband, who, without blinking, also took a bite. Instantly, both realized they were naked and felt ashamed of each other, meaning that sin, which had been invented by Lucifer in that invisible place (remember?), had entered Earth. God then, in his infinite mercy, had no choice but to curse Earth, creating death, thorns, poisonous fruits, parasites, mosquitoes, cockroaches, spiders, scorpions, viruses, bacteria, in short, everything that in Nature is disgusting and dangerous, to put human beings through Hell. All the pain and misery that exist in the world is the result of Eve letting herself be fooled by a talking snake and the man buying the woman's snake oil. So, after taking away man's immortality, the Creator devised a plan to make him immortal again. Only it wasn't going to happen right away, it was going to take a little while. About 1,650 years after the bite on the forbidden fruit, God regretted he had made man. So he sent a flood that wiped out all life on Earth, with the exception of eight people who, along with specimens of all the animal species in the world, got into a boat that took a hundred years to build by a five-hundred-year-old man. Later, God chose a people to be his people, but that people did everything not to be his people, so he always punished his people. On the top of a smoking mountain, God wrote ten commandments on two stone tablets, so that his people would finally know that stealing and killing is wrong. Every time God got angry, which happened often, the folks had to sacrifice animals, because God loved the smell of burning flesh. Who doesn't like a good barbecue, right? So, all human beings, including you, like it or not, carry the guilt of Eve and Adam for taking a bite on the forbidden fruit. It's what some call original sin. It doesn't matter if you and me weren't born yet, we're guilty too, OK? Well, since everything has its price, man's salvation wasn't going to be cheap. It had to be paid with enormous suffering and lots and lots

of blood. About two thousand years ago, God sent his son, who…
is himself, here to Earth to be tortured and shed his blood on a
cross. His name was Jesus Christ. He had no biological father, because when his mother was twelve years old she was impregnated
by the Holy Spirit, who… is himself. There are folks who say the
mother of God was a virgin until she died, but that is a subject for
another conversation. So, God, I mean, Jesus was a different human being, because he did things no human being does, like read
people's thoughts, walk on water, turn it into wine and raise the
dead. Oh, and he also didn't commit a single sin, not even in
thought! So that we never forget the horrendous suffering we
caused the son of God, two thousand years ago, for the sin of disobedience, which we committed in the garden, six thousand years
ago, copies of the cross of Christ, with Jesus hanging with a crown
of thorns on his head, with blood gushing from all sides, are
nailed on walls around the world. Many people even carry a
miniature of it around their necks. Well, on the third day after the
death of his son, God resurrected him and he wandered invisibly
through the region, from time to time appearing to his followers.
After that, he returned to that invisible place and went to sit again
on his throne, to the right of the throne of his father, who… is
himself. Those who go to Heaven can touch the scars of Jesus'
hands and feet. Just before he died, he told his followers that he
would soon come back in the glory of his father, who… is himself,
accompanied by a bunch of angels. So soon that some of his followers would even see that happen. But on another occasion he
had said he'll come back as a thief, on a day that nobody knows.
Because of that, it's been two thousand years that he's about to
come back at any moment. Every day is Jesus' return day. So, all
that and much, much more is written in this book here, called
Bible, a collection of texts inspired by God, written two thousand
years ago and found in caves of the deserts of the Middle East.
Those who believe in what is written in the Word of God, will go
to that invisible place, where they'll receive a golden crown, a mysterious food, called manna, a white stone, with their name en-
graved on it, and a mansion of gold. But those who don't believe
will live with a dragon (remember the talking snake?), in a place

where there's neither peace nor love. There's fire. And what a fire! That place is called Hell, and there the disbelievers will weep and gnash their teeth and burn and roar with pain forever and ever. In a few years, there'll be a world war between Jesus, the dragon and two beasts: one in the sea and another on the earth. The one in the sea has seven heads and ten horns with ten crowns and the one on the earth has only two horns, but speaks like a dragon. Afterwards, God will destroy this rotten world and remake the garden he planted for Eve and Adam. The folks who went to Heaven will live eternally on the New Earth, where the lion will eat straw like the ox. God wants everybody to be saved, but there's a little problem. The Bible is easy to understand, but not without help. It's because God doesn't give anything on a silver platter, you know? One has to make an effort and seek the help of God's representatives here on Earth. And that's where the church comes in. The problem is that the Devil doesn't want people to be saved. So, he keeps creating confusion. Because of that, there are some 40,000 different Christian denominations spread around the world, but only one has been empowered by God to interpret the Bible the right way. But don't worry. You don't know how lucky you are. I'm part of the true church that interprets the Bible the right way. Here, take this leaflet with the times of our meetings, where we explain the Bible bit by bit. Whew! I had to leave out a lot of details, otherwise I wouldn't finish today. Isn't it amazing how all this makes sense? Well, then… do you want it?".

While wiping the sweat from his forehead and from the back of his neck, the missionary does not take his eyes off you, anxious for a reaction. How would the dear reader react? Remember: you had never heard anything even close to it. Now, go on the internet, search for religions, pick any one and find out what it teaches. Then answer in all sincerity: Does the religion the missionary offered you seem to you more logical, reasonable, coherent, plausible, or, if you prefer, less absurd than the one you picked on the internet?

This exercise demonstrates that Christianity is as logical or irrational, conceivable or implausible, serious or laughable as any other religious belief. From a distance, all religions are absurd. How, then, to explain why so many people follow Christianity, despite its evidently bizarre elements?

Of the various reasons, I think socio-cultural factors are the principal ones. Because it is passed from parents to children, we are perfectly accustomed to the predominant religion of the country in which we were born. In Brazil, of those who claim that they no longer follow any religion the great majority was Christian. Therefore, if they go back to believing the chances they will return to Christianity are huge and the chances they will convert, for example, to Islam or Hinduism are tiny. Another reason seems to be the need of many people to feel protected and supported, which is satisfied by the conviction that Jesus cares for them. Furthermore, Christianity gives meaning to the lives of its adherents, because it makes them think they know where they came from and where they are going. And by convincing them they belong to the people chosen by none other than the Creator of the Universe to hold the truth, Christianity also makes them feel special. This feeling of exclusivity may, by the way, be stronger in small denominations, whose small size is seen by their members as evidence of incorruptibility, leading them to consider themselves the true followers of Christ, set apart to preserve and preach the genuine Christian message.

The eagerness of many people to find answers to their doubts related to a supposed transcendent is such that they gladly submit to those who claim to have them. That would explain why it is so easy to impose oneself as a spiritual leader and attract disciples. It would not be wrong to say that followers of religious groups and spiritual leaders are insecure people who seek security in religion.

Until the Middle Ages, it was possible for a scholar to master almost all the academic knowledge in the world. Since then, knowledge is expanding at an accelerated rate. Modern Science has just begun to crawl. Astronomer Edwin Powell Hubble discovered, only about one hundred years ago, that the Cosmos is not limited to our galaxy. On that day, the Universe, which for us was already unmeasurable, became incommensurable. Despite this, we have already elucidated several of its mysteries. The most intriguing one is, however, also one of the most difficult to unravel. Finding life, especially intelligent one, somewhere else in the cosmic immensity would revolutionize our thinking and turn upside down practically everything religions preach.

After bravely accomplishing its mission to visit Jupiter and Saturn, the space probe Voyager 1, launched in 1977, continued its journey without return, from then onwards also without destination. Forty long years after its departure, Voyager 1 has just crossed the doorway's threshold of our home, the Solar System. Although cruising the interstellar space at the astonishing speed of 38,000 miles per hour, it will take 40,000 years for the probe to "approach" another celestial body, a sun from which it will pass far. That allows us to get an idea of how distant the stars are from each other. Yet, the distances between stars are ridiculous when compared to the space that separates galaxies.

The Universe is not, then, just gigantic. It is unimaginably more than super colossal: dimensions that our minds have no capacity to process. The Hubble eXtreme Deep Field photograph, taken by the Hubble Space Telescope and published in 2012, points to the existence of, at the minimum, 200 billion galaxies, each containing billions of solar systems. It is estimated that there are at least one septillion (1 followed by 24 zeros) planets. In view of this, how could the conception of most Christians that only Earth is inhabited be coherent?

The vastness of the Universe prevents us from being able to search for intelligent beings in other solar systems. Notwithstanding, the probability that life exists on other planets is far greater than the probability that gods, angels and demons exist, because, if they exist, extraterrestrials belong to the natural world. In contrast, spirits are not things that can be observed or detected by instruments, and Heaven and Hell are not places that can be visited by probes or spaceships.

Earth is likely to be the only region of the Solar System to harbor intelligent life, but nonintelligent life may exist in places as unlikely as Jupiter's atmosphere and the ocean beneath the thick layer of ice that covers Enceladus, a moon of Saturn. Extraterrestrial life is perhaps the most extraordinary discovery Humanity could make, because, even in the form of a simple bacterium, it would transform our view of ourselves and of the Cosmos. Yet, how much interest do the dear reader, your friends and acquaintances have in this subject? On the other hand, if you are religious, especially Evangelical, you dedicate several hours a week to the study of things that do not belong to the natural world, such as God, Devil, angels, demons, Heaven and Hell, and you find that natural.

We are part of the Universe, but day in and day out we live completely indifferent to what exists and goes on just above our heads. Conscious that in the present state of our technology an effective search for little green men is almost impossible, it is normal that we do not waste time speculating about the existence of beings from other planets. We accept this limitation quite naturally. However, in the existence of extraterrestrials it is not necessary to have faith. Either they exist or they do not. So, if we do not worry about things that, if they exist, are part of the natural world, why should we worry about those that belong to the supernatural world? If Humanity accepted the lack of evidence of the existence of deities as naturally as it accepts the lack of evidence of the existence of aliens, religions would not exist.

By the way, if he exists, why does God need to belong to the supernatural sphere? Existing, his existence should be so obvious that there would be no need to have faith, because no one would be able to doubt. There would be millions of pieces of evidence of a god, not thousands of religions demanding faith in thousands of gods. The believer who claims God exists, but cannot be seen or detected because he is part of the extranatural world is admitting that God's existence is not at all obvious.

In the end, having faith is of little or no value, because religions themselves teach that believing in God is not enough. It is necessary to believe in the true god, follow the true religion, be member of the true church and practice the right way. The absurdity of this conception is evident, especially because each religion claims to be the true representative of the true god. To make matters worse, among practitioners of the same belief there is often no consensus about the right way to worship their god and execute his orders. Because of this, the Christian religion has always been divided.

Already in its beginnings, there were several rival sects and groups. The Great Schism, which split the Catholic Church into Roman and Orthodox, and the Protestant Reformation were only its greatest divisions. Today, there are some 40,000 Christian denominations that more or less despise, antagonize and combat each other.

Idea for a documentary scene. Ask two Christians from different churches: "Which is the true church: yours or yours?".

If believing in Jesus really were the only thing that mattered, not only would there not be so much antagonism between churches but it would not make the slightest difference whether a Christian goes to church or to which one he goes. By the way, would the practice of Christianity not be less monotonous, if, instead of always having to attend the same church, Christians felt perfectly comfortable going every week to a church of a different denomination? However, how would Lutherans feel in a Pentecostal church? And how would Pentecostals feel in a Catholic church? Although Christians like to think Christianity is the most logical religion, its fragmentation into innumerable branches shows just the opposite.

One characteristic of monotheistic religions is exclusivism. Christianity did not abolish the Jewish doctrine of chosen people, it only transferred its validity to believers in Christ. However, even on that the Christian community differs widely. There are Christians who believe that only those who believe in Jesus go to Heaven. Tough luck for those who have never heard of him: they go to Hell all the same. Others argue that believing in Christ is not enough: Christians of the false church also go to Hell. Some say that in the chosen people of God are included the adherents of all other religions: the Christian god acknowledges their sincerity, has mercy on them and forgives their ignorance. A small caveat: if they heard of Jesus and refused to follow him, they go to Hell. There go also all those who practice the sin of not believing in any deities: the atheists. By the logic of these Christians, Jesus prefers worshipers of rival gods to atheists. Other Christians are of the opinion that no one will be lost, not even atheists: Hell does not exist, and in the End Times all people will be reconciled with God. Exclusivist, inclusivist and universalist Christians: all base their arguments on the same book and consider them perfectly logical.

I particularly do not believe Christian inclusivism and universalism are the conceptions most coherent with what the Bible, as a whole, teaches. In my view, they are nothing more than attempts to make Christianity seem more sympathetic, but to no avail, because they presuppose that the Christian religion is the true one, thus reaffirming its exclusivist character. Furthermore, apostle Paul himself leaves no doubt about the destruction of non-Christians: "This will happen when the Lord Jesus is revealed from heaven in blazing fire with his powerful angels. He will punish those who do not know God and do not obey the gospel of our Lord Jesus. They will be punished with everlasting destruction" (2 Thessalonians 1:7-9).

It is worth remembering that, according to the Bible, two men who did not believe in Christ enjoyed the privilege of not dying and went to Heaven: Enoch and Elijah. In Hebrews 11, we have a list of people who were not Christians, but nevertheless have a guaranteed place in Paradise. Interestingly, for 4,000 long years no one needed to believe in Jesus to be saved. After his birth, however, faith in Christ became an indispensable requirement for someone to qualify to go to Heaven.

Atheists understand why many people feel the need to believe in deities, but for believers it is unimaginable that anyone could have reasons not to believe. Because of this, many of them see atheists as people who, motivated by sheer rebellion, deliberately refuse to believe in a god whose existence supposedly is obvious. For religious people, disbelieving is a vile act. Yet, the real reason why they have an aversion to atheists resides in the discomfort it causes them having to admit that nonbelievers are just as good, fulfilled and happy people as believers, who spend their lives striving to do everything their religion dictates.

It is central in Christianity and Islam the idea that disbelief is rebellion. As History proves, that makes them the most intolerant religions, which most persecuted or persecute skeptics. For Christians, what is in the Bible is true, and if it says that there is no excuse for not believing in the biblical god, then there is not:

> Since what may be known about God is plain to them, because God has made it plain to them. For since the creation of the world God's invisible qualities — his eternal power and divine nature — have been clearly seen, being understood from what has been made, so that people are without excuse. For although they knew God, they neither glorified him as God nor gave thanks to him, but their thinking became futile and their foolish hearts were darkened. Although they claimed to be wise, they became fools.
>
> (Romans 1:19-22)

In their arguments against Atheism, Christians like to use this passage, but few realize that Paul is not even referring to atheists. It suffices to read the following verses to see it is about an accusation against idolaters, people who refuse to recognize the biblical god in Nature, preferring to worship deities in the form of objects.

In any case, the apostle's words have no rational basis. It is not true that Nature points to the existence of a god along the lines of the biblical god. There is no historical evidence whatsoever that the worship of a single god was the primordial form of worship. On the contrary: many researchers are of the opinion monotheism is an evolution of animism and polytheism. It has always been common to worship Nature itself, like the Sun, the Moon and the planets, and to conceive and revere deities responsible for different aspects of it, such as the thunder, the fire and the forests.

Furthermore, scholars agree that, initially, the Jewish people themselves were not monotheistic, but polytheistic. According to the *Jewish Encyclopedia*, at first Yahweh was only one of the several deities worshiped by the Hebrews. It was Moses who exalted Yahweh to the rank of Creator of the Universe and induced his people to consider him superior to the other gods. From Moses until the Babylonian Captivity, the Israelites practiced, at most, monolatry, the belief in the existence of several deities, of which one was the highest and, therefore, the principal one. The second commandment of the Decalogue — "You shall have no other gods before me" — even admits the existence of other deities in the religious tradition of the Hebrews, who, by the way, regularly succumbed to the temptation to return to their polytheistic roots. That aroused the religious ardor of prophets, who by means of threats persuaded the Hebrews to stick with the deity whom Moses had established as the official god of the nation of Israel. The most zealous of these prophets and a fierce defender of monotheism was Elijah, whose name even means "My God is Yahweh". In short, making Yahweh the only god of the Jewish people was a gradual process that took several centuries, completed only after the return from the Babylonian Exile.

It does not take a genius to discern sadism in the conception that God hides himself from the human being and, through threat of eternal torture, nevertheless demands that the human being believe in his existence, as if coercing people to believe were normal. The Creator has reasons to hide himself, but the human being, who did not ask to be born, much less in a world of sin, is denied having reasons not to believe in a god who hides himself. No one should feel bad and be seen as evil for not believing, because doubting the existence of a deity who hides himself is perfectly natural. After all, that is exactly why, with the greatest naturalness, Christians doubt the existence, for example, of Brahma, the Hindu god.

Apostle Paul says we are "inexcusable". Assuming that the reasons God has for hiding himself are legitimate, he still communicates with Humanity. The Bible, which was written over a period of several centuries by several people, is the best example of that. Many are the Christians who believe God speaks to them by means of signs, dreams, visions and apparitions, and all are convinced he addresses his people through not only spiritual leaders, such as the Pope, but also through ordinary clergymen, such as priests and pastors. That being so, if the human being has no excuses not to believe in God, what excuses does God have not to reveal to the human being, for example, the formula to cure cancer?

The exuberance of Nature is often used by religious people as an argument to prove the existence of God. According to them,

Nature could not be so spectacular by chance. When they harp on that, the most they prove is the incoherence of religious thought, since they give Nature human qualities and focus only and exclusively on the positive ones. That is like eating from a panettone only the candied fruits.

If Nature evidences the existence of God, then not only through what we in it consider positive, beautiful and charming, like flowers, butterflies and birds, but also negative, ugly and disgusting, like poisonous plants, scorpions and cockroaches. The repugnant vultures and the revolting centipedes are as much a part of Nature as the cute kittens and the sweet ladybugs. If there is a divine intelligence behind the bees, it is the same that is also behind the carnivorous plants, of whose menu, incidentally, the bees are part.

While the majority of spiders weave intricate webs and patiently wait for their dinner to stick to them, a more active species, measuring only 0.6 inch and with terrible eyesight, employs an unusual strategy. At night, it hangs from the underside of tree leaves and weaves a silken thread, at the end of which it forms a sticky ball. From a hole in its abdomen, the bolas spider exudes an imitation of the pheromone that attracts male moths, its favorite dish. When one flies toward the arachnid, similar to a cowboy lassoing an ox the spider swings the ball and throws it in the direction of the enamored lepidopteran, which gets stuck to it. Now, it is just about pulling the line and having dinner.

One of the definitions the *Aurélio Dictionary* gives for the term "sin" is evil. According to the Christian conception, there was no evil in the Garden of Eden, which had been created perfect, that is, without sin. Harmony among living beings was ideal. Consequently, the animals did not eat each other. Not having the need to fight for their survival, they were not created with the necessary skills to prevail in an imperfect Nature, in which the law of the strongest rules.

If before sin animals did not eat each other, what was the need for God to, with the fall of the man, make many of them start killing each other? After all, the ox continued to eat grass. Why, then, did the lion have to be reprogrammed to eat meat? If fallen

Nature has nothing against oxen eating grass, why should it be a problem for it that lions also eat grass, especially when that is what they ate before sin? By the way, what did the bolas spider eat in Paradise? And why does it deceive and kill exclusively moths, and not other insect species as well?

The animal and plant kingdoms would not be what they are, if in Nature the art of deceiving, cheating, tricking, pretending and disguising, so indispensable for the survival of most species, were not common. Theologically, what that little spider does with the moths is fruit of sin, therefore an evil. If it is true that Nature proves the existence of a Creator, who, if not he, taught the bolas spiders to practice the evil of decoying their victims?

A Gallup survey, published in 2014, showed that 42% of Americans believe the biblical account of creation. In other words, 135 million of them are creationists. According to a 2010 Datafolha survey, in Brazil 50 million believe that God made everything in six days. Well, if Nature is imperfect and there was no evolution, this imperfection must have its origin in God. As the only being capable of creating and changing Nature, it was God who adapted the physiology, anatomy and behavior of millions of species of animals and plants, providing each one of them with the necessary sagacity to be able to survive in a hostile world, equipping them with the most varied predatory and defense strategies, such as thorns, stings and poisons. Every particularity of the gigantic transformation from a harmless Nature to a threatening and violent one, the smallest indispensable details to maintain its imperfect state in balance, were not developed, adjusted and adapted over millions of years, but, as if by magic, became the way we know them at the exact moment Adam bit the forbidden fruit.

It is as if the creation of the world were a play in two acts, without intermission and with an abrupt change of scenery. At the instant of the bite on the fruit, God pressed a button, the scenery of the perfect Nature sank into the trap room, the scenery of the imperfect Nature, set up in the background, was quickly pushed forward and the second act began.

If there was no evolution, then the predatory guile peculiar to each species of living being was conceived by the Creator himself and implanted in animals and plants like a chip is implanted in a computer. In the blink of an eye, God reprogrammed Nature to be the imperfect way we know it, with everything that in it is also revolting, deceitful, dangerous, harmful and destructive. Add to that the natural disasters, such as earthquakes, volcanic eruptions, hurricanes and asteroid impacts, since none of that was programmed to exist in an impeccable world. Without evolution, God is the creator of all the imperfection that exists not only on Earth but also in the entire Universe, such as inhospitable planets, black holes, supernovas and gamma ray bursts capable even of eradicating life. God must be behind also all the bacteria and viruses that cause disease and be the programmer of animal instincts that disturb us because they seem to us cruel, like that of lions, which, when they conquer the leadership of a group, kill their predecessors' cubs.

In any case, Christians live in a paradox. Those who accept Evolution have less difficulty understanding the dynamics of Nature. However, since for them God still is the cause of all things, there is no way it does not discomfort them knowing he is the cause also of everything that in Nature, from the human point of view, is bad.

Fundamentalist Christians, those who believe every word of the book of Genesis and, therefore, reject Evolution, live in an even bigger paradox. They believe the Devil is responsible for everything that is wrong and bad, consequently also for all the negative aspects of the world. Like it or not, they give Satan powers that make him a mini-god with the capacity to change Nature and the course of events. In their conception, with the entrance of sin God sort of handed Earth over to the Devil, reason why apostle John calls him "prince of this world", who then had carte blanche to transform paradisiacal Nature into one that reflects his perverse mind. This, by the way contradictory, argumentative juggling is necessary for them to be able to sustain the idea that a loving, but especially perfect, god has no way to produce anything that is fruit of imperfection, that is, sin.

When a cat catches a mouse, it does not kill it immediately. It gives the feline pleasure to make its prey suffer first, releasing it and grabbing it innumerable times. But that is nothing compared to what orcas do to seals. The killer whales visibly delight in martyring them, throwing them all over the place until they tear them apart. There is no apparent reason for orcas to inflict such suffering on seals. They could kill them instantly, but instead prefer to maul them to death. If Evolution is a lie, who taught these predators to play like that?

The hymn *All Things Bright and Beautiful*, much sung in the Protestant world, resembles someone who eats from a panettone only the candied fruits. In using Nature to prove that God exists, Christians choose from it only what is most pleasant. The refrain and the first verse of this hymn, which ends by emphasizing that God "made all things well", say:

All things bright and beautiful,
all creatures great and small,
all things wise and wonderful,
the Lord God made them all.

Each little flower that opens,
each little bird that sings,
he made their glowing colours,
he made their tiny wings.

Annoyed by this naive bias, the British comedy group Monty Python composed a satirical version of this hymn, entitled *All Things Dull and Ugly*:

All things dull and ugly,
all creatures short and squat,
all things rude and nasty,
the Lord God made the lot.

Each little snake that poisons,
each little wasp that stings,
he made their brutish venom,
he made their horrid wings.

All things sick and cancerous,
all evil great and small,
all things foul and dangerous,
the Lord God made them all.

Each nasty little hornet,
each beastly little squid.
Who made the spiky urchin?
Who made the sharks? He did!

All things scabbed and ulcerous,
all pox, both great and small,
putrid, foul and gangrenous,
the Lord God made them all.

Judaism does not preach the existence of a heavenly creature who, by rebelling against God, became the inventor of sin. Jews believe that, since everything that exists must have its origin in Yahweh, the biblical god is the author of both good and evil. The conception that the brightest of all angels was expelled from Heaven, since then fights against God and is "the god of this world" (2 Corinthians 4:4), over which he has almost absolute dominion, being capable of possessing the bodies of people — and animals —, was introduced by Christianity. In it, Satan is the causer of all kinds of evil, from the smallest to the greatest, and responsible for all misfortunes, catastrophes, diseases, violence and misery. His objective is to do as much damage as possible, turning the world into a real hell.

While the *New Testament* has a fixation with the person of the Devil, referring to him many times, the *Old Testament* almost never mentions him. In the book of Job, the most prominent allusion, we clearly read that Satan not only is not God's enemy but also has no power at all, acting only and exclusively under divine permission and commission. Crucial to the Jewish conception of the divine origin of evil is what Isaiah 45:7 says: "I form the light and create darkness, I bring prosperity and create disaster; I, the Lord, do all these things". Assuming that the Universe was created by a single god, the idea that he is the author not only of good but also evil, as the Jews believe, is more coherent.

Religious fundamentalists loathe Evolution, but Nature is exactly the way one expects from a nature that developed slowly. The "cruelty" among living beings, diseases, volcanoes, earthquakes, tsunamis, asteroid impacts, solar flares and explosions of stars are consistent with a universe that evolved. In one created by a perfect deity, all things would have to make sense and have a purpose. Yet, what would be the purpose, for example, of comets and asteroids, objects that can cause enormous damage, including the extinction of life? If Earth was created, why are there volcanism and earthquakes? What sense does a solar system with eight planets make, if seven of them are inhospitable? What is the purpose of stars collapsing and starting to spin 700 times a second? Why does a perfect god, giver of eternal life, create stars with a limited lifetime? In every galaxy, every year a sun dies. From which it follows that, in a universe with 200 billion galaxies, more than 6,000 stars die every second.

As incredible as it seems, the classic explanation biblical literalists give to questions like these is: "Sin". Galaxy collisions? Sin. Seaquakes? Sin. Sin explains all the bizarrenesses of Nature. Well, to claim, for example, that stars are swallowed by black holes as a consequence of a bite on a forbidden fruit is to demand a superhuman simplemindedness from those who reason.

When, in a conversation, I mentioned the black holes, an Evangelical interrupted me shouting: "That's mad scientist stuff!". Another got upset because I said the uncountable craters on the Moon are incompatible with a created universe. Biblical literalists run away from many scientific themes like the Devil runs away from the cross, because they embarrass them, scratch their conception of God and raise doubts. The fact that stars are devoured by black holes does not prove the nonexistence of God, but incites to reflection. However, reflecting on the biblical conception of God is, for the majority of Christians, the same as doubting him, and those who doubt him go to that invisible place where doubters are roasted on coals.

Apropos of that, those who want to disconcert, perhaps even irritate, a biblical-fundamentalist Evangelical do not need to wear themselves out articulating long sentences. Similar to an experiment in which one studies the reactions of individuals to certain stimuli, loud and clear they can exclaim "Dinosaurs!" and stare at the believer to see how he will react. In fact, Jurassic reptiles are one of the factors that most perturb promoters of the creationist doctrine. There are not a few Christians who seriously believe that, when destroying Earth with a flood, God took the trouble to preserve specimens of the dinosaurs in a boat, only to deliver them to extinction as soon as they left it.

Since for Christians the biblical god can do only good, they need another being to be responsible for evil. This is where the talking snake enters the story, a cosmic battle, with God on one side and the Devil on the other. As he is not omnipresent, Satan alone would not be capable of causing all the evil in the world. Because of this, it is necessary to imagine him with henchmen; many, many henchmen. It is not known how many demons "exist", but since in the Christian conception every human being is a constant target of temptations, there must be at least one demon for every earthling. If that is true, what will happen the day humans outnumber demons? Will there be a decrease in the amount of sins committed? Or will Satan's henchmen work harder to compensate?

I have found myself trying to imagine how boring a demon's life must be. Millennium after millennium, having nothing to do but pester people. And for what, if the war is already lost? I do not know, but if I were a demon I would certainly suffer from deep depression. By the way, can demons commit suicide? If not, being a demon must be a torture. If yes, how do they do to commit suicide? Do they throw themselves into a black hole? If they have no way to commit suicide, does one or the other sometimes throw up his hands and bellow: "That's it, I've had enough!", and go take a little break in the back of beyond? When he has nothing else to do, does the Devil, just for fun, instigate a demon to do good?

As one can see, I have several doubts about Devil and demons. All of them very serious. As I understand it, they go through walls.

If not, how do they get into my apartment to tempt me? Through the windows? It has happened to me that the doorbell rang, I opened the door and did not see anyone. Did I open the door for a demon? If they can go through walls, demons can go also through floors and ceilings. Would it not be funny, if we could see their heads going up through the floor and their feet going down through the ceiling? Would it not be even funnier, if it were the other way around? If they go through everything, how do they do to stand on the floor or sit down? Oh, demons do not stand or sit, they are always floating? If they go through everything, how do they do to possess the body of a person? To get rid of the demon, a possessed person just needs to run away, right? The demon that was tasked with taking possession of a parkour practitioner is certainly the one who swears the most. Can demons pass through each other too? And how about a demon being possessed by another demon? In this case, who would perform the exorcism? Beelzebub? When a demon wants to travel from Brazil to Japan, does he take a shortcut through the center of Earth? Since they are not subject to the laws of Physics, do demons travel at a speed greater than that of light? Are there demons on airplanes, pestering the passengers? Worse: the pilots? Do demons fight each other for the right to work in the first class? Are there demons in space stations, making the lives of the cosmonauts hell? And when the astronauts went to the Moon, did any demon go with them to tempt them there? To what kind of temptation is an astronaut on the Moon subjected? Get naked in public?

From that, one can get a glimpse of how absurd the idea of Devil and demons is. I never understood how a demon does to induce someone to sin. By telepathy? Whispering in his ears? Through electromagnetic waves, which he, striking a magician pose, radiates through his hands? The religious conception of temptation makes no sense at all. By the way, as far as I know, all Christian denominations preach that Satan cannot even read people's minds. Therefore, he has no power to implant in them sinful thoughts.

This is the definition that the *Collins Dictionary* gives for connivance: "Willingness to allow or assist something to happen even though you know it is wrong; passive cooperation, as by consent or pretended ignorance". God is omniscient, Satan is not. God is omnipotent, Satan is not. Thus, whatever the Devil has power to do, nothing happens that God does not know beforehand and does not tolerate and permit. Consequently, if the Devil has power to cause evils and God knows the future and has power to prevent them, but does not, the biblical deity is an accomplice of Satan.

Although omnipotent, the god of the Bible also has assistants. This is probably because with good angels contrasting with bad angels the story gets more exciting. More than that, it gets hilarious, because if it is not like one sometimes sees in comedies — a person being nagged in one ear by a demon and in the other a good angel saying: "Don't pay any attention to him!" —, then what is it like? If it really is like that, then the good and the bad angels are only inches away from each other. I am curious to know if they sometimes fight with punches and kicks. And what happens when a bad angel wins and the person sins? Does the good angel cry, or does he get angry and send the demon to Hell? And speaking of crying, is it true that Jesus cries, as many Evangelical parents use to tell their children to psychologically terrorize them? I keep trying to imagine the size of the tears of a being who created a universe with a diameter of many billions of light years.

Anyone who has an eternity at his disposal does not need to hurry. In view of this, it took God six days to create everything, which he found not just good but "very good". One realizes, therefore, a colossal disproportionality in God, because of a mere bite on a fruit, throwing in the garbage all his "very good" Nature, being forced to practically remake it, so radical and profound was the transformation it had to undergo. Would it not have been much easier to recreate the first couple?

It is common for Christians to answer this question by saying that God did not kill Eve and Adam in order not to get the reputation of a tyrant. However, this argument is unfounded, because the Bible clearly shows that it did not cause him any embarrassment to kill anyone. There was no rebuke or second chance. The divine punishment was immediate. God killed people, for example, for simply complaining, and it is undeniable that he exterminated also innocent people, as he did with the Egyptian children. It is illogical for him to transform a paradisiacally perfect world into a cruel one for fear of being labeled as evil, since bringing suffering and pain on billions of innocent people for thousands of years is not only worse than making a single couple disappear but even confirms the evil character of God. If he can everything, with a snap of his fingers God could have made the totality of his creation, including Heaven, with all its angels, disappear. There would be no one to demand from him an explanation. Then it would be just about starting from scratch. In any case, if those who die repentant go to Paradise, by killing Eve and Adam following the bite on the forbidden fruit God would have catapulted them straight to Paradise, exactly where they already were. End of the story. There was no need to make innumerable generations of innocents suffer.

The Bible says that God is love and the biggest proof of that is his Plan of Salvation. Assuming that everything Christianity preaches is true, it took God 4,000 years to send his son — who is himself — to Earth to be sacrificed and thus pay for Eve and Adam's apparently unforgivable mistake of listening to a talking snake. One gets a better idea of how long 4,000 years are when one says "four thousand years" very slowly. Four. Thousand. Years. So, why make Humanity live so long in a world full of suffering? Would ten years not have been sufficient to teach the first couple a good lesson? OK, then, how about a hundred? A hundred years is quite a long time, is it not? All right, let us be generous: a thousand. Ignoring the incoherence of punishing children for the errors of their parents, a thousand years of illnesses, catastrophes, injustices, conflicts and deaths would have more than sufficed to punish Eve, Adam and their offspring.

God of love, Yahweh did not forgive his children for taking a bite on a fruit. Mere human being, I forgive my child for doing much worse things. Need I say more?

As if 4,000 years were not much, another 2,000 years have passed since Jesus came to give proof of God's love: to die on a cross — just like thousands of people before and after him. Two. Thousand. Years. On what logical basis did the sinful state of the world have to be prolonged, if the Plan of Salvation had already been executed? Should the world not have ended two thousand years ago? For 6,000 years the world has been agonizing under the effects of the curse that God cast on Eve and Adam. This disproportionality between transgression and punishment makes the penalty unjust and evidences the mythological nature of the biblical account.

Idea for a documentary scene. At the door of a Catholic church, ask the faithful coming out of Mass: "If Jesus had been hanged, would you carry around your neck a gallows miniature?".

Religion and doubt are incompatible. Because of this, religious people have justifications for each of the innumerable incoherences and contradictions of their belief. These excuses are heard and repeated so many times that, although evidently unsatisfactory, they regard them as plausible. When we question, for example, the reason for God to kill the priests Nadab and Abihu, on top of that in such an extreme way, making fire fall from the sky, Jews and Christians answer: "Because God is love, but also justice". When it is not possible for them to answer in a way with which they themselves are satisfied, as when faced with the question why God does not reveal to a devout scientist the formula to cure cancer, believers resort to the greatest and vaguest of all their excuses: "How unsearchable his judgments, and his paths beyond tracing out!" (Romans 11:33), which is nothing more than a simple "God knows what he is doing". The human being is never excusable; God, always. "God knows what he is doing" is the red emergency button that religious people press whenever their minds is in danger of starting to reason.

It is practically impossible for a believer to scrutinize ("examine carefully and minutely, in order to discover, perceive, know" [*Houaiss Dictionary*]) his religious convictions, because where there is devotion there is no critical eye. Since it tends to annihilate faith, doubt is the principal enemy of religions, reason why they instill in the minds of their followers that to doubt is to affront God. The truth is that doubting is the most natural thing in the world, so natural that it even is easy to make a Christian have religious doubts without feeling he is challenging God. It suffices to tell him, for example, that Islam is the true religion. The Christian will not only doubt, but even laugh. To doubt his own religion is a sin. To doubt the religion of others is a duty.

If the mind of someone who believes with all his heart and soul in any ideology is conditioned to defend its incongruities, how much more so the mind of someone who professes a religion, which indoctrinates its adherents to see doubt as rebellion. The submission to its dogmas must be total, otherwise it does not make sense to follow it. One cannot have only 95% faith, not even 99.99%. As Jesus said, it is all or nothing: "Whoever is not with me is against me, and whoever does not gather with me scatters" (Matthew 12:30). If faith is 100% belief, that is, absolute certainty, then where there is faith there is no free reflection. To truly reflect is to seek the naked truth, whatever it may be, and not a preestablished one, the confirmation of a belief. It is not counting the hits and ignoring the misses, but taking everything into account.

When he has no evidence, there is no problem with a police officer being convinced of someone's guilt. He will be a good police agent if, despite his conviction, he remains aware that he may be wrong. His commitment is to the truth, which he suspects, but does not know what it is. The good policeman wants to find the culprit, whoever he is, and not do everything to make the person he most suspects be the culprit.

Unless one has been indoctrinated from the cradle up, believing is a decision. Anyone who believes has decided to believe. Facts do not matter, incoherences and absurdities are justified. Everything that goes against his belief is ignored by the believer's wishful thinking. In view of this, it does not take a brilliant mind to recognize that religions have nothing to do with reason. In order for the eyes of reason to open, a disenchantment must first occur. Mine was the result of my beginning to realize discrepancies between what the Bible says and reality. One beautiful day, the biblical accounts came to sound like mythological tales, dogmas such as Original Sin and Expiatory Sacrifice to seem irrational to me. At the same time, I began to feel that the religiosity demanded by the denomination to which I belonged was excessive, to realize that I was member of a church that, although it sells itself as modern, is fundamentalist, a club of alienated people, stuck to conventions, people who, for observing a superfluous set of rules, consider themselves special, privileged, chosen. Having my mind conditioned by both a religion and a religious organization had come to seem to me unnatural and, consequently, wrong.

In many people, there is, to a greater or lesser degree, a predisposition to be enchanted by beliefs, creeds, doctrines, dogmas, faith, ideals, ideas, ideologies, philosophies, teachings and theories of all kinds. No matter how incoherent, weird, ridiculous, absurd or vile a system of ideas may be, there will always be people willing to follow and defend it. Even psychopaths have no trouble attracting people who are willing to do anything for them, including killing and committing suicide. If we accuse a religious leader of being deceitful, fanatical or intolerant, his followers will defend him, accusing us of persecuting him.

Christians believe that Christ is about to come back at any moment. Every day is Jesus' return day. Paradoxically, they live as if that will never happen, striving as much as any non-Christian to prosper and ascend socially. How could this not be evidence that they themselves are little or not at all convinced of their Master's return?

Jesus stated he will return only after his followers have knocked on the door of all houses, warning all Humanity of his imminent return and the destruction of the world. The fact is that 2,000 long years have already passed since the Nazarene conditioned the end of everything to the preaching of the Gospel and, despite the enormous efforts of the 40,000 Christian denominations, the world insists on not ending. Not only that: in spite of all the wrong things, in many respects the world today is better than in the past. Those who disagree should build a time machine and go to live, for example, in the Europe of 300, 400 or 500 years ago.

The more Humanity progresses, the more the religion that preaches regression, worsening, ruin, destruction (preconditions for Christ's return), loses credibility. One should note that radio transmissions have been existing for about 95 years and television broadcasting, 65 years. For more than 25 years the masses have had access to the internet. Thus, with so many churches, missionaries, religious radio and television programs, Christian sites and the countless number of ecclesiastical publications, it is almost impossible that there are still people who have never heard of Jesus. Why, then, does he not come back? What is he waiting for?

Let us imagine that no one had ever heard of the Bible. Not a single human being, as if the world had always existed without it. Let us imagine that someone started to spread the word that he discovered some parchment scrolls that talk, among other things, about a mud doll that became a man, a rib that became a woman, invisible beings with wings on their backs wielding swords of fire, a boat in which animals from all over the world lived for more than a year, a chariot of fire that came down from the sky to pick up a man who had made fire fall from the sky, a man who walked on water and with five loaves and two little fish fed an enormous crowd and a 1,380 miles high cubiform city made of gold. How would we react? What would we think of the discoverer of these scrolls, if he claimed to believe everything that is written in them? Would we consider him mentally sane? Would we find plausible the accounts contained in these parchments?

Why, then, for so many people do these stories not sound like nonsenses, hallucinations, insanities? It is simple: we grew up hearing them. We are used to the biblical supernatural. Because of this, even if someone does not believe, for example, in Devil he will not call abnormal a person who believes in him, since billions of people believe in invisible beings with wings on their backs. If someone tells a disbeliever that he from time to time sees angels, that is hardly a reason for the disbeliever to avoid relating to him. On the other hand, the disbeliever probably will be afraid to be friends with someone who swears he sees werewolves. How would we regard someone who is convinced that some people are aliens who have taken over human bodies? However, we do not label as insane those who daily talk to a being no one sees, by whom they wish to be possessed and for whose return they long, so that he takes them to a place no one knows where it is.

On a bus, we are very likely to change seats if we sit next to a person who tells us he believes that a certain Xenu, the dictator of the Galactic Confederacy, using a mixture of alcohol and ethylene glycol, froze, 75 million years ago, billions of inhabitants of 75 planets and brought them in DC-8 airplanes to Earth, where they were unloaded around volcanoes, which he then exploded with hydrogen bombs, killing the aliens, whose spirits were captured, taken to movie theaters and forced to watch a 36-day-long movie that implanted falsehoods in the minds of these spirits, who since then take over human beings, causing them much harm, but who can be cast out, if the possessed are willing to pay for many years of auditing in the organization that has the capacity to liberate them: the Church of Scientology. On the other hand, unless he stinks, we will not distance ourselves from a person who believes in the cosmic battle between Jesus and Satan.

One of the principal reasons why so many people believe the evidently fantastic stories of the Bible is the fact that it is an ancient book. If it had been written these days, an overwhelming majority would not think twice before considering it a work of fiction. Another reason is tradition. The Book of Books is rooted in European and American cultures because for hundreds of years it is being passed down from generation to generation with the label of sacred. Conversely, no Christian believes what religious texts even older than the Bible say, since, although ancient, in the Occident they were not labeled as sacred and as such passed on from parent to child.

Those who consider true everything the Bible says cannot find it foolish to believe in dragons. One of these beasts, from whose nostrils "smoke pours as from a boiling pot over burning reeds. Its breath sets coals ablaze, and flames dart from its mouth", is described in rich detail in Job 41. Based on the *Midrash*, a compilation of rabbinical exegeses, Orthodox Jews believe this dragon exists.

Everyone has the right to believe in whatever he wants. However, it is very unlikely that a person who believes in the Chupacabra will be offended by criticism or jokes. In contrast, with religious people there is no relaxation. The moment the subject is religion, things get serious, very, very serious. This severity is notorious especially in the Semitic religions Judaism, Christianity and Islam, of which the imposition of fear through threat of punishment is a fundamental part. For example, the biblical god "cannot be mocked" (Galatians 6:7). Or, as Brazilian Evangelicals like to warn: "God is not to be played with". No wonder:

> The Lord is a jealous and avenging God; the Lord takes vengeance and is filled with wrath. The Lord takes vengeance on his foes. [...] His way is in the whirlwind and the storm, and clouds are the dust of his feet. He rebukes the sea and dries it up. [...] The mountains quake before him and the hills melt away. The earth trembles at his presence, the world and all who live in it. Who can withstand his indignation? Who can endure his fierce anger? His wrath is poured out like fire; the rocks are shattered before him.
>
> (Nahum 1:2-6)

Once, in Austria, a female friend, receptive to a variety of spiritual currents, told me she believed in spirits. I asked her why I did not see them. She answered: "Because you are not open to them". In other words, spirits exist, but they appear only to those who believe in them. Interesting, is it not? Some time later, I bumped on the street into a female acquaintance whom I had not seen for many years and has a Master's degree. At the café on the corner, where we went to catch up with each other, I was surprised to discover she had become an esotericist. At one point, she fell silent and stared at me with a smile. I asked her the reason why she was looking at me that way and she told me it was because she was seeing an angel sitting next to me. I did not know what to say or do, but I confess that I considered faking a trip to the bathroom and getting out of there.

In all the years I was an Evangelical, no angel appeared to me or to the multitude of believers I met, including pastors and the devout faithful. Cherubim did not manifested themselves even to evangelist Billy Graham. Asked if angels still appear, the reverend replied: "I'm convinced they do, on occasion, although sometimes we may not even be aware of them, because they have chosen to appear as ordinary human beings". In other words, the perhaps greatest of the Protestant world's icons has never seen a heavenly messenger, and if one had appeared to him Graham would not have realized it, since anyone who crossed his path could have been an angel.

If angels exist and are as portrayed in Daniel 10, you had better hope you are not visited by them, because the chances of a cardiac arrest are enormous:

> I looked up and there before me was a man dressed in linen, with a belt of fine gold around his waist. His body was like topaz, his face like lightning, his eyes like flaming torches, his arms and legs like the gleam of burnished bronze, and his voice like the sound of a multitude.

Despite all secularism, billions of people are still of the opinion that religious beliefs are a natural part of life and without them it is not possible to live well. Indignation about the finitude of life, yearning for a paradisiacal one and longing for someone to tell them what they must do to achieve it lead many people to exempt religions from rational scrutiny, as if spirituality enjoyed a privileged position and it were normal for it to be above reason.

Religions offer "answers" to people who think that not having answers is bad. There is just one little problem with the "answers" offered by religions: they are not answers. Followers of religions and of spiritual leaders live, then, in the illusion of knowing the answers. A religious person may call "To Heaven" the answer to the question "Where do I go after I die?". It is not. It is conjecture, on top of that a perverse one, because there is no Heaven without Hell. Those who were induced to believe in Paradise were induced also to find it normal that people be tortured in a lake of fire and brimstone.

No matter the question, there is nothing wrong with not knowing the answer. Saying "I don't know" is noble, since it is honest.

I leave the dear reader with what, in an interview from 1965, said Richard Feynman, winner of the Nobel Prize in Physics:

I can't believe the special stories that've been made up about our relationship to the Universe at large, because they seem to be too simple, too connected, too local, too provincial.

How do you find out if something is true? And if you have all these theories of the different religions and all different theories about the thing, then you begin to wonder.

Start out understanding religion by saying everything is possibly wrong. Let us see. As soon as you do that, you start sliding down an edge which is harder to recover from.

With the scientific view or my father's view, that we should look to see what's true and what may not be true, once you start doubting, which, I think, to me is a very fundamental part of my soul — to doubt and to ask —, when you doubt and ask, it gets a little harder to believe.

I can live with doubt and uncertainty and not knowing. I think it's much more interesting to live not knowing than to have answers which might be wrong. I have approximate answers and possible beliefs and different degrees of certainty about different things, but I'm not absolutely sure of anything. And then many things I don't know anything about, such as whether it means anything to ask why we are here and what that question might mean. I might think about it a bit and then, if I can't figure it out, I go on to something else. But I don't have to know an answer. I don't feel frightened by not knowing things, by being lost in the mysterious Universe without having any purpose, which is the way it really is, as far as I can tell, possibly. It doesn't frighten me.

3

Myth

"God made first the man,
the woman was born afterwards.
That's why the woman
works always for both."

— Carlos Lyra
(*Maria Moita*)

MEMBER OF A Christian denomination imported from the United States, therefore belonging to the conservative segment of the Protestantism with Puritan roots, my mother taught my brothers and me to have deep respect for the Bible, which had to be handled with a zeal that bordered on superstition. No other book or anything else could be placed on it. The Book of Books had to be always on the top.

For someone who grows up hearing the world is corrupted by sin and will soon be destroyed, that our home is not here, but in Heaven, the only safe place to store up treasures, because there they are consumed neither by moth nor by rust, nor are they stolen, where everyone will have his own mansion of gold, and that the noblest of all objectives is to lead as many people as possible to believe in Christ, so that they too be rewarded with mansions of gold, it is natural to think that no profession can be more important than that of a church pastor. Thus, although, as a child, I dreamed of becoming a comic book and animation artist, at the age of twenty I moved to São Paulo and entered the Faculty of Theology of the church to which I belonged. At the end of the fifth semester, in July 1989, I abandoned studies and, with the purpose of earning money to buy an airplane ticket to Europe, went from door to door selling Bibles. Two months later, with the ticket in my hand and 600 dollars in my pocket, I crossed the skies of the pond (the Atlantic Ocean) with a vague idea of what I wanted to do.

No one loses overnight the desire to go to church. Distancing oneself from it is a gradual process, especially for someone who "grew up in the church" participating in its programs and activities. Because of this, despite my doubts, in Europe I attended church for two more years, but more for social than spiritual reasons.

There are believers who disagree with the way some things in the Bible are interpreted by their church, but, because they are convinced it still is the right religious movement, they remain in it as discontents or rebels. Others change denomination and some start their own church. In my case, the problem was both the Bible and the church. At a certain stage of the game, I began to have difficulty reconciling with reality what the Holy Scriptures teach. The creation of the world in six days, the Flood, the plagues of Egypt, the pillar of fire in the desert, fire that falls from the sky, chariots of fire, apparitions of angels, resurrections of the dead, miracles and everything else supernatural that is related in the Bible, including bizarre tales, such as of Balaam's talking ass and of the two hundred foreskins that David brought to Saul, so that he could become his son-in-law. One beautiful day, all that came to sound like cock-and-bull stories.

The great majority of Christians, consisting of Catholics and European Protestants, do not interpret the whole Bible literally. They are believers who generally do not combat Science, notably the Scientific Theory of Evolution. Biblical literalists are a minority, most of whom are found in the Third World, precisely where the population's level of education is low. However, although a minority, we are talking about many millions of fundamentalists. In Brazil alone, about 50 million people believe, for example, that the prophet Jonah spent three days in the belly of a whale and are certain that at Joshua's request God made Earth stop spinning just so that Israel could destroy its enemies.

Once founded on biblical literalism, churches no longer have a way to abandon this foundation. If the dear reader is a member of one that from the beginning has taught, for example, that prophet Elisha's floating axe is a true story, how likely is it that its pastor will begin a sermon by saying: "Dear sisters and brothers, today's sermon is about the lessons we can learn from the Flood… uh… legend"? True to the doctrines of your biblical-fundamentalist church, you spent your life combating Evolution, accusing it of being a demonic doctrine. How, then, would you feel, if, in view of countless scientific evidence, your church admitted Evolution is true? Even if History, Archaeology and Science show them that they are wrong, fundamentalist churches will continue to be fundamentalist.

The *Pentateuch*, the first five books of the Bible, took its present form about 2,500 years ago, but from even older oral traditions and text fragments. Since the *New Testament* was written, almost 2,000 long years have passed. Well, anyone endowed with common sense recognizes that 2,000 years is too much time to expect veracity of every account and accuracy of every word from a compilation of copies of copies of more copies of rags of fragments of parchments from the Iron Age containing narratives also from the Bronze Age. If this is so with books that are just centenary, would it not be so with an anthology that is millenary?

If the god who created trillions of galaxies wanted to reveal something to his creatures, would he do it through, of all things, a work so imperfect, since it is imprecise, obscure and susceptible to errors of writing, copying, translation and interpretation, like the compilation of oral traditions and copies of manuscripts that we call Bible? How likely is it that a deity is on the one hand so intelligent and powerful as to create the Universe and on the other incapable of finding a way to reveal himself in such a manner that his revelations do not cause even a single confusion, but are unequivocally understood by all people of all times and cultures?

Can God be holier than his angels? No. Holy is holy. If angels are holy, they are as holy as God. No more, no less. So, if it is because of sin that God cannot appear to humans to speak directly to them, as he did in the Garden of Eden, when he walked among the trees, why are angels, who also are holy, not subject to this limitation? The Bible relates several apparitions of angels. What, then, would happen, if these celestial messengers, with the traditional wings on their backs (jaw-dropping aerospace technology made in Heaven), appeared floating three feet above the ground in public squares, beaches, companies, schools, airports, in short, places where they could be seen by all people? If angels showed themselves to everyone, saying: "The God of the Bible sent us", in a single instant any and all doubt about the existence of the deity of the book with the black cover would disappear, all the theological, historical and scientific divergences generated by it would once and for all be "sent into space" (Brazilian expression that means destroyed). Churches would become obsolete. The billions of dollars in tithes and offerings to maintain temples (and enrich pastors) around the world would be redirected to social projects. Even without showing his face, it would be extremely easy for God to prove his existence. However, the creator of centillions of stars and planets preferred to do it by means of the book that aroused the most conflicts, still today provokes discord and caused the death of millions of people.

The literal interpretation of the Bible is an incoherence even for historical reasons. Anyone who, like me, has walked the streets of Jerusalem knows the frustration of being informed that the places where Jesus has been are not historical, but only symbolic, accepted by tradition. This is true even for the places that are venerated as of his birth and crucifixion.

The Bible says Jesus did exceptional things, reason why he was followed by large crowds. Besides curing lepers and making the lame walk and the blind see, he raised the dead. Imagine, dear reader, a man who gives life to corpses, even to those that have already started to stink. Would you not expect a man like that to be the most talked about on the planet? Would there not be several books about him, written by people from different places? Would he not, at the very least, be mentioned in innumerable letters from eyewitnesses? It is, therefore, more than natural to find it strange that the personality who made the greatest impact on the history of Humanity is not mentioned by any historical source of his time. The Gospels themselves, of which, by the way, no original exists, were written several decades after the death of Christ.

The earliest extrabiblical allusions to the man who multiplied loaves are no more than two simple mentions in the vast work of Roman-Jewish historian Flavius Josephus, too small to be worthy of a figure who caused such a commotion. If the historian was sure that Jesus existed and performed all the miracles related in the

Gospels, especially that of making the dead walk, would he not have dedicated whole pages to these incredible events? Moreover, in view of so many undeniable and astonishing wonders, would one not expect that Josephus had become a Christian? Yet, not only was he always Jewish, he was also one of Judaism's greatest apologists.

Besides the brevity of these mentions contrasting with the magnitude of Jesus and the extent of Josephus' work, when the historian was born the Nazarene had already died. If he really re-ferred to the Master of the Christians, he did so six decades, or 60 long years, after his death. To make matters worse, the oldest copy of *Antiquities of the Jews* is a Latin translation made about 400 years later. For these and other reasons, there is broad consensus among historians and exegetes that these allusions to Jesus are nothing more than fraudulent additions. As a devout Jew, who at the age of nineteen had become a Pharisee, Josephus' objective was to glorify Jewish culture by means of a monumental literary work that would impress Greeks and Romans. In light of this, it is easy to recognize that he never could be the author of these words:

About this time, there lived Jesus, a wise man, if indeed one ought to call him a man, for he was one who performed surprising deeds and was a teacher of such people as accept the truth gladly. He won over many Jews and many of the Greeks. He was the Christ. And when, upon the accusation of the principal men among us, Pilate had con-demned him to a cross, those who had first come to love him did not cease. He appeared to them, spending a third day restored to life, for the prophets of God had foretold these things and a thousand other marvels about him. And the tribe of the Christians, so called after him, has still to this day not disappeared.

Was the coming of the Creator of the Universe himself to Earth not the most important of all happenings? Why, then, all this mystery surrounding the existence of the man-god who was none other than the Savior of Humanity? Why was precisely the event that changed the course of History not widely documented by Jewish, Roman and Greek eyewitnesses?

Even before he was born, it was known that he would be someone special. A supernatural being informed his mother that the child she was to conceive would not be a mere mortal but would be divine. He was born miraculously, and he became an unusually precocious young man. As an adult he left home and went on an itinerant preaching ministry, urging his listeners to live, not for the material things of this world, but for what is spiritual. He gathered a number of disciples around him, who became convinced that his teachings were divinely inspired, in no small part because he himself was divine. He proved it to them by doing many miracles, healing the sick, casting out demons, and raising the dead. But at the end of his life, he roused opposition, and his enemies delivered him over to the Roman authorities for judgment. Still, after he left this world, he returned to meet his followers in order to convince them that he was not really dead but lived on in the heavenly realm. Later some of his followers wrote books about him.

About whom, dear reader, is the above text talking? Obviously, about Jesus, right? Wrong. It was written by Bart Ehrman, a professor at the University of North Carolina and one of the most respected authorities on *New Testament*, and reproduces exactly what was spread about Apollonius of Tyana, a Greek philosopher who supposedly was a contemporary of Jesus, but in present-day Turkey. Like the Nazarene, one is not absolutely sure if Apollonius really existed. Even so, and as incredible as it seems, there is more historical evidence of him than of the Son of God.

The fact that there are no eyewitness references to the Nazarene is not a bagatelle. In fact, this lack of historicity is the principal reason why several scholars conclude that he is a myth. And among the experts who believe Jesus existed, some, like Ehrman, are of the opinion that, by virtue of their innumerable differences and errors, the Gospels are not reliable historical sources. Consequently, if there was a historical Jesus, much of what is attributed to him is legend. Certainly, he was an ordinary man, that is, without superpowers. Otherwise, it is incredible that, despite being constantly followed by crowds and closely observed by Jews, Romans and Greeks, no one has written even a single line about his spectacular deeds.

If the Nazarene really existed, should his existence, the most important thing for the largest religion in the world, not be so obvious as to be ridiculous to debate about it?

What do Moses, Buddha, Jesus and Mohammed have in common? The dense cloud of obscurity that surrounds them. Historically, that is, outside their own religious traditions, absolutely nothing can be known about the principal figures of the large religions. Zero. Coincidence? Why does religion have to be a mysterious thing? It is simple: because without mystery there is no religion. Clearly, religions live from uncertainty.

Millions of Christians are convinced stories like that of Hananiah, Mishael and Azariah, who walked unharmed through the flames of Nebuchadnezzar's furnace, are real, but it does not seem strange to them that similar things do not happen outside the Bible. Of the great figures of the Protestant Reformation who were put to burn in bonfires, none came down from the pole, shook the ashes off his scorched clothes, said "My, this fire made me so thirsty! Can someone give me a glass of water, please? Very kind of you. God bless" and went home. The biblical god delivered the three Hebrews from the oven of Babylon's king, but not a single reformer.

In 2014, after being severely beaten, Shama and Shehzad, a Pakistani Christian couple, from the locality of Kot Radha Kishan, were thrown into a bonfire, accused of blasphemy by a crowd of Muslims chanting: "God is great!". Neither the woman, who was pregnant, nor the husband survived. Would that not have been an excellent opportunity for God to show all disbelievers that the biblical accounts of divine intervention are true, and all religious people that Christianity is the true religion? Similar to what he did for Daniel's friends, it would have sufficed that God made the couple stand up and walk out of the fire. From that day on, what Muslim would dare to touch Christians?

The flight of the Hebrews from Egypt, or the Exodus, is one of the most important biblical narratives for the Judeo-Christian faith and fundamental to the historical identity of the nation of Israel. It is commemorated every year on Pesach, or Passover, one of Judaism's principal festivals. In 2014, Stephen Rosenberg, a senior fellow at the Albright Institute of Archaeological Research, in Jerusalem, published an article in *The Jerusalem Post* entitled *The Exodus: Does Archaeology Have a Say?* The first sentence of the article is short: "No!". According to the Bible, more than 600,000 men, with wives, children, animals and belongings, in addition to a multitude of non-Hebrews, exited Egypt. If each man was accompanied by one woman and only one child, we have a total of at least 1.8 million people who left the Pharaonic lands. Two children for every couple increase this number to 2.4 million, excluding the non-Israelites. Imagine more than 2,400,000 people wandering in the desert. Some Bible passages say the Israelites lived in Egypt for 400 years; others, 430. Despite this almost half millennium of Israelite presence in Egypt and the four decades in which more than two million people camped in the desert, Rosenberg states that there is not a single piece of archaeological evidence to support the biblical accounts: "Nothing on the slavery of the Israelites, nothing on the plagues that persuaded Pharaoh to let them go, nothing on the miraculous crossing of the Red Sea. Nothing at all". "It's embarrassing", says the researcher. The same conclusion reached Israel Finkelstein, another prominent Israeli archaeologist, professor at Tel Aviv University. According to Finkelstein, the Israelites have never been in Egypt.

Curious to know what Jewish religious authorities think about the literal interpretation of the Bible, Andrew Silow-Carroll, editor-in-chief of the *New Jersey Jewish News*, asked the following question of five influential rabbis, whose answers he published in December 2007: "Does belief in Torah mean every word is true?". Rabbi Richard Hirsh, then executive director of the Reconstructionist Rabbinical Association, responded:

Since the Bible is an anthology of collected writings of human beings over a period of 1,000 years, we should not expect and will not find consistency, and we often find contradictions, which sort of makes it hard to believe in every word. There are parts of Scripture from which I happily dissent, such as stories that imagine God commanding the Israelites to commit genocide (see Deuteronomy 20:17) or parents to stone a rebellious child (Deuteronomy 21:18-21).

As for rabbi David Nelson, associate director of the Association of Reform Zionists of America, he stated:

> If I believe the Bible literally? Certainly not. I believe that the Bible is a product of human authorship, and to the extent that all human creativity is driven by God, then I see God's hand in its pages. But that does not make it all true.

Although belonging to the conservative wing of Judaism, Rabbi Joyce Newmark said:

> I don't believe that the Torah is necessarily factual. I certainly don't believe that the world was created in seven days some 6,000 years ago. I do believe that God created the world and everything in it, and that the specific process He used and the exact time frame aren't really important.

If not even rabbis, that is, those who know better than anyone what we call *Old Testament*, a book written by their people, interpret the Bible in a literal way (with the exception of the small ultra-Orthodox minority), why, then, this obsession of Evangelicalism with biblical literalism? Do Evangelicals want to reinvent the wheel? Is the literal interpretation of the Bible not the reflection of the fundamentalists' simplistic view and the proof that their faith is based purely on fear of displeasing God? Besides a convenient escape from reality to the comfortable illusion of certainty of knowing all the answers, taking the Bible literally is nothing but superstition and idolatry.

In his stand-up comedy *Red, White & Screwed*, Lewis Black, a well-known Jewish-American comedian, speaking about then-President George W. Bush, who is a creationist, said:

> I never thought that during the course of my life, a president would be elected who didn't believe in Evolution [...]. He believes that the Earth was created in seven days [...]. And why does he believe that? Because he read it in the *Old Testament*, which is the book of my people, the Jewish people. [...]

And yet, every Sunday I turn on the television set and there's a priest or a pastor reading from my book and interpreting it, and their interpretations, I have to tell you, are usually wrong. It's not their fault, because it's not their book. You never see a rabbi on TV interpreting the *New Testament*, do you?

Was the Earth created in seven days? No. For those of you who believe it was, for you Christians, let me tell you that you do not understand the Jewish people. We Jews understand that it did not take place in seven days, and that's because we know what we're good at, and what we're really good at is bullshit. This is a wonderful story that was told to the people in the desert in order to distract them from the fact that they did not have air conditioning.

I would love to have the faith to believe that it took place in seven days, but I have thoughts. And that can really fuck up the faith thing. [...]

And then there are fossils. Whenever anybody tries to tell me that they believe it took place in seven days, I reach for a fossil and go: "Fossil!", and if they keep talking I throw it just over their head.

There are people who believe that dinosaurs and men lived together, that they roamed the Earth at the same time. There are museums that children go to in which they build dioramas to show them this. And what this is, purely and simply, is a clinical psychotic reaction. They are crazy. They are stone cold fuck nuts. I can't be kind about this, because these people are watching *The Flintstones* as if it were a documentary.

The nonliteral interpretation of the Bible is not a recent phenomenon, as fundamentalists like to believe. An analysis of Judaism's history shows that the figurative, metaphorical or allegorical interpretation of the biblical texts has always been part of the Jewish tradition, even before the Christian era. In the Middle Ages, Moses Maimonides, known as "the second Moses of Judaism", to this day one of the most respected rabbis, who was also a philosopher, jurisconsult, astronomer and physician, argued that the Bible should be taken literally as much as possible, but never to the detriment of reason. According to the *Jewish Encyclopedia*, Maimonides responded to a query about astrology, stating that "man should believe only what can be supported either by rational proof, by the evidence of the senses or by trustworthy authority".

The rabbi ended the letter with the sentence: "A man should never cast his reason behind him, for the eyes are set in front, not in the back".

An example of one of Maimonides' deviations from biblical literality is the wrestle that Jacob had with an angel, related in Genesis 32. Since to the rabbi it seemed irrational that a man could fight with a celestial being, for him that fight did not happen in reality, but in dream.

Many Christians look at other religions with disinterest; sometimes, disdain. Although their faith depends on a Jewish literary work, the majority of them have no idea how Jews view the book written by their ancestors. For Jews, Jewish tradition, consisting of the Oral Law, compiled in the *Mishnah*, which over the centuries received innumerable complementary elaborations, gathered in the *Gemara*, part of the *Talmud*, and the commentaries of many notorious rabbis, such as Rashi and Maimonides, is as valuable as the biblical texts themselves. Therefore, not even Orthodox Jews, whose mother tongue is Hebrew and who from an early age learn ancient Hebrew, regard the Bible as sufficiently clear or precise to be understood without auxiliary explanations. For them, rabbinical interpretations are indispensable.

A in my view positive aspect of Judaism is that in it the "truth" is not monolithic. Rabbis enjoy the freedom to diverge from each other, sometimes even diametrically. Believe it or not, there are Jews, for example, who eat pork.

A literary work that generates so much disharmony simply cannot be inspired by God, unless his objective was precisely to have fun with the arguments and discords it provokes. However, would God find funny, for example, the wars between Catholics and Protestants, the result of different ways of interpreting the Holy Book? In view of this, I can only classify as sadomasochism the fixation that fundamentalist Christians have with the literal interpretation of the Bible.

Religious dogmatism annihilates critical sense, without which there is no discovery, learning and development. Devoid of a reflective mind, we become automatons. A person who practices a religion whose principle is to follow a book to the letter is a spiritual robot without self-confidence, a healthy feeling transformed into pride and rebellion by the negativism of fundamentalists.

Unless we are children, or retards, when we are told a story we instinctively feel whether it is plausible or fanciful. Instinctively, Christians feel that the stories told by the holy books of other religions are fantastical. Yet, as incredible as it seems, they do not sense the smell of fantasy of the stories told by their own holy book, more or less like someone who is used to his own foot odor.

The Gallup survey, that I mentioned, conducted in 2014, shows that 42% of Americans believe the story of Eve and Adam. In Germany, this number drops to 12.5%, according to a 2005 survey by the Gesellschaft für Sozialforschung. A huge difference. Even so, it is about ten million Germans, citizens of one of the most developed countries of the so-called First World, who believe the woman was made from the rib of a mud doll, a snake induced her to eat a magic fruit and that this is the cause of all the evils in the Universe. These surveys show also that the lower the level of education, the more the Bible is interpreted literally. 46% of Americans with a high school education are creationists, compared with only 27% of those with a college degree. Among Germans with a college education, only 5.8% are biblical literalists. Clearly, education reduces fundamentalism.

Millions of fundamentalist Christians marvel as much as non-Christians at the scientific progress that makes space probes land on planets, moons and comets and send to Earth images from the confines of the Solar System. Yet, these biblical literalists, who every day take medicine and ride in cars and airplanes, thereby placing their trust in Science, are the same ones who ridicule it because of Evolution.

Fundamentalists suffer from cognitive dissonance so severe that many of them like to brag by citing geneticist Francis Collins, director of the Human Genome Project, as an example of a Christian scientist, even though Collins is an evolutionist and, in an interview with the site *Beliefnet*, said:

> The evidence supporting the idea that all living things are descended from a common ancestor is truly overwhelming. I would not necessar-

ily wish that to be so, as a Bible-believing Christian. But it is so. It does not serve faith well to try to deny that.

Idea for a documentary scene. Visit Francis Collins in his laboratory and thank him for confirming that the evidence proves that Evolution is true. While Collins, flattered, is smiling, ask him: "Why does a mind as brilliant as yours believe in such primitive things, like the Devil and Hell, of which neither you nor anyone else has any evidence?".

After mastering the languages of the natives sufficiently to be able to communicate with them, what did the Portuguese and Spanish conquistadors, settlers and missionaries think when they heard the indigenous beliefs' creationist accounts? Most likely something like: "Our Lady of Navigators, what a naivety! How can they believe these fables?". I suppose the supernatural stories told by the indigenes motivated the invaders to consider it a noble duty to induce them to abandon the belief in fictional narratives and start believing the "true" stories of the Bible, such as of Eve and Adam and the talking snake.

When I imagine myself in the role of a person who has never heard of the Bible and reads the first two chapters of Genesis, this is what leaps to my eye and evidences the fabulous character of this account:

- God rests.
- God makes a mud doll, breathes into its nostrils and it walks.
- God plants a garden.
- God calls a tree Tree of the Knowledge of Good and Evil.
- God warns the man that if he eats of the fruits of this mysterious tree he will be punished with death.
- God makes the animals of the field and all birds parade before the man, who gives names to all of them.
- God operates on the man and from him extracts a rib, from which he forms the woman.
- The serpent is as intelligent as humans and talks.

- Eve and Adam realize that they are naked and sew themselves aprons of leaves.
- God walks in the garden, talking.
- God does not know, or pretends not to know, where Eve and Adam are hiding.
- God curses the serpent and condemns it to eat dust.
- God makes coats of skin and clothes Eve and Adam.
- The fruits of a second mysterious tree, called Tree of Life, give eternal life to those who eat them.
- To prevent humans from eating of the Tree of Life, angels guard it wielding swords of fire whose flames whirl in all directions.

If the biblical text presents enormous difficulties of interpretation already in its original languages, how much more in translations. How many people master, for example, Hebrew? Only five million worldwide have it as their mother tongue. Notwithstanding, it would be of little advantage for a Christian to be fluent in this language, since modern Hebrew has little to do with the Hebrew of the Bible. Trying to read the original *Letter of Pêro Vaz de Caminha to Manuel I of Portugal* gives us a little idea of how an Israeli feels when reading the Dead Sea manuscripts. Yet, if only 500 years made Caminha's letter almost unintelligible to current Portuguese speakers, what to say of the more than 2,000 years that separate an Israeli from the biblical fragments found at Qumran?

It is practically impossible for a compilation of copies of manuscripts from the Iron Age based on oral traditions also from the Bronze Age and written by different people at different times not to contain discrepancies, incoherences, contradictions and absurdities. Nothing better than the biblical account of creation, responsible for leading millions of Christians to ridicule and combat scientific evidence, to exemplify that.

Beginning of My Analysis of Chapters
1 to 3 of the Book of Genesis

1) "In the beginning God created the heavens and the earth" indicates that the Universe was created on the same day as our planet. Those who base themselves on the biblical texts to calculate the age of Earth claim it is 6,000 years old. Consequently, all the many billions of galaxies would be the same age as Earth, which has no way to have even a shred of foundation. While the nearest galaxies are already millions, the most distant galaxies are billions of light years away from us. So, when we contemplate these far-off island universes, we see them in a very remote past, in the state they were millions or billions of years ago.

2) For three days, Earth was the only celestial body to exist in the entire Universe, since the stars were created only on the fourth day.

3) The account indicates that the Universe was created for the human being, reason why the great majority of Christian denominations teach that life exists only on Earth. However, if the Universe was created by God and everything he created has a purpose, what is the purpose of a space of unimaginable size containing two trillion galaxies with centillions of planets devoid of life? The cosmic dimensions themselves and the more than stunning number of celestial bodies evidence the absurdity of the conception that all this exists because of the human being. On the cosmic scale, Earth is an atom. Anyone who has seen the photograph Pale Blue Dot, taken in 1990 by the Voyager 1 space probe, knows what I am talking about. In the 16th century, to the Dominican friar Giordano Bruno it was inconceivable that, in view of such a colossal universe, life is restricted to Earth. For preaching the plurality of worlds, that is, the existence of intelligent beings also on other planets, Bruno was condemned for heresy and burned at the stake.

4) "The earth was without form", yet we know that all celestial bodies over 300 miles in diameter are turned into spheres by the force of gravity. If "without form" means just "a chaos", then why do so many translations say "without form", instead of "a chaos"? Did the translators forget to ask for divine guidance to translate correctly or is it the Creator of the Universe who has difficulty expressing himself accurately?

5) "The Spirit of God was hovering over the face of the waters." One of the attributes of the biblical god is to be all-powerful. Nothing limits him. Consequently, God cannot have a body, because a body is a limit. Not being limited by anything, God is also omnipresent, that is, he is everywhere at the same time. In consequence, there cannot be a single yoctometer (one septillionth of a meter) in the Universe in which God is not. God occupies, that is, fills the Cosmos completely. Passing through all things, nothing can be outside God and he cannot be outside anything. God, therefore, has no way to hover over the water.

(Apropos of that, the dear reader remembers Bento, Benito, Bendito, Benedito, yes, Baruch, of whom I spoke at the beginning, one of the principal precursors of the Enlightenment? According to Baruch Spinoza, "*Quicquid est in Deo est, et nihil sine Deo esse, neque concipi potest*", or "Whatever is is in God, and without God nothing can be, nor be conceived". Judaism, Christianity and Islam say the same. God is the source of all things. So, where did the matter from which stars and planets are formed come from? Well, there being no other source, it came from God. Therefore, everything that exists must be constituted of the same substance of which God himself is constituted. From this it follows that no distinction can be made between God and the things that he created, or rather, that came out of him. In other words, God and Nature are the very same thing. Unintentionally, Jews, Christians and Muslims worship a god whose attributes, such as unity, incorporeality, omnipotence and omnipresence, make him identical with Nature.

In the title of a documentary about his life, Spinoza is called "apostle of reason". If his philosophy still today sounds daring, in the 17th century it was a true blasphemy. Despite the relative religious freedom that the Dutch enjoyed, Spinoza ran the risk of being sentenced to death for heresy. Because of this, his masterpiece *Ethics, Demonstrated in Geometrical Order* was brought to press only after his death.

If his older brother had not died so soon, Spinoza would not have been forced to leave yeshiva, the talmudic school, to help in the family business and would most likely have become a rabbi. When Spinoza was 23, his ideas reached the ears of the rabbis of the Portuguese synagogue in Amsterdam. Despite still being in a primordial stage of formulation, they already were sufficiently radical to earn him excommunication and an exemplary curse, known as Herem, the most severe banishment imposed by Judaism:

> With the sentence of the Angels and the ruling of the Saints, we banish, exclude, curse and condemn Baruch de Espinoza, with the consent of the Blessed God and that of all this Holy Congregation, before these holy books, with the six hundred and thirteen precepts written in them, with the curse with which Joshua cursed Jericho, with the curse with which Elijah cursed the young men and with all the curses that are written in the Law. Cursed be he by day and cursed be he by night, cursed be he when he lies down and cursed be he when he rises up, cursed be he when he goes out and cursed be he when he comes in. The Lord will not want to forgive him. He will fume his wrath and zeal on this man, upon whom will lie all the curses written in the book of this Law. And the Lord will eliminate his name under the sky and separate him to his own evil from all the tribes of Israel, with all the curses of the firmament, written in the book of this Law. [...] Warning that no one may speak to him orally or in writing, nor do him any favor, nor be with him under the same roof, or in less than four cubits, nor read any text written by him.

One of Spinoza's most striking characteristics is his acuity, which impresses even other philosophers. Speaking about the art of reasoning, Georg Friedrich Hegel, one of the greatest German thinkers, wrote: "Thought must place itself in the Spinoza point of view. This is the essential beginning of all philosophizing. When one begins to philosophize, one must first be a Spinozist".

God and Nature being the very same thing, there is no brain behind the Universe. Nature, then, cannot and even should not be worshiped. The relationship with it is purely a "*amor Dei intellectualis*", or intellectual love for God. To know and love God is to know and love Nature.

The belief in an anthropomorphic god, like the one of the Bible, presents the believer with several dilemmas. The greatest one is the impossibility of rationally harmonizing the idea of an omnipotent, omniscient and loving deity with the suffering that exists in the world. To claim, for example, that the biblical god, who, although all-powerful and knower of the future, allows children to be kidnapped, tortured, raped and murdered, is a god of love is more than perversion: it is madness.

When God is not a being distinct from Nature, contradictions like these disappear. In the Spinozist conception, the good that happens to us is not a divine blessing or reward and the bad that happens to us is not a punishment from God or the work of the Devil. Everything has natural causes. Evil diminishes as people exercise reason, which counteracts passions, the source of destructive impulses. According to Spinoza, people moved by reason understand that their own happiness increases in proportion as they make other people happy.)

6) "And God said." Apparently, the biblical god likes to talk to himself, because when he "said" no one was there to listen to him. By the way, why did he need to speak for something to come into existence? Would snapping his fingers not have been sufficient?

7) God specifically called into existence the light, the firmament, the "dry land", the vegetation, the Sun, the Moon, the stars and the animals. However, the space, the Earth and the water were not given any order to exist. The same is true for the air, which must be understood as having been created together with the firmament.

8) Also on the first day, God made the light and separated it from the darkness, two things that by nature never mix and, therefore, do not need to be separated. Even if this is figurative language for the creation of the day and the night, the Sun, which is known to be our source of light and, along with Earth's rotation, indispensable for days and nights to exist, was created only three days later.

9) "God saw the light, that it was good." If we start from the assumption that the biblical god is perfect, he has no way to create something imperfect. Therefore, God would be neither surprised nor delighted with the things he invents. Besides, what other light was there for him to compare and realize that the one he had just created was good?

10) On the second day, God created a firmament, which he called sky. Strangely, the sky was made "in the midst of the waters" and was firm like a glass dome. Some of the ocean water God placed over the sky, forming a second ocean above the celestial vault. Besides being weird, it took him a whole day just to do that.

11) On the third day, God created the plants and the trees. Days later, when creating the man, God stated: "I have given you every herb that yields seed which is on the face of all the earth". However, chapter 2 says that before Adam was created "no shrub had yet appeared on the earth and no plant had yet sprung up". In what follows, one reads that the reason why there were no herbs is that there was no one to till the ground, but also, and principally, because "God had not [yet] caused it to rain". Here, there are several discrepancies:

- When God created the man, the herbs already existed (chapter 1).

- When God created the man, the herbs did not yet exist (chapter 2).

- The herbs did not exist because it did not rain. (Interestingly, the trees and the plants had no problem existing without rain until the Flood, or for about 1,650 years.)

- It did not rain, "but a mist went up from the earth and watered the whole face of the ground". (It was, therefore, not indispensable to have rain for the herbs to exist.)

Needless to say, vegetation depends on sunlight to exist. The herbs and the trees were created on the third day, but the Sun only on the following day. The vegetation, then, was created one day before the Sun. Even if we say that for the plants it was not a big problem to wait 24 hours for the solar rays, this inversion of the logical order reinforces the fantastical character of the account.

12) On the fourth day, God said: "Let there be lights in the firmament of the heavens to divide the day from the night", creating the Sun, the Moon and the stars. However, on the first day God had already created the light, separating it from the darkness. Bizarrely, for three days there had been light on Earth, although the Sun did not yet exist.

It is curious that the Moon is called light and was created "to rule the night", because it has no light of its own and appears also during the day. However, even more curious is that God needed six days to make Earth, but all the trillions of galaxies, with their centillions of suns, he created in the blink of an eye: "He made the stars".

"God set them in the firmament of the heavens to give light on the earth" indicates that Sun, Moon and stars are at the same distance from Earth, fixed in the glass dome, and that the stars too illuminate our planet, which we know is impossible.

13) God created the marine animals and the birds on the fifth day, closing it with the command: "Be fruitful and multiply". The following day, when creating the terrestrial animals, the man and the woman, God said "Be fruitful and multiply" to Eve and Adam, but not to the animals.

14) In chapter 1, God created the man and the woman in the same instant: "Let us make man [...]. So God created man [...]; male and female he created them". However, in chapter 2 the man was created alone, without woman.

If the animals were created in pairs of males and females, it is illogical for God to create the human being only male. Therefore, the first version, in which the man and the woman are created at the same time, makes more sense, but it is not the one that is accepted by Christians. In chapter 2, one realizes that God did not even intend to create the woman. It was not part of the plan. Proof of this is that when God forbade Adam to eat of the Tree of the Knowledge of Good and Evil, Eve did not yet exist. The phrase "but for Adam there was not found a helper" confirms that Adam spent a long period alone, looking for his better half. Only after noticing Adam's loneliness and realizing that "it is not good that man should be alone" does God decide to create the woman.

As soon as he created the man, "God saw everything that he had made, and indeed it was very good", but later he realized that "it is not good" that the man should be alone. Clearly, the plan of creation was not perfect, because it contained something "not good", an error that needed correction: the creation of the woman.

Idea for a documentary scene. At the door of churches, say to women coming out of Mass or worship service: "If the man had not missed a helper, God would never have created the woman", and film their reaction.

If the woman had not been created, Adam had eaten of the forbidden tree and, as Christianity teaches, redemption is possible only through the sacrifice of God himself, he would have had to come to die for a Humanity consisting of only one human being: Adam, who would be forced to nail Jesus to a cross.

15) In chapter 1, the man was created after the animals; in chapter 2, before.

16) God sometimes speaks to one or more equally divine and creating beings: "Let us make man in our image, according to our likeness". Jews believe that God addressed the angels. However, besides having to assume that they existed before the Universe was created, angels have no creating power. Christians, on the other hand, believe that God the Father was speaking to God the Son and God the Holy Spirit. For fear of causing a short circuit in their brains, adherents of Christianity never ask themselves how it is possible for someone to talk to two people who are himself. Others see in these verses indications of the existence of more than one god.

17) "Of every tree of the garden you may freely eat; but of the tree of the knowledge of good and evil you shall not eat, for in the day that you eat of it you shall surely die." It is almost impossible not to smell a fable in the story of a tree with an enigmatic name and producing mysterious fruits that should not even be touched. Furthermore, in this prohibition there is cruelty, by the way a common element in legends. If the dear reader has children, imag-

ine putting in front of them different kinds of cookies and saying: "My children, you can eat all the cookies, but do you see this one? This one I forbid you to eat. All the others you can eat, just not this one. Do you understand? If you eat this cookie here, I will have to kill you", without explaining to them the motive why you are putting them to the test or the reason why they have to be punished in such an extreme way for eating a simple cookie.

What justification could there be for God to make all Humanity suffer because of such an ingenuous transgression? This already enormous discrepancy becomes irrational when we remember that God, being omniscient, knew that Eve and Adam would not pass the test.

I never forbade my son to do something just to test his obedience, I find it hard to imagine a father would feel the need to do that to his children and it is impossible for me to conceive that he makes them suffer and kills them, if they do not pass the test.

Besides its punishment being disproportionate, this test of obedience is unjust, since by planting the tree "in the midst of the garden" and revealing that it is called "Tree of the Knowledge of Good and Evil" God piqued the curiosity of the first couple. In a world without evil, Eve and Adam were like ingenuous children in the bodies of adults who had no idea what good and evil were. Curiosity, however, is inherent to human nature, especially when one is a blank page, like the first humans, who certainly walked around in the garden dazzled by everything they saw, including the sparkling dental arches of the tyrannosaurus rex, which at that time was as meek as a lamb. That the first couple would fail was more than predictable.

There is contradiction in God concluding the creation of Paradise with a "very good" and at the same time forbidding Eve and Adam to eat the fruits of a single tree. The first couple had no way to understand the reason for this prohibition, because it was not possible for them to imagine what could be wrong with those fruits, since they ate all the others.

Not only the punishment but also the test of obedience itself is disproportionate. On one side, an eternal, omniscient and omnipotent god, creator of trillions of galaxies; on the other, a newly created couple of humans.

Creationists scoff at the scientific evidence of Evolution, but have no problem in, without evidence, accepting and teaching that Humanity comes from incest, that we are descendants of women who had sex with their own brothers, by the way something considered immoral by the biblical god and that at his behest was punished with death. To make matters worse, Jewish tradition says Eve and Adam had 33 sons and 23 daughters. It is assumed, then, that some of the daughters had sex with more than one brother.

If the dear reader and your partner lived in a beautiful and wonderful place, free of evil and diseases, and overnight were chased out of there to a hostile, dangerous and sickly place, would you want to have children? Because they did not know evil, the first couple was naive, but not dumb. If they were made by the hands of none other than the Creator of the Universe himself, Eve and Adam were very intelligent. Thus, knowing that their descendants were condemned to all sorts of suffering, it is to be expected that the first couple had decided not to have children. Would God force them? Let us not forget that Christians believe God had already elaborated his famous Plan of Salvation even before the fatal bite on the forbidden fruit. Eve and Adam only needed to wait for it to be executed.

Imagining this possibility reveals the childishness of the Plan of Salvation. If Eve and Adam refrained from having children, would Jesus still have to come to Earth to be tortured and killed, in order to save the couple? If so, Eve would have to be Jesus' mother and he would have to be martyred and nailed to the cross by his own stepfather.

The synthesis of the biblical account of creation is not only that the world was created by God but also created perfect. However, this conception suffers from illogicality. Where there is perfection, there is no sin; where there is no sin, there is no wickedness of any kind. If God created the world perfect, Eve and Adam were perfect. Consequently, they did not possess even the slightest predisposition to think wickedly. So, when he ordered Adam (Eve had not yet been created, according to chapter 2) not to eat of the forbidden fruit, there was no need for God to threaten him with death, because in the total absence of propensity to act wickedly, he had no way to feel the desire to disobey God. The threat "you shall surely die", which through the infliction of fear aimed to repress in Adam an eventual will to disobey, made to him no sense, since fear, a feeling that is fruit of imperfection, is something that his perfect nature could not feel.

Free will, an argument used by believers to try to explain why God allows evil, is much debated in both philosophical and scientific circles. Several neuroscientists claim free will is an illusion. Experiments show that it is possible to predict someone's decisions several seconds before he makes them. From a theological point of view, free will presents the believer with enormous obstacles that force him to spend a lot of energy in unconvincing argumentative acrobatics, because if God is omniscient and knows the future, how can the human being be free to choose?

We can only choose what exists to be chosen. If evil did not exist, no one could choose to practice it. Moreover, the woman in no way deliberated to disobey God. As I said, because they were immaculate, Eve and Adam had the nature of children who see no evil in anything. In view of this, when the serpent said to Eve: "You will not surely die", in her inability to discern evil she reacted in accordance with her childish nature, believing the words of the ophidian. There was, therefore, on Eve's part no intention to go against God. By the way, the Bible itself admits that Eve was deceived. Well, being deceived is never a deliberate action, much less an evil one, but always the result of ingenuousness and credulity. When someone believes a lie, would it be rational to say that he knew it was a deception, intentionally allowed himself to be deceived and committed a transgression deserving the death penalty? How, then, could the innocent, ingenuous and credulous Eve be made responsible for the entrance of sin into the world and for all the suffering that there is in it simply for believing the words of the talking snake?

Christians never ask themselves if what the serpent said to Eve was a lie. This is what the serpent said: "You will not surely die.

For God knows that in the day you eat of it your eyes will be opened, and you will be like God, knowing good and evil". And this is what happened: "The eyes of both of them were opened [...]. Then the Lord God said: 'Behold, the man has become like one of us, to know good and evil'". As we can see, what the snake said and what Eve believed was true. Therefore, neither Eve, nor Adam, nor the serpent deserved to be punished, because they committed no evil. In fact, God was the one who lied: "In the day that you eat of it you shall surely die". It is incredible that Christians spend their lives reading and hearing this story and never realize these details. How could this not be proof of the conditioning of the mind by religion?

Unlike Jews, Christians believe the talking snake was an angel expelled from Heaven, whom they call Satan, who goes also by the names:

Accuser, Adversary, Angel of the Bottomless Pit, Anointed Cherub, Antichrist, Beast, Beelzebub, Belial, Deceiver, Demon, Devil, Dragon, Enemy, Evil One, Fallen Angel, Fallen Light Bearer, Fallen Star, Father of Lies, Lawless One, Lucifer, Mammon, Murderer, Prince of the Power of the Air, Prince Satan, Roaring Lion, Ruler of the Darkness, Ruler of this World, Serpent of Old, Son of Perdition, Son of the Dawn, Son of the Morning, Son of Wickedness, Tempter, Thief and Wicked One.

Think, dear reader, of a fruit that does not exist. Were you able to? Your imagination had to strive to invent one. However, although invented, this unknown fruit is composed of known elements. The shape, color, smell, consistency and taste that your mind gave to this fruit exist. Like Adam, Lucifer was created in a perfect system, in which negative feelings, fruits of imperfection, such as arrogance, boastfulness, haughtiness, presumption, vanity and pride did not exist. Where there is perfection, imperfection has no way to arise. Just as we cannot imagine unknown elements, we cannot have unknown feelings. How, then, could Lucifer feel what did not exist to be felt?

18) "I have given you every herb that yields seed which is on the face of all the earth, and every tree whose fruit yields seed; to

you it shall be for food." In a world without sin, or perfect, nothing died. That being so, why did the woman and the man need to eat? And what would happen, if they did not eat anything? The same thing with the air. If death did not exist and Eve and Adam were created to live eternally, why, then, did they need to breathe? After all, angels neither breathe nor eat. At least that is what one of them told me.

In Paradise, no plant or fruit could cause death. As soon as Eve and Adam took the legendary bite on the forbidden fruit, God introduced into the vegetation the toxic substances that turned poisonous many plants and fruits. Since he did not provide a list of them, many people had to get sick and die in order for us to have knowledge of their poisons. In his anger, God punished the living beings with the elimination of immortality and the man with hard life. There was, then, no need for this extra, for God to inject poison into the vegetation. In doing so, he demonstrated his sadistic character. According to the National Capital Poison Center, in the metropolitan area of Washington alone about 600 children under the age of six are every year treated for plant and mushroom poisoning.

19) "Your desire shall be for your husband, and he shall rule over you." It is more than evident that the intention of this account's author is to create a legitimization, that is, an excuse for the male domination of women, by establishing it as the will not of men, but of God, which they are obliged to obey. Clearly, this artful curse has the objective of taking away all feelings of guilt from husbands who treat their wives as inferior and preventing women from even thinking about rebelling. In fact, even if the woman had not been condemned to be inferior to the man, this hierarchy had already been established by God when he created Adam first, and Eve only later. Furthermore, God made the woman from a piece of the man and to end man's loneliness and serve him as a helper.

End of My Analysis of Chapters
1 to 3 of the Book of Genesis

Six thousand years after the expulsion of Eve and Adam from Paradise, in the 21st century there is still great acceptance of this hierarchy as something instituted by God, reason why in the Catholic Church and in most of the innumerable branches of Evangelicalism women cannot be ordained and exercise pastoral ministry. However, and as incredible as it seems, Christian women themselves seem to have no problem with the divine curse that condemned them to be dominated by men. Quite the contrary: they obey willingly, because they rejoice in doing what they think is the will of God.

In the Ten Commandments, the biblical text that supposedly was written by the infinite and perfect being himself who created trillions of galaxies and the female sex in his own image and likeness, the woman is a possession of the man as much as his oxen, donkeys and slaves, but even so not the most important one, which, as one reads in Exodus 20:17, is his house.

By biblical law, if a man does not want to risk going through the embarrassment of receiving a "No!" from a girl's father, he can rape her. After being violated, the girl will be forced to marry her rapist. All the man now has to do is pay his victim's father "the bride-price for virgins" (Exodus 22:16).

Some Christians try to deny it, but it is indisputable that the biblical god considers the woman less valuable than the man:

> The Lord said to Moses, "Say to the Israelites: 'A woman who becomes pregnant and gives birth to a son will be ceremonially unclean for seven days [...]. Then the woman must wait thirty-three days to be purified from her bleeding [...]. If she gives birth to a daughter, for two weeks the woman will be unclean [...]. Then she must wait sixty-six days to be purified from her bleeding.'"
>
> (Leviticus 12:1-5)

Giving birth to a boy makes the woman unclean, which forces her to ritually purify herself. However, giving birth to a girl brings double uncleanness on the woman, demanding from her twice as much purification. *Niddah 31b*, in the *Babylonian Talmud*, relates that the disciples of the sage Simeon bar Yochai, one of the most illustrious rabbis in the history of Judaism, questioned him as to why the woman's period of uncleanness is twice as long for giving birth to girls. The master replied that during labor pains the woman vows never again to have sexual relations with her husband, but since everyone rejoices at the birth of a boy, a week later she already regrets what she said. On the other hand, since what the birth of a girl causes is indignation, it takes double the time for the mother to regret her vow.

Even though they are portrayed disparagingly in the Bible and the Koran, women are more religious than men. According to a 2014 survey by the Pew Research Center, in Washington, there are more women than men in all American Christian denominations, including in the Catholic Church, in which women are prohibited from being ordained to the priesthood, and in Mormonism, notwithstanding its known polygamous past. In particular, it is striking the fact that there are 15% more women than men among the patriarchal Jehovah's Witnesses. In a speech in Oakland, United States, in 1971, Samuel Herd, a member of the Governing Body of Jehovah's Witnesses, made clear what the biblical God expects from women:

Scientists say that the cranial capacity of a woman is 10% smaller than that of a man. So, now this shows that she's just not equipped for the role of headship. Her role is one of subjection to the man. Her role is that of submissiveness, and that means that she should recognize that she is a woman and be glad to be a woman […]. Sometimes we hear her say: "Oh, if I were a man, I'd do this and I'd do that", as if to be wishing to be something that she is not designed to be. Do you know what that borders on? That borders on homosexuality.

Whenever this subject is brought up, embarrassed believers try to reason, mumbling phrases such as "It's not like that". The truth is that the Bible does not mention the subjection of the woman as a mere reflection of the customs of the time, limited to the Jewish culture, but presents it as an express divine will established in creation and consolidated in the *New Testament* by the apostles, therefore valid for all generations of Christians:

Wives, in the same way submit yourselves to your own husbands
[...]. Your beauty should not come from outward adornment, such as
elaborate hairstyles and the wearing of gold jewelry or fine clothes. 4
Rather, it should be that of your inner self, the unfading beauty of a
gentle and quiet spirit [...]. For this is the way the holy women of the
past who put their hope in God used to adorn themselves. They submitted themselves to their own husbands, like Sarah, who obeyed
Abraham and called him her lord. You are her daughters if you do
what is right and do not give way to fear.

(1 Peter 3:1-6)

Under divine inspiration, apostle Paul explains what it means
for the woman to have been created from a rib of the man:

But I want you to realize that the head of every man is Christ, and the
head of the woman is man [...]. A man ought not to cover his head,
since he is the image and glory of God; but woman is the glory of
man. For man did not come from woman, but woman from man; neither was man created for woman, but woman for man.

(1 Corinthians 11:3,7-9)

In an act of extreme benevolence, Paul allows the woman to
learn, as long as she shuts her mouth. He says the woman must be
subject to the man not only because she was created after him and
for him but also as a punishment for having allowed herself to be
deceived by the talking snake, reason why the woman is a lost
soul. Not wanting to sound too harsh, the apostle consoles her,
saying there is a way out. The woman can achieve mercy through
childbirth, but only if she does not stop being submissive:

A woman should learn in quietness and full submission. I do not permit a woman to teach or to assume authority over a man; she must
be quiet. For Adam was formed first, then Eve. And Adam was not the
one deceived; it was the woman who was deceived and became a
sinner. But women will be saved through childbearing — if they continue in faith.

(1 Timothy 2:11-15)

How women who cannot or do not want to have children will be saved God only knows.

In light of how women are seen by apostle Paul, it is not surprising that Martin Luther spoke about them thus:

> Weeds grow fast, that is why girls grow faster than boys. Men have wide breasts and narrow hips, reason why they have also more intelligence than women, who have narrow breasts and wide hips and butt, so that they stay at home, sit quietly in the house, do household chores, bear and raise children.

If the biblical god does not consider the woman inferior to the man and the misogyny of the Bible was valid only for the times of its authors, as some Christians like to preach, why on earth did John Knox, the greatest star of the British Reformation and founder of Presbyterianism, write a book entitled *The First Blast of the Trumpet Against the Monstruous Regiment of Women*? In it, the reformer says things like: "God, by the order of his creation, has spoiled woman of authority and dominion" and "Their sight in civil regiment [government] is but blindness; their strength, weakness; their counsel, foolishness; and judgment, frenzy".

Basing themselves especially on Paul's words, the overwhelming majority of Evangelical denominations condemn homosexuality. Why, then, in many of these churches are women allowed to hold leadership positions, preach or even be pastors, if by doing so they disobey the same apostle who reproves homosexuals? If Paul was inspired by God to censure homosexuality, was he not inspired also when he wrote this?

> Women should remain silent in the churches. They are not allowed to speak, but must be in submission, as the law says. If they want to inquire about something, they should ask their own husbands at home; for it is disgraceful for a woman to speak in the church.
>
> (1 Corinthians 14:34-35)

The greatest figure of Christianity condemns homosexuality and the woman who speaks in church, yet only the condemnation of homosexuals should be taken literally, not that of the woman?

Ask a Christian what he thinks of Islam and he will most likely mention the submission of the woman, although the Bible also in this respect is no different from the Koran. Ask a Muslim what he thinks about this and he will deny it saying: "It's not like that", just as Christians do with the Bible. Apropos of that, Mohammed had a vision of Hell and noticed that in it there are more women than men. When asked about the reason for that, the prophet answered: "Because they are ungrateful to their husbands".

It is beyond me why a book that propagates such a negative image of women, such as the Bible, should be considered scientific authority and taught in classrooms. In hundreds of American schools, thousands of children and young people are being taught, for example, that a 600-year-old man built a ship out of tree trunks on which specimens of all species of animals, including dinosaurs, spent a year, while outside God killed men, women, pregnant women, children, babies, the elderly and the sick and destroyed the world by means of a flood.

"But what harm is there in teaching this in schools?", ask the fundamentalists. Of the various reasons, I give three:

- It is ridiculous to use as a source of scientific information a book that claims that snakes talk and a magic trick turned a man's rib into a woman.

- The Bible is a compilation of oral traditions from the Bronze Age written in the Iron Age, 3,500 years after the supposed creation of the world and 1,800 years after the supposed Flood. My common sense tells me it is bizarre to make use of a collection of millenary texts to teach Science.

- Is the Bible, also called the Word of God, not a religious book and the foundation of Christianity's dogmas? In a laic State, favoring one religion is unconstitutional. If the Bible should be admitted in classrooms, the same privilege needs to be granted to books and traditions of other religions. By the way, in the case of countries like Brazil and the United States, should the beliefs of the indigenous peoples not have priority over one imported from the Middle East?

Due to the growth of Evangelicalism in its various forms, in Brazil more and more fundamentalist Christians are entering politics with the objective of creating and approving laws based on their religious convictions. Every now and then, an Evangelical congressman presents a bill aiming to make compulsory the teaching of Creationism in schools. At the same time, the majority of Christians abhor religious fundamentalism in countries such as Afghanistan and Iran. Well, is the fanaticism of the Muslim nations not a result precisely of the fact that in them there is no real separation between Church and State?

Let us remember that Islam is a Semitic religion, therefore related to Judaism. Many biblical characters appear also in the Koran and no one can be a Muslim if he does not believe Jesus was a prophet. Consequently, Islam is related also to Christianity. Well, are Christians not horrified by news, for example, of stoning in Islamic countries?

> If your very own brother, or your son or daughter, or the wife you love, or your closest friend secretly entices you, saying, "Let us go and worship other gods" (gods that neither you nor your ancestors have known, gods of the peoples around you, whether near or far, from one end of the land to the other), do not yield to them or listen to them. Show them no pity. Do not spare them or shield them. You must certainly put them to death. Your hand must be the first in putting them to death, and then the hands of all the people. Stone them to death, because they tried to turn you away from the Lord your God, who brought you out of Egypt, out of the land of slavery.

Question of the day, worth a superspecial prize. Where do the dear listeners think I took that text from: from the Bible or from the Koran? Hurry up! You have only one minute to answer! The first one to call 555-2368 and who knows the answer will win a ticket to Ark Encounter, the Christian theme park with the largest replica of Noah's Ark. Oh, we already have a caller on the line. So, where did I take that text from: from the Bible or from the Koran? What? The connection is bad. Please, repeat that. Koran? Did you say Koran? The answer is… [suspenseful music] wrong! What a pity, what a pity… The right answer is Bible. Bible! You didn't win the ticket to see the big boat, but don't be sad, because tomorrow there's another… [music] Bible or Koran-an-an-an-an!

That's right. The above verses were taken from the Holy Bible, the Book of Books, the Holy Scriptures, more precisely from Deuteronomy 13:6-10, and are, therefore, an indivisible part of the Word of God, a book inspired by him, which reveals his will, in which is found the creation account, taken by many literally and which some think should be taught in schools.

Believe it or not, despite being still today a legal form of punishment in some Islamic nations, stoning is in no way taught by the Koran, the Holy Book, the Word of Allah, the Bible of the Muslims. Stoning is part solely of *Sharia*, the Muslim code of conduct based principally on Islamic traditions. According to the survey *The World's Muslims: Religion, Politics and Society*, published in 2013 by the Pew Research Center, only half of all Muslims believe that *Sharia* was inspired by Allah. The number of Muhammadans in favor of it being the official law of the country varies enormously from nation to nation: 99% in Afghanistan versus only 8% in Azerbaijan. Put simply, the more fundamentalism, the greater the desire for Sharia to be applied with rigor.

As for the biblical god, he explicitly orders punishment by stoning. In Deuteronomy 22:13-21, one reads that the punishment for a man who defames his wife, falsely accusing her of not having married as a virgin, is a few lashes and to pay a hundred silver coins to the father-in-law. However, the burden of proof is on the accused. If she has no way to prove that her husband is lying, the woman must "be brought to the door of her father's house and there the men of her town shall stone her to death".

And how about the solution given by God to the problem of children's disobedience?

> If someone has a stubborn and rebellious son who does not obey his father and mother and will not listen to them when they discipline him, his father and mother shall take hold of him and bring him to the elders at the gate of his town. They shall say to the elders, "This son of ours is stubborn and rebellious. He will not obey us. He is a glutton and a drunkard." Then all the men of his town are to stone him to death.
>
> (Deuteronomy 21:18-21)

Passages like these prove that the Bible has nothing divine about it. Not only Judaism and Christianity but any religion is a reflection of the mentality of the time in which it was invented. Supposing that God exists, I simply cannot imagine him with the despotic nature of a tyrant who finds it natural to command the stoning of people, let alone of women for not bleeding on the wedding night and of children for being rebellious. Those who are not afraid to reason recognize that the gods of the sacred books of religions were created by the human being in his image and likeness.

The fundamentalist Christian who prides himself on following the Bible to the letter, but does not obey every one of the 613 commandments of the *Pentateuch* and the 1,050 of the *New Testament*, deceives himself and lives in incoherence. Biblical literalists use passages like Leviticus 20:13 — "If a man has sexual relations with a man as one does with a woman" — to condemn homosexuality, but ignore in them God's command to kill homosexuals. The second half of this verse says: "They are to be put to death; their blood will be on their own heads". Yet, has the dear reader ever seen pastors who preach against homosexuality exhort the faithful of their churches to obey this divine ordinance and murder homosexuals?

From this it follows that pastors and believers who, because it is abhorred by the god of the Bible, combat homosexuality are hypocrites, since they regard the first part of the verse as in force, but the second part — "They are to be put to death" — as expired. Well, the Christian who sees no problem in ignoring the second half of the verse should see no problem in ignoring also the first half.

John Joe Thomas, a 28-year-old resident of Pennsylvania, United States, followed the Bible to the letter when he, in 2011, murdered 70-year-old Murray Seidman with a sock full of stones, claiming he had been making sexual advances to him. Thomas told police the Bible orders the stoning of homosexuals and, after praying asking for divine guidance on how to proceed, God commanded him to kill Seidman with stones.

Others who followed the Bible to the letter were brothers Benjamin and James Williams, fundamentalist Christians from Palo Cedro, California. In 1999, they burned down an abortion clinic and three synagogues and murdered a gay couple. In an interview with *The Sacramento Bee* newspaper, Benjamin stated:

> I'm not guilty of murder, I'm guilty of obeying the laws of the Creator. You obey a government of man until there is a conflict, then you obey a higher law. It's part of the faith. So many people claim to be Christians and complain about all these things their religion says are a sin, but they're not willing to do anything about it. They don't have the guts.

As one can see, the Williams brothers had courage. Asked about the death penalty, the most likely in his case, Benjamin said he was not worried, since dying as a "Christian martyr" would inspire others to attack Jews, homosexuals and other people.

Apropos of that, right after the massacre of 49 people in a gay nightclub, in Orlando, in 2016, two pastors from two different American Evangelical churches rushed to praise the Muslim shooter for doing the will of God and what, according to them, should be the obligation of the State. When it suits them, Christians regard Muslims as friends, which, in this case, is bizarre, because, unlike the Bible, no verse in the Koran orders the murder of homosexuals.

It is easy to prove that the Bible teaches madnesses. If we ask Christians what they think of killing women for not bleeding on the wedding night, children for rebelliousness and people because of their sexual orientation, the majority will answer that it is madness.

What tends to happen when religious fundamentalism is endorsed at constitutional level? Freedoms of conscience and religion end. That is what occurs in several Islamic republics. In 1992, Farag Foda, an Egyptian author and professor, critical of fundamentalism in his country, was murdered at his home's gate by members of an Islamic group disappointed with the delay of the authorities in arresting him. The charge: blasphemy. After serving a 20-year prison sentence, one of the killers stated in an interview:

"The punishment for an apostate is death, even if he repents. [...] Any citizen is entitled to carry out Allah's punishment".

Let us imagine that the number of Evangelical politicians continues to increase and they come to constitute the majority in the Brazilian National Congress. Let us imagine also that, one beautiful day, full of the religious zeal and ardor of biblical characters such as King Josiah, who commanded the assassination of leaders of other religions (episodes to which the Jehovah's Witnesses' *Watchtower Online Library* gives the title *Teach your children: Josiah chose to do what was right*), these politicians feel called by God to cleanse Brazil of everything that is not Christian and, following the example of what the Muslim republics do with *Sharia*, institute the Bible as the code of conduct to "teach, rebuke and correct" (2 Timothy 3:16). The day the fundamentalist Christian political majority, followers of a Semitic religion related to Islam, decides to legislate Brazil in full conformity with the commandments expressed in the Word of God, the Christian Theocratic Republic of Brazil will be born.

Exaggeration? Brazil has never been a truly laic country, but the infiltration and influence of Evangelicalism in politics have taken on alarming proportions. For abruptly ending a plenary session, in May 2016, parliamentarian Waldir Maranhão, then president of the Chamber of Deputies, was surrounded by colleagues who demanded the reopening of the debates. "Give me two to three minutes just with myself, so I can talk to God", Maranhão said. "Three minutes with God?", interpellated a surprised deputy. "Two minutes with God, my supreme being", asked the president.

Those who have been in a church know that no one is expelled for not kneeling or not standing. If the dear reader is of the opinion that Brazil is not in danger of becoming a Christian republic along the lines of the Muslim ones, it is because you have not yet heard of the case of Regis Bencsik Montero, who, in 2012, was expelled by the police from the plenary of the Piracicaba City Council for refusing to stand up for the Bible reading, an expulsion considered unconstitutional by the Order of Attorneys of Brazil.

If Brazil is not yet a theocracy, it has already had a theocratic municipality. In 2015, the Council of Novo Gama, a city 25 miles from Brasília, passed a law that made a crime any critical stance towards Christianity. Adherents of Afro-Brazilian religions were harassed by Christians. To the *Correio Braziliense* newspaper, a merchant of Umbanda items stated having been the target of threats. "As it is, in a few days I may be forced to close my shop", she said. Pressured, since it is unconstitutional, a year and a half later the mayor revoked this law.

To make Christianity uncriticizable is to admit that it teaches such nonsense that it becomes necessary to protect it by law.

While many people insist on ignoring that Brazil is little by little being transformed into a theocracy, the reality is that Evangelical politicians no longer keep secret that this is their objective, as proven by the words of then-minister Marcelo Crivella, bishop of the Universal Church of the Kingdom of God and nephew of its multibillionaire founder Edir Macedo, spoken in 2011: "I don't know if it will be in our generation, when it will be, but Evangelicals will elect a president of the Republic who will work for us and for our churches". In 2016, Crivella was elected mayor of Rio de Janeiro with 59% of the votes, despite having commanded exorcism rituals, written stupidities like "medicines and doctors treat the effects, but the cause of all illnesses, which is spiritual, can be treated only with the power of Jesus" and preached imbecilities like "Women should obey men more, after all they are a piece of men". In his book *Plano de Poder (Power Plan)*, the owner of the Universal Church does not beat around the bush: "The moment is opportune for the divine project of nationhood".

Those who think that only Evangelical politicians threaten the laicity of the State are sorely deceiving themselves. At a presidential rally in the city of Campina Grande, in 2017, Catholic Jair Bolsonaro vociferated: "God above all. There is no such thing as a laic State. The State is Christian, and the minority that is against it should move country. The minorities must bow down to the majorities". It was precisely Bolsonaro's Taliban discourse that catapulted him from being one of the most mediocre congressmen, with only two unimportant projects approved in 26 years, to being seen by Evangelicals and fanatical Catholics as sent by God to save Brazil. Enchanted, in 2018 over 70% of Evangelicals chose the sexist, homophobic, pro-guns, pro-dictatorship and pro-torture candidate, electing him president.

The more religious, the more manipulable.

It is important that the believer becomes conscious of the fact that biblical literalism was not practiced in the early Christianity of the so-called Church Fathers with as much dogmatism as it is today by the Evangelicalism that Americans exported to the Third World. Actually, literalism was introduced in the 16th century by Martin Luther, the Father of the Protestant Reformation, the same one who in everything saw the Devil and preached the extermination of witches, the beating of peasants to death, the murder of Anabaptists and the burning of synagogues.

In his article *On the Heresy of Literalism*, thus expresses himself Dr. Kevin Lewis, professor in the Department of Religious Studies at the University of South Carolina, United States, about following the Bible to the letter:

> Thus did literalism teach the "letter" to drive out the "spirit" of the biblical writings, effectively misusing the text in order to promote a corrupted theological agenda. The effect is a rigid constriction of the inspiring Word. [...] There are better, more legitimate, less blasphemous ways than this to affirm that the Bible is the Word of God. The Word is to be affirmed without the heresy of divinizing each word of Scripture as though it fell from Heaven a perfect expression of the mind of God. The drive for certainty in a skeptical age is more dangerous to our faith than we might suppose. It leads away from "faith" to a calculating "belief" not satisfied with the promises of God, but restless to prove, verify, and guarantee those promises with scientific precision.

Those who believe the Bible should be interpreted literally have, after reflecting on everything I wrote, four options:

- Continue living in the illusion that they follow the Bible to the letter.
- Start following the Bible really to the letter, in its entirety, obeying all divine orders exactly as they are expressed.

- Acknowledge that following the Bible to the letter not only is impossible but also madness and that literalism is the foundation of religious extremism.

- Acknowledge that the Bible teaches insanities and, therefore, has nothing divine about it.

4

Diversity

"One half full, one half empty.
One half sadness, one half happiness.
It's always good to remember
that an empty glass is full of air."

— Gilberto Gil
(*Copo Vazio*)

DOES THE DEAR reader like to travel? So do I. I have had the opportunity to set foot in almost all countries of Europe, some of South America, in the United States, Russia, Turkey, Israel, Malaysia, Australia and Japan. Not very exotic trips, I admit. To go to the end of the world, so far the money has been tight. Yet, with the magnificent sales of the phenomenal bestseller the dear reader holds in his hands, that will change. Thank you for purchasing my literary work and being part of the many millions of people who contribute to the financing of my future trips to exotic places, which I will finally be able to explore — from the balcony of the presidential suites of the five-star hotels in which I will stay. If you give me your address, my secretary will send you a postcard. I promise.

Seriously, why do we like so much to travel? Is it not because sometimes we get tired of seeing and feeling the same things? Maybe because the diverse fascinates and stimulates us, the unusual challenges and educates us? When it comes to places more distant than usual, other regions of the country or abroad, enjoying the different landscape is a great motivation for me to take a trip, but not the principal one. More interesting is seeing how people live, hearing their language or accent, knowing a little about their way of thinking and expressing themselves, their customs and traditions, listening to their music and tasting some of their food. However, if one lives in a large country he does not need to travel abroad to have experiences along these lines. Brazil, for example, is so large that one already can feel a taste of adventure when one goes from one state to another.

It is improbable that the dear reader goes to the country of Socrates and Plato to eat sausage and drink *Weißbier* in one of the many *Biergärten* that, due to the large number of German tourists, there are in some parts of Greece, and it is unlikely that you travel to the land of Picasso and Miró to eat fish and chips and drink Guiness in one of the many pubs that, owing to the large number of British tourists, there are in certain regions of Spain. Such places usually leave a sad impression of mischaracterization. People of good taste appreciate the diverse and value the authentic.

Does the dear reader remember the movie *Highlander*, with Sean Connery and Christopher Lambert? Do you remember also the tagline of that film: "There can be only one"? Well, that is the unofficial motto of many religions and of all Christian denominations. Apart from delusion, power and money, why would, for example, a Christian found a church if not to convince people that it is the true one? Every church is, therefore, established on the presumption of being the true representative of God on Earth. Since only one can be the holder of the truth, the intent of each one is, then, not only to be bigger than the others, but the only one.

Let us imagine that, after many decades of energetic missionary work, one church achieved its longed-for objective of convincing the entire world that it is the true one. All of Earth's population converted, say, to the Mormon Church. Not a single person is an atheist or has a different belief. The whole world, including the inhabitants of the most inaccessible regions, such as the nomads of the Tibetan Plateau and the islanders of Tristan da Cunha, came to follow Mormonism. All have been persuaded that the Mormonic religion is the true one, just as it has long preached. Let us imagine almost eight billion people hearing the same messages, reading the same books and singing and listening to the same songs. Let us imagine all facets of the cultures of different peoples, from their peculiar ways of thinking to their arts, customs, traditions, festivals, foods, dress and tastes, being infiltrated, altered and shaped by the way of thinking, being and living that is inevitably exported along with religions, in this case Mormonism, and imposes itself as ideal to be followed.

In Brazil, many denominations originate in the United States, and the Brazilian ones imitate the American ones. In the one to which I, by force of childhood indoctrination, went, the majority of the hymns are American and the ones composed by Brazilians copy their musical style. Having learned that everything that is not from the church is worldly and, therefore, despicable, I grew up alienated from the world of arts and culture. Fundamentalists go neither to theaters, nor to circuses, nor to shows, nor to dances, nor to concerts, nor to operas. Yet, if an American Evangelical band comes to perform in Brazil they will organize caravans to go and see it, whatever the cost. At home, we did not listen to worldly music, except by chance, when the radio was on. Out of our stereo came only Christian music and most of my records were imported from the United States. Since works of fiction deprave the believer's mind and the philosophical and scientific ones distance him from God, practically everything I read came from the church press, whose publications usually are translations of American authors. Add to all that the frequent visits to Brazil by American preachers, with their sermons in English, and the sending of many Brazilian pastors to the United States to study in Christian colleges. Thus, it is no wonder that many Brazilian Evangelicals are so fascinated by the United States.

Going back to our example, if everyone converted to Mormonism schools would teach that dinosaurs lived on other planets, since that is what Mormonites believe. When these celestial bodies were destroyed, God reused their debris to form Earth. That is how the fossils of the Mesozoic reptiles ended up getting here. On the other hand, if all people started to profess a single religion, it would not make the slightest difference if it dictated, among other things, what has to be taught in schools, because there would not be anyone who would find that preposterous.

Imagining the world like that sends shivers down my spine. It is similar to watching a science fiction horror movie like *Invasion of the Body Snatchers*. If the dear reader visualized all the inhabitants of Earth following the same religion, then you must have sensed how absurd and frightening the idea of universal religious truth, advocated by the innumerable branches of Christianity and by Islam, is. Wanting an end to bad things, like poverty and violence, and for all people to live well does not mean consenting to transform our planet into a gigantic church.

This imagination exercise makes us see the delirium that evangelizing is, regarded by Christians as natural. However, how could it be natural to knock from door to door to convince people to believe in things of which the missionaries themselves have no evidence, urging them to join a group of people who cultivate wishful thinking? Worse: How could it be natural to pay to be part of such a group?

Members of one denomination see members of other denominations and followers of other religions, irreligious and atheists as wanderers in necessity of guidance or lost people in need of salvation. I remember that, when I was an Evangelical, it seemed natural also to me to think that people who did not believe as I did needed to be conducted to the truth. Because it is one of the foundations of their religion, Christians do not realize that this worldview is arrogant. Christianity is so perverse that it makes its adherents feel guilty even for not spreading it. They are led to believe God makes people cross their path exclusively for them to guide these people to Jesus. Evading evangelizing them can mean the eternal damnation of many of them.

Believers usually think they enjoy an emotional advantage over disbelievers, as if in people without religion a cog of the gear responsible for producing happiness were missing. Because of this, the objective of missionaries is not only to save people from the flames of Hell but also grant them the privilege of being happy. Well, not believing in deities and not following religions is precisely what makes atheists happy. Despite this, has anyone ever seen atheists knocking from door to door to share with believers the happiness that exists in disbelieving in invisible beings and places, offering them help to liberate themselves from their beliefs and churches?

If there is an expression religious people like to use to label atheists, it is "empty people", by the way a good example of concepts that are passed on without critical examination. In psychology, "emptiness" is a term that is employed to define what a person feels who no longer sees meaning in things. It is, therefore, a feeling that is associated with depression. Thus, to say that atheists are empty people is to claim that all atheists suffer from depression, which is ridiculous, not least because depression is not an emotional disturbance to which believers are immune. I know Evangelicals who have been treated for depression.

The question that almost no believer asks himself is: "What the hell is an atheist?". We know that atheists do not believe in the existence of gods, and for a very simple reason: lack of evidence. The supposed "evidence" presented by believers is not free from errors of reasoning. On the contrary: it is full of contradictions. Ignoring for a moment that the burden of proof lies on the one making a claim, just as it is not possible to prove the existence of supernatural beings it is not possible to prove their nonexistence. This is as true for a deity as it is for Saci Pererê (a character in Brazilian folklore with only one leg and a magical red cap). So, technically every atheist is an agnostic. But only technically. In the same way the probability that Saci Pererê exists is so minuscule to the point of bordering on zero, so for the atheist that God exists. It is not impossible that God exists, just extremely unlikely. It is not certainty of impossibility, but of improbability, the same certainty that believers have of the nonexistence of Saci Pererê, although no one can prove it. On a scale of 1 to 10, on which 1 represents the certainty that God exists and 10 that he does not exist, convinced atheists rate themselves a 9.

Those who believe in a supernatural being cannot have difficulty believing in other supernatural beings, such as angels, demons, witches, spirits, ghosts, apparitions and hauntings, nor in superstitions, conspiracy theories and folkloric figures, such as the Headless Mule, by the way a legend based on a woman who supposedly was cursed by God. Those who believe in God cannot find it wrong to believe in the existence, for example, of the Werewolf and Chupacabra, since they can very well be diabolical manifestations. Christians and Muslims are fully convinced that demons exist. On what rational basis could they, then, contest the existence, for example, of vampires? In contrast, a person who does not believe in deities and demons is immune to all kinds of old wives' tales.

The list of atheists who have contributed and contribute in an extraordinary way to the progress of Humanity is long. To conceive that a man who restored the sight of thousands of citizens in several countries was an empty person is almost impossible, and really impossible that a man whose initiatives led more than a million people to see will go to Hell just for not believing in the existence of deities. When the atheist ophthalmologist Fred Hollows died, the chief minister of the Australian Capital Territory said: "An egalitarian [advocate of equal rights and opportunities for all human beings] and a self-named anarcho-syndicalist who wanted to see an end to the economic disparity which exists between the First and Third Worlds and who believed in no power higher than the best expressions of the human spirit found in personal and social relationships".

"Empty person" is also a figurative expression used to characterize someone as frivolous, vain or futile, whose life is useless, worthless or meaningless. Well, the notion of what the meaning of life is can only be individual. Thus, when we judge that a person's life is meaningless, we use our own parameters, which are different from his. Someone may live a life that everyone around him considers exemplary, while he himself regards it as meaningless. Hitler, for example, may have felt that no life had more meaning than his. Furthermore, if only the life of someone who believes in God has meaning, what meaning does the life of someone have who believes in God and lives on the streets?

Let us say that by labeling them as empty the believer is actually saying atheists are unhappy people. Anyone who says that has never asked himself these two little questions: Is every believer in God happy? Is every atheist unhappy? Just as it is impossible to know if every Christian is happy (full), it is impossible to determine if every atheist is unhappy (empty).

When we talk to someone who is sad, we can feel if his sadness is small or great, but of two people with depression it is impossible to specify how much sadder one is than the other. It is unlikely, however, that the intensity of the sadness of both is the same. If the disbelief in God causes emptiness, the size of this emptiness has to be the same in all disbelievers, which is impossible, because, just as some people are sadder than others, some people are emptier than others. From this it follows that different empty people would need different amounts of what fills their emptiness, which according to the believer is God. Moreover, if doubting the existence of God makes someone empty, or unhappy, all Christians should always be full, or happy. In fact, just as the day repels the night and the night the day, without one extinguishing the other, except temporarily, so happiness and sadness constantly alternate. In consequence, believing in God can never bring fullness, since fullness is a permanent state of absence of emptiness, something unreachable. Actually, if I were constantly happy, I would not know it, since we can only know what happiness is because it comes interspersed with moments of sadness.

If what ends emptiness is fullness, but it can never be reached, then Christians themselves are never free of the feeling of emptiness they say is exclusive to atheists. Besides, a person who had reached fullness would no longer have any notion of what "feel an emptiness" means. Because of this, when a religious person calls an atheist an "empty person" he is proving that he himself feels an emptiness.

Apropos of that, if Christians are full and atheists are empty, what are believers in Vishnu, Osiris, Zeus, Allah, Odin, Thor and Nhanderuvuçu? And what about a person who invents his own god?

Fullness is an unattainable state, since it is perfect. However, even if believers were "fuller" than disbelievers, why are they not extraordinarily better than disbelievers also in other respects? I myself am proof that those who believe in the biblical god are not much different from those who do not believe in him. My belief was sincere. I prayed, studied the Bible daily and tried to live according to the guidelines of the church, in whose activities I was engaged. I certainly was not a bad Christian. Even so, the practice of Christianity never significantly improved the way I was. Aggressiveness, anger, anguish, antipathy, anxiety, arrogance, coldness, disappointment, disillusionment, distress, envy, fanaticism, fear, frustration, hatred, haughtiness, hostility, impatience, intolerance, ire, irritability, jealousy, pride, rancor, resentment, resignation, sadness, selfishness, worry, in short, every negative feeling that exists in disbelievers existed also in me.

Where are those almost saintly, enlightened Christians, free of negative feelings and worries, the kind who visibly appear to be not of this world? As fervent as I was, I was not like that. Nor have I ever met a believer who was. Likewise, the conviction that I belonged to the true church did not make me a better Christian than the members of the false churches. By the way, the Bible says that "Enoch walked with God", which was sufficient for the Creator to rapture him to Heaven. I do not know what millions of devout Christians do differently from Enoch, because I have never heard of a single one whose devotion earned him the privilege of being teleported alive to Paradise.

It is true that religions can serve as an impulse to free people from alcohol and drugs, but when it comes to emotional disturbances beliefs can worsen them, since it is in their nature to induce believers to trust divine help more than that of men. Thus, instead of seeking professional help for their psychological problems, believers often seek guidance from priests, pastors and gurus who, apart from spiritual advice and prayers, have nothing to offer. The root of the problems remains untouched.

To follow a religion is to live in paradox. At the same time that they strive to convert the entire world, all denominations know that this target is unattainable. After all, it goes against the Bible itself. If one church managed to convince all Earth's inhabitants, the apocalyptic prophecies would not be fulfilled, because the world would not degenerate into a state of complete chaos and, consequently, would not head for its end. According to the Bible, in the End Times there will be a great physical war, called Armageddon, between the forces of good and evil. For the prophecies to be fulfilled, it is necessary not only that many people reject the message of the missionaries but even that many Christians abandon Christianity. This apostasy is a precondition for Jesus to return to Earth and destroy it. Missionary work is, therefore, a Sisyphean task.

The social projects of the churches and the charitable works of the Christians are another contradiction. Jesus commanded his followers to do good, helping the poor and feeding the hungry. Well, to combat poverty is to improve the world, contribute to its progress. Yet, the Jesus who said "If you want to be perfect, go and sell all your possessions and give the money to the poor" is the same one who promised to come back only when poverty and hunger worsen. In other words, Christ commanded Christians to combat something he will increase, so that his predictions be fulfilled and he can return. This is the same as saying: "While you obey me and fight against misery, I will see to it that your efforts are in vain". Not quite what I would call a motivational message.

Many Christians ignore that the End Times and the return of Jesus are dogmas also of Islam. Both religions preach that God will destroy the world and renew it. It is more than four billion people ardently wishing for Earth to be as soon as possible made into ruins. As far as Christianity is concerned, the End Times is, however, one of the many proofs the Bible is a confusing book, because not even on something so essential is there a consensus among Christians. Quite the contrary: some churches preach that Christ's return has already occurred, others that it will be symbolic, some that it will be visible, others that the entire Universe will be destroyed, some that only Earth will be destroyed, others that Paradise will be spiritual and some that it will be physical and here on Earth.

To make matters worse, Jesus told his disciples they would see him come back "with power and great glory" before they died, which, unless I am in Hell dreaming that I am writing this book, evidently did not happen. Since Christians cannot admit that the Bible contains errors, much less that out of Jesus' mouth came nonsense, they have no other way out than to struggle with their Master's words, trying to decipher what he meant, for which there are various interpretations.

Does the dear reader get indignant when you see someone throw trash in Nature? I once dissuaded a boy from tossing a potato chips package from the top of a beautiful waterfall. If Earth is about to be destroyed by God, why should Christians care about pollution? Should they not be giving a damn about trash? And what about the overexploitation of natural resources? Would it not even be coherent for Christians to engage in devastating the world to anticipate its end, thus hastening the coming of Jesus?

> The heavens will disappear with a roar; the elements will be destroyed by fire, and the earth and everything done in it will be laid bare. Since everything will be destroyed in this way, what kind of people ought you to be? You ought to […] look forward to the day of God and speed its coming. That day will bring about the destruction of the heavens by fire, and the elements will melt in the heat. But in keeping with his promise we are looking forward to a new heaven and a new earth.
>
> (2 Peter 3:10-13)

In view of this, is it a coincidence that churches offer seminars on engagement, family, addictions, financial success and sexual morality, but never workshops on topics related to the environment?

And speaking of financial success, this is perhaps the greatest contradiction with which people who believe in the end of the world live. While rooting for the fulfillment of the prophecies, looking in the newspaper headlines for evidence that Humanity is already heading for the longed-for chaos that will precede the return of the one who comes to destroy this corrupt, perverted, depraved and degenerated world, believers run after material success in the same way as nonbelievers, as if the world would never end. Not only have I never met a Christian who followed his Master's advice to sell all his possessions and give the money to the poor but also the churches that grow the most are precisely those that promise a wealthy life, and that despite everything Jesus said against the accumulation of material goods and the apostle Paul's admonition that "the love of money is the root of all kinds of evil".

If there is a field of human activity that aims to create conditions for all citizens to live well, it is politics, defined by the *Aurélio Dictionary* as "the art of governing the peoples well". Even if a ruler is bad, this does not change the fact that the purpose of politics is to make society advance, progress, prosper, evolve. How, then, could there be compatibility between politics and a religious belief whose followers do not even consider themselves citizens of this world and which depends on the world's destruction to have its veracity confirmed? An Evangelical who holds political office suffers from severe cognitive dissonance, because, at the same time that he is being paid, and by the way very well, to improve the living conditions of his fellow citizens, he believes the world needs to worsen so that his god can come back.

The best example one can have of the deep cognitive dissonance from which a religious person suffers when entering politics is neurosurgeon Benjamin Carson, a member of the Seventh-day Adventist Church and, in 2016, a candidate for the presidency of the United States. Carson lives on two levels of contradiction: for being a Christian and for being an Adventist. Despite being a follower of a deity who taught that "the meek shall inherit the earth" and "the peacemakers shall be called the children of God" and preached love, forgiveness and nonviolence, as president Carson would have to be open to involving his country in military conflicts not only of a defensive but also offensive nature. It is no secret that "clean war" is an illusion and all armed conflict causes the death of thousands of innocent people, many of them children. (It is estimated that the invasion of Iraq, led by Evangelical George Bush and "The Right Honourable" and Catholic Tony Blair, in 2003, killed about half a million Iraqis.) In an interview, Carson stated that the first thing he would do as president would be to "seal the borders" of the United States to prevent the illegal entry of immigrants and "turn off the spigot that dispenses all the goodies, so we don't have people coming in here", thus going against what the Bible and Jesus teach about how foreigners should be treated, but especially the poor and needy. This Adventist even suggested that drones bomb caves on the border. Yet, what is worse is that the church to which Carson belongs preaches that one of the beasts of Revelation is the Papacy and the other the United States government itself, and that in the End Times, which for Adventists has already began more than 170 years ago, the two beasts will unite in the service of Satan. When that happens, one of the things the Catholic Church and the United States will do will be to force all Earth's inhabitants to worship the Pope and keep Sunday, which will trigger a persecution of Adventists, God's chosen people who keep Saturday. Had he been elected, Carson would bizarrely take the place of one of the apocalyptic beasts that will persecute the very church of which he is a member. Carson several times stated he had been called by God to run for president. However, God must have changed his mind, since he did not engage at all in the Adventist's campaign. Not having the slightest chance of winning, the doctor whose religion preaches that the world is already ending gave up stating: "I will still continue to be heavily involved in trying to save our nation".

Does the dear reader know a single Christian who does not do the opposite of what the Bible teaches and Jesus commands? In other words, do you know a single Christian who is not a hypocrite?

According to several denominations, the End Times have already begun, the world will soon deteriorate to unbearable levels and before long be destroyed by God, who will gift with resplendent mansions of gold those who have interpreted the Bible correctly. Well, would gold have any value to the being who created trillions of galaxies? Could the material of which a house is made have importance to those who live in a perfect world? In a city where all houses were made of gold, it would have the same value as a brick. Imagine, dear reader, that we lived on a planet in which, instead of water, it rained diamonds. That is exactly what, due to their atmospheric conditions, most likely happens on Saturn and Jupiter. Every single day. If mansions of gold are not proof that the biblical god is fantasy, then I do not know what they are.

What fundamentalist Christian politicians really like to do is oppose. In general, they oppose the laicity of the State, social programs, gender and race equality and the right to abortion, euthanasia and homosexual marriage. Notwithstanding seeing themselves as ambassadors of biblical morality, the site *Transparência Brasil (Transparency Brazil)* published, in 2012, that more than half of the political representatives of the Brazilian Evangelical population have pending court cases. According to the blog of journalist Paulo Lopes, "the lawsuits investigate charges such as embezzlement, administrative improbity, electoral corruption, abuse of economic power, tax evasion and criminal conspiracy". The following year, the *Veja* magazine article entitled *Vinde a Mim os Eleitores (Come to Me the Voters)* revealed that more than one-third of the Brazilian Christian congressmen "respond to lawsuits before the Federal Supreme Court. There are some accused of corruption, embezzlement, electoral crime, use of false documents, money laundering and swindling. There is even one sentenced to prison".

Apparently, administering two trillion galaxies does not stress God sufficiently to the point of not finding the time also to bother himself with the sexual orientation of his creatures, reminding them by means of his representatives on Earth that homosexuality is an aberration. Silas Malafaia, a Prosperity Theology televangelist and religious leader who often uses his popularity to help Evangelical candidates get elected, as he did with his brother, is the best-known of the Brazilian pastors who wage war against same-sex marriage. In 2012, in a TV program, this illustrious representative of the religion of Christ's love stated that "The Catholic Church should come down hard on these guys [homosexuals], beat the hell out of them, to teach these guys a lesson". A year later, in an interview, this Assembly of God authority said: "I have nothing against homosexuals, but I love homosexuals as I love criminals". The site *BuzzFeed Brazil* found that, from March to September 2014, in his Twitter messages the pastor mentioned the vocable "gays" 87 times, but "Jesus" only 59. In 2016, the moralist Malafaia was the target of a police investigation for receiving R$ 100,000 (around US$ 30,000) from a lawyer accused of illicit enrichment. To the police the man of God declared that it was an offering of gratitude for a prayer.

If for Christians who long for the end of the world homosexual relationships are immorality, and moral degeneration is one of the principal preconditions for Jesus' return, why, then, do they combat homosexuality with such ardor? By the Bible's own logic, the

Christian who fights against homosexuality is being used by Satan to prevent the fulfillment of the prophecies.

I remember already in my adolescence having difficulty understanding the determinism embedded in the apocalyptic predictions, which reveal Satan's actions in the End Times and what will happen to him. Imagine, dear reader, that you were not only the most evil person in the world but also the most intelligent, thousands of times more than the greatest of all geniuses. Imagine also that many people were writing and talking about you and you could read what they write and hear what they say. The word on the street is that, in the near future, you will act motivated by desperation, suffer a humiliation of cosmic proportions and be punished through the ages of the ages. Besides seeming bizarre to you that your actions are predetermined, would you not be enraged with these people for wanting to see you dead? Would you be willing to live up to their expectations, or would it not give you an immense desire to frustrate their predictions by doing the exact opposite of what they say you will? Well, if Satan knows the biblical prophecies, why would he want to act in accordance with them, making them come true? Now, if they must be fulfilled at any cost and the Devil cannot frustrate them, then he has no will of his own, but was programmed like a robot and is nothing but a puppet in God's hands.

Without the dogma of free will, Christianity could not exist, because Lucifer could not have chosen to rebel against God. However, this supposed freedom of the most intelligent creature in the Universe to practice evil is one of the greatest contradictions of the Christian belief. Just as Christians think that with the vocable "God" they explain the origin of the Universe, they think that with the term "free will" they explain the origin of sin. The truth is that these words are nothing more than labels that clarify neither one nor the other. Free will does not explain how a perfect being could have the impulse to feel, think and act in an imperfect way, since, as I have shown, it is not possible to have feelings that do not exist. Even if we sidestep this incongruity, Christians believe that in Heaven, or Paradise, the saved will live infinite centillions of years without ever sinning, because the history of sin must not repeat itself. Ever again! Well, if Lucifer could choose to sin, it is evident that eternal sinlessness can only be guaranteed if the Creator reprograms his creatures to never again do evil. Simply put, if angels and humans can choose to sin, God will extirpate from them this faculty.

The curious thing about the doctrine of celestial rebellion, which resulted in the expulsion of Lucifer and his partisans, is that it is assumed it was a unique episode. If angels really have free will, after that one there may have been other rebellions. It would not stop being mythology, but at least it would sound more natural. Otherwise, it seems that either the angels were afraid of God or he, to make new insurrections impossible, extinguished the freedom of choice.

Satan is a very contradictory character. On the one hand, he is the most intelligent creature in the Cosmos, but on the other he is an incredible jerk. The being endowed with the most brilliant mind should know that waging war against someone who has no way to be defeated is to play the role of the perfect cosmic idiot. Unless, of course, his intention is, in a suicide mission, to demonstrate to the Universe that the Creator is a dictator. If free will exists and the Devil is free to act as he wishes, and not a robot programmed to execute divine commands, he could embarrass God. It would suffice that Satan make the prophecies fail. For that, he would have several options. Since his war really is lost, he could, for example, commit suicide. Oh, the Devil is a spiritual being and has no way to die, he is forced to live forever? If someone cannot choose not to live, where is the free will? And how about Satan shouting "I don't give a damn!" and folding his arms? If idleness bores him, what prevents the Devil from doing good? Could Satan not pack his bags and go to live, for example, on Venus? With its 900 degrees Fahrenheit (475 degrees Celsius), the Morning Star certainly is a more pleasant place for demons than Earth. Oh, the Devil is bound to Earth? Interesting. What kind of bars and chains hold beings that have no bodies?

An Evangelical minority preaches annihilationism: instead of sempiternally fried, Satan and his co-workers will, together with the wicked, be roasted to death. Well, if spiritual beings cannot die, apparently the reason why the Devil does not commit suicide, how can demons be destroyed? If they do not interact with matter, how can the fire of Hell burn them? Or are the infernal flames reserved for the torture only of murderers, rapists, thieves, homosexuals, atheists and the like? And if the dear reader is starting to find these questions ridiculous, is it not because they demonstrate that this whole story is a tremendous nonsense?

As any child knows, Hell is one of the principal dogmas of Christianity. Whenever Jesus wanted to strike fear into his listeners, he mentioned the lake of fire and brimstone. I have the impression the Catholic Church, maybe to appear a little modern, nowadays harps less on Hell, allowing it to be an almost exclusive theme of the Evangelical churches. Perhaps this was not the smartest of decisions, because scaring with the Devil and threatening with Hell still is one of the best strategies to soften the hearts of sinners, as we can see in the vertiginous growth of Evangelicalism. Be that as it may, let us try to imagine a place where people are afflicted, agonized, burned, mortified, penalized, punished, scourged, tormented, tortured and wounded for a long time. No, not ten thousand years. Not ten million years. Not ten billion years either. Caramba, but ten billion years is a long time! I know, I know, but I am talking about a period in which billions of billions (funny, writing this made me think of Carl Sagan) of years are not even the blink of an eye: eternity. That's right. Billions of people weeping and gnashing their teeth in a colossal furnace for infinitillions of years. Forevermore forever and ever!

Was the dear reader able to imagine that? Hell is the stupidest dogma of Christianity and Islam and the one that best evidences the perverse character of these religions. As American author and former pastor Daniel Edwin Barker said, "Any system of thought or any religion that contains such a threat of physical violence is morally bankrupt". Hell is irrational already because of its atrocious disproportionality. Although they live an average of 65 years, human beings are tortured for all eternity. (Of the thousands of Christian denominations, only a handful preach that Hell is not eternal.)

Like all human beings in the past, present and future, you, dear reader, are condemned and lost. But do not despair: you can be saved. It suffices that you admit being an unworthy sinner, in need of salvation, and accept Jesus as your savior. Apostle Paul wrote: "If you declare with your mouth, 'Jesus is Lord,' and believe in your heart that God raised him from the dead, you will be saved. [...] Everyone who calls on the name of the Lord will be saved" (Romans 10:9,13). Based on that, imagine a man who is so wicked, but so wicked, that when he looks at flowers they wither. Wherever he steps, not even a mother-in-law's tongue sprouts. His life is dedicated to the practice of all that is evil. He lies, cheats, traffics, beats, robs, kidnaps, rapes, tortures and murders. However, in the last seconds of his life the thug repents of all his sins and "calls on the name of the Lord". Consequently, he goes to Heaven to spend eternity chanting praises in the paradisiacal garden of his gleaming mansion of gold. On the other hand, an acclaimed cardiologist who consecrates himself to the salvation of poor patients' lives and, for promoting dialogue between nations, is awarded the Nobel Peace Prize goes to Hell to spend eternity roaring in pain on the satanic grills simply for not having believed in any invisible being.

Let us further imagine a man who does nothing but preach the Gospel. Year after year, decade after decade, Bible in hand, he goes around the world propagating Jesus. He founds churches, writes books and speaks on radio and TV. In the four corners of Earth, his magnetic charisma attracts multitudes to football stadiums and thousands of people are baptized. Yet, one beautiful day the Christian doctrines start to seem to him absurd. Surrounded by doubts even about the existence of God, bang! A fulminant heart attack. Assuming that Heaven and Hell exist, where does this evangelist of the masses go: up or down? As a result of his tireless missionary work, thousands of converts are gifted in Paradise with little palaces of gold, without, however, being able to thank the one who converted them, because the televangelist's spiritual vacillation teleported him straight to that gigantic brazier that roasts vacillating evangelists along with those who dedicated their lives to the practice of all that is evil, lied, deceived, trafficked, beat, robbed, kidnapped, raped, tortured and murdered. From not very far away, the pastor hears the screams of Hitler, Stalin, George Bush and Vladimir Putin. If he is unlucky, the Devil mistakes him for a Brazilian congressman and puts him to be grilled with the Evangelical Parliamentary Front.

Things get even more bizarre when one tries to imagine how the inhabitants of Paradise will be able to enjoy eternal life knowing that billions of human beings are being "tormented day and night for ever and ever" (Revelation 20:10). Having the soft twittering of birds as background music in the backyard of his mansion of gold, what will a citizen of Heaven feel when he stretches out in his hammock to savor paradisiacal grapes and suddenly remembers his daughter, who, for having rejected Christianity, is being tortured in the infernal oven, begging to die? Will he shrug his shoulders and say: "Too bad for her!" or "I warned her!"? Or will he lose his appetite? Or will God have reprogrammed the saved not only to never again sin but also not to think about their lost family members?

The Bible does not specify whether the punishments to which the wicked are subjected in Hell are proportional to the sins they committed. Assuming they are, is Tartarus divided into departments, one area reserved for murderers, another for thieves, another for rapists, another for homosexuals and so on? And if someone was a murderer, thief, rapist and homosexual, where does he fit in? And what to say of someone who was an atheist, but committed only petty little sins? Will his sentence be as severe as that of a genocider?

In the 1997 movie *Deconstructing Harry*, Harry Block, a character played by Woody Allen, pays a visit to the Devil. Hell is divided into levels, by the way a concept derived from the Koran. While the elevator descends, a female voice announces:

Floor five: subway muggers, aggressive panhandlers and book critics. Floor six: right wing extremists, serial killers, lawyers who appear on television. Floor seven: the media. Sorry, that floor is all filled up. Floor eight: escaped war criminals, TV evangelists and the NRA. Lowest level: everybody off.

The Morning Star, the brightest of the angels, the most intelligent creature in the Cosmos, had full consciousness not only that a created being cannot be "like the Most High" (Isaiah 14:14) but also that a rebellion against the Creator of the Universe is doomed to failure. It would be more or less like an amoeba trying to defeat a brontosaurus, but with a small aggravating factor: the brontosaurus is everywhere at the same time, has infinite powers and does not die. That alone is more than sufficient to expose the irrationality of this doctrine.

Idea for a documentary scene. At the door of churches and mosques, ask the faithful: "Did you know that God already knows if you are going to Hell?".

How is it possible that there are people willing to believe tales as fabulous as this one? Why do so many continue to believe these myths even after reaching maturity? Is it not also because of the almost irresistible seduction of the occult and supernatural? I have always liked and still today am drawn to mystery tales, such as those of Edgar Allan Poe, and fantasy, horror and superheroes movies. The extranatural fascinates us because it stimulates our imagination and satisfies our desire to escape reality. However, I do not know anyone who, because he likes superheroes, believes Superman exists.

How many people does the dear reader know who believe in vampires? Only 250 years ago, most of the inhabitants of the Balkan Peninsula believed vampires were real. So much so that the army of the Habsburg Monarchy, based in Vienna, Austria, was forced to send to Serbia, one of its provinces, a commission to investigate several cases of alleged vampirism. In present-day Serbia, no one believes in bloodsucking undead anymore, which for today's Serbs are nothing more than a curiosity of their folklore. In contrast, under threat of eternal punishment, more than four billion people are persuaded by Christianity and Islam to believe supernatural tales that are not 250, but between 1,300 and 3,500 years old.

According to Gallup International's 2012 *Global Index of Religiosity and Atheism*, 23% of the world's population is composed of nonreligious and 13% of atheists, which amounts to almost three billion people who do not feel even the slightest need to believe in the supernatural stories of the holy books. After all, if only 250 years ago it was common to believe in witches and vampires, what to say of the worldview of the time when these millenary books were written? Would it still today be natural to believe in the product of societies that in everything saw gods, demons, spirits and fantastic beings?

It is evident that churches feel it is increasingly difficult to convince people to believe the biblical accounts. Hence the need to simulate modernity, be led like companies and advertised like brands to make religion and themselves attractive to the most varied segments of society. However, does a being that created a universe with trillions of galaxies need to be propagandized by means of marketing strategies and its message commercialized?

I remember how common it was, in the 1980s, for the church to which I belonged to offer seminars for smokers. One or another participant always ended up converting. Today, many denominations make use of broadcasting to sell themselves. For churches, in a country where millions of poorly educated people, therefore with little critical sense, spend an average of six hours a day staring at a TV set, television is a blessing.

Tired of seeing more and more of its sheep running into the arms of Evangelical pastors, the Catholic Church decided to counterattack with singing priests who present themselves not as clerics, but in the style of artists of popular music and are frequent special guests of talk shows. The songs and these padres' way of singing and preaching are clearly copied from the Evangelicals.

Some years ago, on the TV channel it owns, the Universal Church of the Kingdom of God advertised what it calls the Congress of Victors (curiously the same name as an assembly of the Communist Party of the Soviet Union, in the Stalinist Era), people who, due to financial problems, suffered from depression, but who after starting to attend the meetings of this CV became happy owners of big houses with swimming pool and two or three cars in the garage. In the publicity, the name of the church is never mentioned and the presenter, who is more of a Wall Street yuppie, with the indispensable gel in the slicked back hair, is never called a pastor.

The Prosperity Theology makes not only the Catholic Church nervous but also some traditional Evangelical denominations, which have been tempted to copy to a greater or lesser extent the neo-Pentecostal style of arousing interest by approaching topics related to success in finance. A search I did on Google for the expression "*sucesso financeiro*" ("financial success") listed in seventh place the page *Sucesso Financeiro em 5 Regras (Financial Success in 5 Rules)*, from a site called *Novo Tempo (Hope Channel)*. On it, one sees a picture of a man not in jacket and tie, but in shirt and with gel in the slicked back hair. In one corner, an upward arrow, like those on financial charts of companies that have made a profit. In another, the logo of a TV program called *Saldo Extra (Extra Balance)*. No allusion is made to any church. One has to scroll down the long page to notice a small logo in almost the same color as the background. Only those who know it know that it is of the Seventh-day Adventist Church. On the right, the advertisement of a book, entitled *Administração Financeira da Família (Family Financial Management)*, does not mention the author. Clicking on it opens the page of the church's publishing house, where one finds out that the author is a pastor and the general director of Novo Tempo, the Adventist company that produces the program *Saldo Extra*, of which the man of God with gel in the hair is the host. The book's description reads: "You will know the antidote to not be contaminated with one of the worst diseases of the modern world, consumerism". Those who want to be cured of consumerism have to consume, that is, buy that booklet. The five rules for financial success turn out to be six: "A sixth and very important step is [...] return to God the tithes and offerings, be faithful and He will reward you".

Idea for a documentary scene. Ask the treasurer of the General Conference of the Seventh-day Adventist Church: "What is the bank name and the account number of the Creator of the Universe?".

Seminars for smokers, alcoholics and drug addicts, financial congresses, radio and TV programs, singing priests and pastors, selling of all kinds of religious items, in short, many are the strategies employed by churches to increase the number of sheep in their flocks.

Religious people like to claim that believing in God is natural, because the Creator implanted in his creatures the instinct to believe in him. If that were true, would there be a need to offer God from door to door and on radio and television programs? Would all people not believe, especially in the same god? However, what we observe is precisely what we would expect from a species whose eagerness to explain the reason for its existence makes it idealize thousands of gods and elaborate innumerable religious beliefs, many of which even combat each other.

If God exists and configured us to seek him, but knowing him is possible only through the true religion, why does he not reveal its name, thus putting an end to all this religious pandemonium? It would be easier than making a galaxy. If it is true that God wrote with his own finger on a wall, as related in the book of Daniel, what prevents him from writing the name of the true church on every wall on the planet? If that is too much to ask, then how about God making everyone have the same dream? If all Earth's inhabitants, on the same night, dreamed the exact same thing, that is, the name of the true religion, would anyone be able to doubt that it was a divine revelation?

Every religion is full of incoherences. Since it is increasingly difficult to deny that, it is now fashionable for followers of a religion to say religion is not important. Once, an e-mail from a Baptist Church pastor appeared in my inbox. It was about his success as a missionary. Although it was not addressed specifically to me, I answered him speaking of my critical view of organized religions and evangelism. The pastor countered: "When I speak of God, I am speaking of a person, Jesus, not of concepts or institutions". I replied: "It is naive of you to claim your missionary work is dissociated from religious institutions. As a pastor, you belong to a church. Thus, the Jesus of whom you speak is Jesus as he is seen by the church for which you work. There is no neutral Jesus, unless you restrict yourself to solely handing people a copy of the Gospels without saying anything, much less inviting them to your church, allowing them to draw their own conclusions".

The movie *At Play in the Fields of the Lord*, by Héctor Babenco, an adaptation of Peter Matthiessen's novel, shows with virtuosity the insanity that evangelization is, especially when the objective is to save the souls of indigenous people, whose customs and traditions are considered primitive, immoral and satanic by Protestant missionaries, who take the opportunity to combat the Catholic evangelizers. The result of that is arrogance, distortion, tension and conflict.

If there is an ideology that should be free of arrogance, it is religion (all the more so because it is based on conjectures). In many religions, humility is a doctrine as fundamental as love and forgiveness. The biblical god, for example, despises arrogant people. Often, the purpose of his punishments was precisely to make people be humble. Paradoxically, however, religions do not make people be humble. The countless religious wars throughout History are proof of that. Still today, individuals, peoples and countries antagonize each other for the simple fact of having different religions. It does not take a genius to realize that it is impossible for the idea of an absolute truth of universal validity, revealed to a people handpicked by none other than the Creator of the Universe, not to generate arrogance.

When I went to live in Austria, I lived for a few months with a family of members of the denomination to which I belonged. One beautiful day, two Jehovah's Witnesses knocked on the door and, contrary to what most people do, the man of the house invited them in. Before long, the three engaged in a debate about different Christian doctrines. Versed in biblical matters, my host was visibly excited at the opportunity to be able to demonstrate his knowledge. He leafed through the Bible in an almost frantic manner, rebutting the arguments of the missionaries with the smile of someone who sees himself at an advantage and takes pleasure in causing discomfort. Clearly, he had no consciousness that he was being presumptuous. In his mind, he was doing the right thing: defending the "truth".

Having no doubt about the things they believe, it is natural for religious people to feel superior to those who do not believe in the same way. If, however, the opponents are atheists, this feeling of superiority is stronger. On social media, it is common for Christians to retort to atheists with threats such as: "One day you will see, but it will be too late!". As incredible as it seems, it does not cross their minds that not only is it ethically wrong to frighten disbelievers, since no one should believe out of fear, but it is also ridiculous to threaten them with a punishment the believers themselves do not know exists.

False certainties are possible only when critical thinking has been suppressed and questioning has ceased to exist, reason why religious people are capable of believing the most baseless things. A good example of that is the prohibition of pork, contained in the Leviticus 11 list of animals that should not be eaten, obeyed by Orthodox Jews and some Christians, such as the approximately 50 million members of the Ethiopian Orthodox Church. Forbidden also by the Koran, 1.8 billion Muslims do not savor the meat of this animal either. However, notwithstanding being consumed for millennia, there is no indication that it causes harm to the point of needing to be declared dangerous, unless you hit someone over the head with a ham leg, which would be more a case of police than Science. Vegetarian nutritionists do not regard pork as worse than other meats, but just as equally harmful. In contrast, among those who say meat should be part of a healthy diet some even favor it over beef or chicken, because it contains less fat and more vitamin B6.

In view of this, no one, not even Orthodox Jews, can explain the reason why Yahweh forbade the consumption of pork. Indeed, the Torah contains several nonsensical commandments, such as the prohibition against trimming the edges of the beard. In light of modern Science, several of the biblical laws related to cleanliness have little or nothing to do with hygiene. Even Shlomo Yitzchaki, better known as Rashi, one of the most famous rabbis and commentators on the *Hebrew Bible*, admits that many of God's decrees, such as the prohibition against eating pork, wearing *shatnez* [clothing made of wool and linen] and the purification procedure effected by the water of purification [water mixed with red heifer ashes], have no rational justification. According to Rashi, the rationality of these commandments should not be questioned. God wants them to be obeyed even if they are not understood, reason why the biblical text says "I am the Lord", explains the rabbi.

When I ask my son not to do this or that, I do not want him to obey me like a robot, but to understand the reason for my requests, which necessarily must make sense. In contrast, Yahweh, or Allah (the same deity, only in a different religion), takes pleasure in blind obedience. Well, is modern Science not sufficiently advanced to find out what is so wrong with pork that justifies it having been forbidden by the god of the Bible and the Koran? Besides being useless, this law caused the death of many people. According to the books of the Maccabees, when he criminalized the practice of Judaism the Syrian-Greek emperor Antiochus IV Epiphanes forced the Jews to eat pork. For refusing, a mother and her seven children were tortured to death and a 90-year-old Hebrew died of scourging, despite being allowed to pretend to eat "forbidden meat". Fourth Maccabees is the work of someone who took the trouble to write an entire book about these nine people, who are portrayed as heroes just because they did not eat a piece of pork steak.

Swine meat is a good example of biblical and Christian incoherence. With no guilty conscience, the great majority of Christians eat pork, because they understand that Jesus abolished the law of unclean animals. However, since it is part of Scripture, which, as apostle Paul said, is "all inspired by God", the law about unclean animals is not an invention of Moses. On the contrary: it begins with a clear "The Lord said". It was, therefore, dictated by the very creator of the pig, Yahweh, who in the Christian conception is Jesus. If Yahweh-Jesus declared that the pig is unclean, reason why he forbade its consumption, how could this animal have ceased to be unclean? Had the pig always been a clean animal and Yahweh pulled a prank on his people? Is Yahweh-Jesus a sadistic god who takes pleasure in giving meaningless orders, just to test the obedience of his servants? Did Jesus, as if by magic, alter the pig's physiology, turning it into a clean animal? In this case, why did he not create it clean? By the way, why did he not create only clean animals? Or do these discrepancies not point to the obvious, that is, that these laws have nothing divine about them, but were made for merely nationalistic-political reasons, with the objective of differentiating and separating the people of Israel from the rest?

Besides the menu for meat eaters, the Creator of the Universe took the trouble to create laws about how to proceed with people with skin diseases, such as leprosy, but, incredible as it may seem, did not bother to pass on to Humanity information that would have saved the lives of millions of people, such as about bacteria and viruses and how to cure the sicknesses they cause. Instead, he limited himself to order that lepers be banished from the camp to, left to their own luck, or rather, bad luck, die alone.

The Almighty constantly acted in spectacular ways, such as making bread fall from the sky, but curing lepers, that he did not do. In the event that the skin disease were not leprosy, which without treatment is incurable, and one or another infected person were lucky enough to get well, Yahweh devoted an almost entire chapter to the rules that the lucky ones had to obey in order to be considered purified, like this one: "The priest is to take some of the blood of the guilt offering and put it on the lobe of the right ear of the one to be cleansed, on the thumb of their right hand and on the big toe of their right foot" (Leviticus 14:14). If this is not proof of how primitive the Judeo-Christian religion is, then I do not know what it is. A bird and three lambs had to be sacrificed and provide the blood with which the priest made propitiation for the convalescent, in order for their sins to be forgiven and the wrath of the biblical god appeased, because diseases in general, but especially the ones of the skin, were considered divine curses.

Apropos of that, when Aaron and Miriam criticized their brother Moses for marrying a foreign woman (I suppose because the foreign women did things the Hebrew ones were forbidden to do), God punished only Miriam, making her hand turn leprous. Aaron received no punishment. Thank goodness, God is not unfair and misogynistic!

Either the Bible was from cover to cover inspired by an infinitely loving, wise and, consequently, coherent being or it was not. However, "Ye shall know them by their fruits" applies only to human beings, never to God. Was it not King David who said: "Taste and see that the Lord is good"? Yet, there are many things in the Bible, said and done by God, which clearly are not good, such as this:

> The Lord said to Moses, "Say to Aaron: 'For the generations to come none of your descendants who has a defect may come near to offer the food of his God [...]: no man who is blind or lame, disfigured or deformed; no man with a crippled foot or hand, or who is a hunchback or a dwarf, or who has any eye defect [...], or damaged testicles. No descendant of Aaron the priest who has any defect is to come near [...]; because of his defect, he must not go near the curtain or approach the altar, and so desecrate my sanctuary.'"
>
> (Leviticus 21:16-23)

No comment.

It is undeniable that the god of the Bible discriminates against people with physical defects, which were considered divine punishment for sins that could have been committed also by their ancestors. On a stone tablet, with his own finger God wrote: "I, the Lord your God, am a jealous God, punishing the children for the sin of the parents to the third and fourth generation" (Exodus 20:5). Yet, since the biblical god is capable of not only regretting but also forgetting, some time later he forgot what he had written and contradicted himself: "He will not die for his father's sin [...]. The one who sins is the one who will die. The child will not share the guilt of the parent, nor will the parent share the guilt of the child" (Ezekiel 18:17,20). This passage goes against the very principle, obviously perverse, on which the Judeo-Christian religion is founded, according to which we children are paying for the sin of our parents Adam and Eve.

If people with physical defects were forbidden to approach the altar, in a much worse situation were those generated out of wedlock or descended from bastards. Those God did not want to see even in the last church pew: "A person of illegitimate birth may not enter the assembly of the Lord; to the tenth generation no one related to him may do so" (Deuteronomy 23:2).

Similar to the case of pork, Christians never ask themselves why God once abhorred the presence of adulterers and their posterities in the church if he later came to have no problem with them. Did the deity who uttered "I the Lord do not change" change his mind?

Strangely, many millions of the same Christians who claim Jesus removed from the pigs the label "Warning: unclean!" do not drink wine because they think God condemns it, when in fact there is no commandment forbidding the ingestion of alcoholic beverages. Quite the contrary: several biblical characters were fond of wine, including the great Noah, whom apostle Peter calls "preacher of righteousness". Fundamentalist Christians even claim Jesus turned water not into wine, but into grape juice, as if drinking grape juice at a wedding party were the most natural thing in the world.

Who would know better whether Yahweh disapproves of alcoholic beverages than the descendants of the redactors of the book that he practically dictated? The renowned Orthodox rabbi, professor and historian Berel Wein (with wine even in his name) wrote: "Wine is considered a holy drink — the only liquid drink that has its own special blessing to be recited before consuming it. Wine is part of all life-cycle events in Jewish life".

What good is it for a Christian not to eat pork, but to eat barbecue, cake and ice cream? What good is it for a Christian not to drink wine, but to drink soda? It is similar to the Christian who does not go to theaters, but watches TV, or to the Christian who does not read novels, but reads Christian fiction books, or to the Christian who does not steal, but shares pirated gospel CDs and DVDs, or to the Christian who gets indignant at the liberalization of abortion but does not get indignant when he sees children living on the streets.

Needless to say, hypocrisy is not something that is found only in religious circles. We are all susceptible to being hypocrites. Yet, among believers hypocrisy superabounds, and that is because of belief itself, since religions are based on the principle of holiness and purity, reason why the god of the Bible gave precise instructions to his worshipers about the things they must not think, do, eat, drink, wear, etc., lest they become unclean. "Be perfect as your heavenly Father is perfect" (Matthew 5:48), said Jesus himself, who, according to the Christian belief, was perfect and did not sin even in thought.

There is something unnatural in the Judeo-Christian religiosity that invariably generates hypocrisy, because the biblical deity demands from his worshipers a conduct that disregards human nature and, especially in modern times, is almost impossible to have, which can range from gossiping to squabbling on a soccer field, from telling white lies to cutting in line, from driving over the speed limit to not declaring goods bought abroad, from feeling antipathy to having sexual thoughts. That would not be a problem, if believers kept their beliefs to themselves. As we, however, know, they claim the Christian moral code is valid for all Earth's inhabitants, although they themselves do not live it as they should. In this way, they do what in German is called "preaching water, but drinking wine".

A 2007 study entitled *A New Generation Expresses its Skepticism and Frustration with Christianity*, conducted by David Kinnaman, president of The Barna Group, a California Christian company, revealed that 85% of non-Christian Americans between the ages of 16 and 29 think Christians are hypocrites. Just 16% have a good impression of Christianity as a whole and only 3% have positive associations in relation to Evangelicals. It is interesting to note that 75% are of the opinion that Christians are too involved in politics. The survey shows also that Christians themselves have a negative impression of Christianity. Half of them see Christians as hypocrites. 34% said Christianity is "old-fashioned and out of touch with reality".

As is the case with most Evangelical churches, the one in which I was raised also condemns going to movie theaters. During the two and a half years that I attended the Faculty of Theology, in São Paulo, I lived in the dormitory of the college, whose rooms had no television. Because of this, the students' thirst for watching movies could only be quenched at a professor's home. When a TV channel announced that it was going to air *Rambo II*, I and a group of classmates quickly planned to go see it, even though we knew it was a violent movie. In it, 69 people are murdered in 96 minutes, that is, approximately one for every minute and a half. However, those who are used to the extreme violence of biblical accounts, which they accept as true, find the Hollywoodian violence of *Rambo II* even amusing. Studying Theology did not take away from us the desire to watch worldly movies. If the church had a problem with movie theaters, we did not have a problem with movies, because at the same time that we were believers we felt the desire to be normal. For many young Christians, it is emotionally draining to live in this dualism. On one side, religion determining everything they should consider bad; on the other, human nature naturally wanting to enjoy life without the feeling of guilt.

In 2011, the same Barna Group published the results of another study, conducted over five years, entitled *You Lost Me: Why Young Christians are Leaving Church*. Kinnaman found that 59% of young American Christians walk away from the church after they turn 15. These are their principal reasons:

- Churches seem overprotective ("Christians demonize everything outside the church", "The church ignores the problems of the real world", "My church is too concerned that movies, music and video games are harmful").

- Experience of Christianity is shallow ("The church is boring", "Faith is not relevant to my career or interests").

- Churches antagonize Science ("Christians are too confident they know all the answers", "Churches are out of step with the scientific world we live in", "Christianity is anti-science", "The creation-versus-evolution debate turned me off").

- The church is simplistic and judgmental in relation to sexuality ("It's tense to live up to the church's expectations of chastity and sexual purity", "I've made mistakes and feel judged", "Teachings on sexuality and birth control are out of date").

- The exclusive nature of Christianity ("Churches are afraid of the beliefs of other faiths", "I feel forced to choose between my faith and my friends", "The church is like a country club: only for insiders").

- The church is unfriendly to those who doubt ("I don't feel safe admitting that sometimes Christianity doesn't make sense", "I'm not able to ask my most pressing life questions", "My faith doesn't help me with depression or other emotional problems").

I find it unlikely that there is a religion that does not impose guilt, but almost impossible that there is one that in imposing guilt beats Christianity. Guilt is the very essence of the religion of Jesus. The first thing many people feel when they leave Christianity is a tremendous relief at the disappearance of the burden of guilt. The Christian religion teaches that all human beings are guilty of the entrance of sin into the world. We all believed the talking snake and bit the forbidden fruit. All human beings are guilty of the death of Jesus. We all pierced his hands and shed his blood. Because of this, we are condemned, whether we like it or not, whether we believe this absurd story or not. As if that were not enough, the father of the one we killed (which is himself) monitors us day and night, night and day. He records all our actions and all our thoughts. We do not have a single second of privacy. Not even in the bathroom. We have no way to refuse, no way to not be part of this absurd story. Even wanting to be left alone is deserving of punishment. And the punishment is not just any one. If the overwhelming majority of Christians are right, those who refuse to believe this absurd story is absurdly tortured for infinite absurdillions of years.

Unless, of course, we turn off common sense, logic, intelligence, believe this absurd story, accept our guilt, repent that, 6,000 years before we were born, we bit the forbidden fruit and beg forgiveness from the one whose hands we, 2,000 years before we were born, pierced and whose blood we shed. That will almost allow us to live in one of the enviable mansions of gold of that 1,380 miles high cubiform city.

Yes, almost, because from then on we need to be afraid only of having had the bad luck not to discover which of the 40,000

Christian denominations is the true one, the one that correctly represents the one whose hands we pierced and whose blood we shed. No Christian is free from being surprised at the Last Judgment with the devastating information that he was a Christian in vain, because he was part of the false church. It is not impossible that on that terrible day, sitting at his old and enormous desk, God, with his voice of thunder, will say to a believer:

— Is this really your name? Eraldonclóbes Santos da Cruz?!

— Y-y-yes, Lord.

God looks the believer up and down.

— All right. Do you remember that leaflet they shoved into your hand on such and such a day there on the pedestrian mall and that you crumpled and threw in the trash?

— N-n-no... I d-d-don't remember... Lord.

— Hmmm... Don't remember, eh?

God snaps his fingers and a gigantic screen with a resolution that is not of this world appears behind him. He turns to it, snaps his fingers again and a hidden camera style video starts playing. In it, a man in a white shirt and black tie and pants is seen on the street shoving a leaflet into the believer's hand. Without stopping walking, the believer looks at the leaflet. The camera zooms in on his face and a contemptuous sneer can be seen. From another angle, the believer is seen crumpling the leaflet and, without looking, throwing it in the direction of a trash can. He misses the target and the little paper ball falls to the ground.

God turns to the believer.

— In addition to throwing the leaflet away, you dirtied the street, Eraldonclóbes.

Terrified, the believer does not know what to say. God continues:

— And that TV program, with that background image with sheep grazing and sunbeams passing through the holes in the clouds, do you remember?

— N-n-n...

God turns to the screen, snaps his fingers and a video shows the believer stretched out on the sofa, looking at the TV and shaking his head in disapproval, indignant at the pastor with the Bible in his hand. The believer presses hard on a button on the remote control and changes the channel.

Without turning to the believer, God proceeds:

— And remember the decal with a church logo on the window of that car parked in front of your house?

— C-c-car?

Another finger snapping, another video. As he leaves home, the believer notices a decal on a car window. Curious, the believer approaches, but when he recognizes the logo of a church he makes a face of disdain and moves on.

While slowly turning back to the believer, God snaps his fingers and the giant screen disappears. He looks at the believer, sighs and says:

— Well, Eraldonclóbes, they were all signs of the true church that I put in your path, but which you ignored, insisting on staying in the false church, believing it was the true one.

The believer sweats as if he had the Iguazu Falls on his forehead, but his mouth is drier than the dunes of Namibia's Skeleton Coast. God then looks down at the huge open tome on the table, licks his finger, leafs back and forth a bit, looks at the believer over his glasses, strokes his long white beard, leafs some more, turns to the side, and, getting up, says:

— Peter. Hey, Peter!

— Speak, Lord, for thy servant heareth.

— Are you busy?

— Yes.

— Look, take a break there and take my place here. I've had enough for today. And see if there's anything you can do for this guy. His name is… Eraldonclóbes.

— What's his name?

— It's not a mistake. This really is his name.

— Christian?

— Yes, but from the false church.

— Jesus! How many today?

— I don't know, I lost count. I sent a bunch of them to Hell.

— Oh, my God!

— I need to distract my mind. I think I'll go cause a little galaxy collision.

— No prob, you can go.

— Look, whatever you decide to do with this guy is fine with me, OK?

— Leave it to me.

As I have shown, it is not possible to choose a religion making use of logical-rational criteria. Any belief can be the right one and all can be wrong. Religious practice boils down to hoping to have been indoctrinated by the parents in the true religion or chosen the true one. Hoping. And nothing more. Therefore, how could anyone consider himself sensible when he seeks to convince others that his religion is the true one? How could anyone regard himself as coherent when he believes that those who refuse to accept his collection of speculations will be punished?

The objective of religions is to uniform Humanity through manipulation. Children are blank pages. Whatever their parents write on them the children believe. Indoctrinated, they grow up accepting the absurdities of their genitors' creeds as unquestionable truths. Accustomed to the irrationality of the beliefs that were imposed on them at an age when they could not defend themselves, they reach the age of majority conditioned to think religion is something indispensable. Unaccustomed to think for themselves, these now adults prefer to be guided. Even at a mature age, they see free thinking as an insult to God, which is a clear contradiction. If it is true that the Creator of the Universe gave us the capacity to think analytically and critically, why would he condemn the analytical-critical thinking that he himself created? How could God be just in demanding from his creatures that they believe in things that to them seem absurd? If to diverge from religious dogmas is to diverge from God, and to diverge from God is susceptible to punishment, then he really created not free people, but little robots. All little robots that do not think the way they have been programmed to think are defective. If they do not allow themselves to be fixed, they must suffer — horribly.

That alone would suffice to conclude that religions are an affront to the intellect. What affronts the intellect has no way to be healthy for the spirit, and what is unhealthy for the spirit must be repudiated.

5

Reality

"I've made more than a thousand promises,
said so many prayers.
It must be that I pray quietly,
because my God doesn't hear."

— Edu Lobo
(*Borandá*)

A FEW DECADES in the future. The media tell the most bombastic news in all of Humanity's history: Science has just discovered that God really exists. There is no longer any doubt. It is true. God exists, yessir. It is proven. Billions of believers almost explode with euphoria. Minutes later, a complementary news: Science discovered that God does not hear prayers and life after death does not exist. Abrupt silence. Shouts of jubilation stuck in the throat. Billions of dropped jaws. From euphoria to deep depression, in a second. Indignant at the nonexistence of Paradise, an hour later the believers start to say that this scientific research is bogus. Illuminati stuff.

Who would want to worship such a god? And what about serving him, a concept so fundamental to monotheistic religions, to the point that many believers take pleasure in saying that they are servants of God? What reason would anyone have to serve this god who now all people know exists, but does not give a damn about them?

Religions boil down to two things: recompense and punishment. What motivation would anyone have to follow Christianity or Islam, if Paradise were not part of their dogmas? And what reason do the Bible and the Koran have to promise crowns and mansions of gold if not to make the reward sound more attractive? Clearly, promising eternal life would not have sufficed. However, as ever more people find it dull to follow a religion that promises only future prizes, there are ever more Christian denominations promising also money and health, yet another incoherence to Christianity's long list of incoherences.

If Christians were 100% convinced that Paradise exists and that they should not worry about tomorrow, they would not spend this life running after money and social welfare, something that their Master, who had "no place to lay his head" and admonished people to sell everything they owned and accumulate "treasures in heaven", reproved. Hence the need for Christianity to promise benefits also for before death.

Personal advantage is, therefore, what motivates many people to follow a religion. A person who, through reflection, finds reasons to believe that there must be a creating force behind the Universe will believe in it on principle, and not to receive benefits, prizes and rewards. Eternal life, Paradise, protection, cure and prosperity are products sold by religions, and in none are they commercialized as successfully as in the Christian one. To follow Christianity is to buy what it has to sell.

I do not know any church that does not associate tithes and offerings with divine blessings. After all, that is biblical doctrine. When asking the Christians in Corinth for financial contributions for poor believers in Judea, apostle Paul does not limit himself to saying: "Folks, our brothers in Jerusalem need your help". Apparently, that would not have been sufficient to motivate the Corinthians to donate. So much so that Paul spends two whole chapters of the Bible on considerations about the importance of giving offerings. It seems that that would not have been sufficient either, because at one point he goes on to resort to promising divine rewards to the givers. Barefacedly, Paul states that "whoever sows sparingly will also reap sparingly, and whoever sows generously will also reap generously" and is not ashamed to say that "God loves a cheerful giver" (2 Corinthians 9:6-7). After that, what Christian would dare not open his wallet?

Soliciting financial help for brothers in the faith evidences that not even the greatest figure of Christianity trusted the biblical promises of divine support, such as that given through Solomon, the most blessed man on Earth: "The Lord does not let the righteous go hungry" (Proverbs 10:3).

It is undeniable that the book with the black cover links divine favor with faithfulness in tithing and generosity in offerings.

When we buy a product or pay for a service, we know exactly what we will receive. If we do not receive it, or if we are not satisfied, it is natural that we get disappointed, and we have the right to complain. With the innumerable biblical promises of protection, deliverance, cure and prosperity, it is not so. No matter how faithful and generous they are, there is no way for the worshipers of the god of the Bible to know if he will keep his end of the bargain, much less to demand of him that he keep it. Worse: if he does not grant what they ask for, it is not God's fault, but theirs. Maybe they are not being sufficiently faithful. Maybe they need a lesson. Whatever it is, God is never held accountable, because he is good and knows what he is doing.

In an attempt to explain why they do not receive what they ask for, it is common for believers to say phrases like "God is not obligated to grant requests". However, several Bible passages make it clear that this is not true, such as 2 Chronicles 7:14: "If my people [...] will humble themselves and pray and seek my face and turn from their wicked ways, then I will hear from heaven [...] and will heal their land". As one can see, God made a covenant with his worshipers: "If you do what I ask of you, I will do what you ask of me". The same thing is taught by the *New Testament*: "We know that God does not listen to sinners. He listens to the godly person who does his will" (John 9:31) and "If two of you on earth agree about anything they ask for, it will be done for them by my Father in heaven" (Matthew 18:19). Moreover, "God is not human, that he should lie [...]. Does he promise and not fulfill?" (Numbers 23:19).

It should not be forgotten that the biblical god is called father. The best example of this is the Lord's Prayer. This is not so by chance. Traditionally, the father's role is primarily to protect, and protection is what believers most expect from a deity.

Many people have difficulty conceiving that the Universe might not have been created. However, to imagine that there is a Creator, but that he is indifferent, does not care about his creatures, is for them much more difficult. Actually, unbearable. Yet, does the idea of a Creator who intervenes in his creation match reality? Is this what is observed? Does he really protect those who call him father?

There is no better way to indoctrinate people than through the use of music. Our brain retains images and read and spoken words, but if there is anything it really likes to retain, it is music. That is why it is so essential in churches and often used in the catechization of children. Thanks to Osiris, I do not remember the content of any of the thousands of sermons I have heard, but not even Thor is able to make me forget the lyrics of hundreds of Christian songs.

If everything that is sung in a church must be in harmony with what the Bible teaches, also the messages of the Christian hymns are regarded by the faithful as true. They do not disagree with or doubt any of their words, such as those of *Tenderly He Watches*, by George Beverly Shea:

Tenderly, he watches over you,
every step, every mile of the way.
Like a mother watching over her baby,
he is near you every hour of the day.

When you're weak, when you're strong,
when you're right, when your wrong,
in your joy, in your pain,
when you lose or when you gain.

Tenderly, he watches over you,
every step, every mile of the way.

Long before time began,
you were part of his plan.
Let no fear cloud your brow.
He will not forsake you now.

These lyrics summarize well the Christian conception of the Father in Heaven who guides and guards his children always, without ceasing and at every instant, "every step of the way".

Would this hymn be sung in churches, recorded and listened to, if it did not match what the Bible teaches?

Now, some examples of what the Holy Scriptures say about how God protects his worshipers and grants their requests:

The Lord is my shepherd, I lack *nothing*.

(Psalms 23:1)

The angel of the Lord encamps around those who fear him, and he delivers them. Taste and see that the Lord is good. [...] Fear the Lord, you his holy people, for those who fear him lack *nothing*. The lions may grow weak and hungry, but those who seek the Lord lack *no* good thing. [...] The righteous cry out, and the Lord hears them; he delivers them from *all* their troubles. The Lord is close to the broken-hearted and saves those who are crushed in spirit. The righteous person may have many troubles, but the Lord delivers him from them *all*; he protects *all* his bones, *not one* of them will be broken.

(Psalms 34:7-10,17-20)

Take delight in the Lord, and he will give you the desires of your heart.

(Psalms 37:4)

Blessed are those who have regard for the weak; the Lord delivers them in times of trouble. The Lord protects and preserves them — they are counted among the blessed in the land — he does not give them over to the desire of their foes. The Lord sustains them on their sickbed and restores them from their bed of illness.

(Psalms 41:1-3)

Cast your cares on the Lord and he will sustain you; he will *never* let the righteous be shaken.

(Psalms 55:22)

For the Lord God is a sun and shield; the Lord bestows favor and honor; *no* good thing does he withhold from those whose walk is blameless.

(Psalms 84:11)

A thousand may fall at your side, ten thousand at your right hand, but it will *not* come near you. [...] *No* harm will overtake you, *no* disaster will come near your tent. For he will command his angels concerning you to guard you in *all* your ways.

(Psalms 91:7,10-11)

But whoever listens to me will live in safety and be at ease, without fear of harm.

(Proverbs 1:33)

Ask and it will be given to you; seek and you will find; knock and the door will be opened to you. For *everyone* who asks receives [...]. If you, then, though you are evil, know how to give good gifts to your children, how much more will your Father in heaven give good gifts to those who ask him!

(Matthew 7:7-8,11)

Truly I tell you, if you have faith as small as a mustard seed, you can say to this mountain, "Move from here to there," and it will move. *Nothing* will be impossible for you.

(Matthew 17:20)

Truly I tell you, if you have faith and do not doubt, not only can you do what was done to the fig tree, but also you can say to this mountain, "Go, throw yourself into the sea," and it will be done. If you believe, you will receive *whatever* you ask for in prayer.

(Matthew 21:21-22)

Whatever you ask for in prayer, believe that you have received it, and it will be yours.

(Mark 11:24)

We know that God does not listen to sinners. He listens to the godly person who does his will.

(John 9:31)

Very truly I tell you, whoever believes in me will do the works I have been doing, and they will do even greater things than these [...]. And I will do *whatever* you ask in my name [...]. You may ask me for *anything* in my name, and I will do it.

If you remain in me and my words remain in you, ask *whatever* you wish, and it will be done for you [...], so that *whatever* you ask in my name the Father will give you.

(John 15:7,16)

My God will meet *all* your needs.

(Philippians 4:19)

Is anyone among you sick? Let them call the elders of the church to pray over them and anoint them with oil in the name of the Lord. And the prayer offered in faith will make the sick person well; the Lord will raise them up [...]. The prayer of a righteous person is powerful and effective.

(James 5:14-16)

Cast all your anxiety on him because he cares for you.

(1 Peter 5:7)

We receive from him *anything* we ask, because we keep his commands and do what pleases him.

(1 John 3:22)

What words leap to the dear reader's eye? Obviously, the ones I italicized, such as *nothing, no, all, not one, never, everyone, whatever* and *anything.* And what expressions are not contained in these divine revelations? Maybe, who knows, eventually, once in a while, if I feel like it and if I am not busy playing throwing stars into black holes.

These extracts, which many Christians know by heart, do not come from just any book, but from the Word of God, the Creator of the Universe. For his worshipers, everything that is written in it is, therefore, true. Several of these passages state that absolutely nothing bad happens to those who serve the biblical god. Yet, contradicting themselves, some say that adversities may occur, but that they are no reason for despair, because God favorably answers all the prayers of his servants and delivers them from all evils, including illnesses.

It does not take a genius to realize that these promises bear no relation to reality.

A bus carrying an Evangelical choir on a tour collided with an oncoming truck transporting iron bars. One of them broke loose, penetrated the bus and impaled a Theology student through the chest. He was an acquaintance of one of my brothers.

The son of an Evangelical couple, friends of my family, poor and very devout people, died of cancer while fulfilling his and his parents' dream of going to college.

A famous gospel singer, whom I knew personally and who took the message of his religion and the name of his church to millions of people, also died of cancer.

In São Paulo, the roof of an Evangelical church collapsed, killing nine and injuring 107 worshipers waiting for the worship service to begin. In recent years, many ceilings of "houses of God", both Evangelical and Catholic, have collapsed, causing deaths and injuries.

In Fortaleza, a priest who dedicated himself to the education of disadvantaged youths was murdered with a shot to the back while fleeing a robbery.

In Curitiba, a pastor was tortured in his home by three men. With a kitchen knife, they cut off his ear and later murdered him with a shot to the head, in front of his wife. The night before, the man of God had had an argument with the three, who were his neighbors.

A two-year-old girl was found floating in the baptismal tank of an Evangelical church in Joinville. She was taken alive to the hospital, but eventually died. The tragedy happened during the worship service, while the child's parents were listening to the sermon.

During a Pentecostal event in Maringá, a church member, father of two daughters, lured to his car a ten-year-old girl who was playing in the parking lot. At home, he raped and, with a plastic bag, suffocated the child. After committing necrophilia, he set fire to her corpse. Following that, the believer returned to the church and helped in the search for his victim. Still free of suspicion, the murderer went to the wake to comfort the girl's family.

When hearing news like this, does the Christian recognize that the biblical promises are at variance with reality? Of course not. His mind is so used to blocking out everything that contradicts what he has accepted as unquestionable truth and to justifying the incoherences of his belief that, instead, in these misfortunes the believer sees the confirmation that this world is under the Devil's dominion, although that does not explain why the Almighty does not fulfill what he promised.

Actually, these examples are not even necessary, because, in a country with almost 90% adherents of Christianity, everyone knows of cases of Christians who died of serious diseases or were fatal victims of accidents or violence. Before the dear reader finishes reading this paragraph, somewhere in the world a child will be sexually abused or murdered, even if his parents are believers. If the overwhelming majority of the world's population follow a religion, then when tsunamis, earthquakes, volcanic eruptions, hurricanes, floods, forest fires, landslides, ground subsidence and asteroid impacts kill hundreds or thousands of people it is obvious that the overwhelming majority of the victims believed in God.

Before any trip, it is common for Christians to pray for divine protection (as if God needed to be reminded of the promises he himself made). Certainly, that is what the 154 Catholics did who, on tour, were returning from religious festivals and lost their lives in the two biggest road accidents in Brazil, in 1987 and 1988. In the biggest one, the pilgrims, who were traveling ironically from Coração de Maria (Mary's Heart) to São Félix (Saint Felix), plunged over a precipice. If God decided to take them, he could have made them die sleeping in their comfortable beds. Yet, for some mysterious reason, he preferred it to be in such a horrible way.

Needless to say, the Judeo-Christian god is not the only deity not to protect his worshipers. In 1954, in the city of Allahabad, India, some 800 pilgrims of Hinduism's largest religious ceremony, the Kumbh Mela, who had come to wash themselves from their sins in a holy river, died trampled in a mass panic. Since 1987, in Mecca, the city in Saudi Arabia that Muslims consider the holiest in the world, more than 5,000 devotees have died especially trampled while worshiping Allah in the Hajj pilgrimage, a religious duty instituted by Mohammed himself and one of the Five Pillars of Islam.

In tragedies like these, it is impossible for a religious person who is in full possession of his mental faculties not to ask the most natural of questions: "Where was God?". Let us remember we are not talking about mere faithful, but about devout people. In the face of such catastrophes, how to pronounce stereotypical expressions such as "God knows what he is doing", or "God's ways are unfathomable", or even "God is love"?

Conceding that God protects his creatures, the misfortunes that befall believers demonstrate that they are no more protected than nonbelievers, from which it follows that divine interventions cannot be attested. Actually, believing that God intervenes generates discrepancies. If Christians really were under constant divine protection, they could experience adversity only if God withdrew his protective hand from them. In consequence, whatever bad happens to Christians is always God's will.

Idea for a documentary scene. When the popemobile, with its bullet-proof glass and surrounded by bodyguards, passes by, raise a sign with the biblical promise "A thousand may fall at your side, and ten thousand at your right hand, but it shall not come near you" and film the reaction of God's greatest representative on Earth.

If when they die, believers die in God, should their families not jubilate rather than lament? Instead of thanking God, should the believers who survive a calamity not be disappointed, even indignant, that he did not take them? After all, not only they continue to be susceptible to suffering but also to temptations that can cause their perdition. If those who died were delivered from the afflictions of the world and taken to Paradise, were they not favored and the survivors discriminated? How to thank God for the rescue, in view of so many deaths and such pain? What to say of the psychological traumas of the children who lose their parents in tragedies? And what does a believer think who survived, but was left with terrible sequels? If to save him was to make him suffer, did God not commit a wickedness?

A heavy rain can bring a city like São Paulo to a halt. When a plane crashes, sometimes we see on TV some passengers thank God for having arrived late and missed the flight. If God sent rain specifically to prevent some from boarding, it is the same one that caused the fall of trees, power outage, landslides, that flooded houses, brought about traffic accidents and led to the death of patients in ambulances that, because they were stuck in the traffic jam, were not able to arrive in time at the hospital.

With regard to diseases, believing in the biblical God does not make anyone immune even to simple colds, much less to tumors. When a church member has cancer, the whole congregation prays for him. If the congregation is large, it is hundreds or thousands of prayers a week. In vain. If the cancer is not treated or, even if in treatment, is in an advanced stage, "the prayer offered in faith will" not "make the sick person well" and "the Lord will" not "raise them up".

It does not cross the minds of the believers that if God answers the prayers of some and protects or cures them, he is an unjust god. To be just, he would have to answer either all prayers or none. If I had cancer, were cured and attributed the cure to God, how could I be grateful to him knowing that, every year, he lets ten million people, including children, first suffer for months, then die of this disease? If a Christian or Muslim father and his son have cancer, implore God to be cured, the father is cured, but the son is not, will the father be able to rejoice in his cure? If the father believes that God took his son to Heaven, will he not ask himself why he let him agonize, and for so long?

If it were true that prayer saves the sick, as the Bible says, Christians would have no need for doctors, medicines and hospitals. Ever and for any malady. The reality is that if a believer catches a simple cold, not even the most fervent supplication of his denomination's world president will make the pain in the muscles, throat and head, the sneezes, the runny nose and the cough disappear. Even praying, the believer will have to wait a week to feel better. If a Christian sprains his foot, prayers will not prevent the intense pain and inflammation of the ankle. Even if he promises God to dedicate the rest of his life to the evangelization of the world, the believer will be unable to walk for several days and it will take weeks before his foot returns to normal. Notwithstanding appearing to be a simple injury, without medical care a sprained ankle can leave sequelae.

If God does not cure simple illnesses, why would he cure serious ones? Furthermore, it is theology of the Bible itself that nothing can happen without God permitting it. Why, then, would he cure people of the diseases he permitted? Such a deity suffers from severe dissociative identity disorder. Worse: those who believe that God cures believe in a sadistic god, because if he cures the sick, but does not extinguish the diseases, he uses them to coerce human beings to worship him. Worse yet: a god who cures only those who implore him is a perverse god. Apropos of that, if cure comes from God, atheists cured from cancer are proof that it is not necessary to believe in him to be cured by him.

A religion derived from Judaism and Christianity, Islam is as irrational (and perverse) as they are. *Kutub al-Sittah*, a compilation of Muhammad's sayings and deeds, recounts that the prophet said: "Allah has sent down both the disease and the cure, and He has appointed a cure for every disease". In its turn, the compilation *Sahih al-Bukhari* relates that Muhammad uttered: "There is no disease that God Almighty has created, except that He also has created its treatment". God is like a physician or pharmacist who creates illnesses to be praised for curing them.

The belief in God not only does not cure but even can lead the sick to death. That is what happened, for example, to musical icon Bob Marley, one of the fathers of reggae. First a Catholic, then a follower of Rastafari and later a member of the Ethiopian Orthodox Church, when he discovered that there was a melanoma under his right foot's big toe nail, for religious reasons Marley did not undergo treatment, nor did he allow the toe to be amputated. Three years later, the artist sought help, but from alternative medicine. Marley died a few months afterwards, aged just 36 and at the height of his career.

Contrary to what the Bible says, Christians do not cure either, unless, of course, they are doctors. If what is related about Jesus is true and he really did all those miracles, why do we not see his followers transform withered hands into perfect ones? Why do we not see Christians make the blind see? Why do we not see Christians with five loaves and two little fishes feed a crowd of thousands of poor people? (By the way, would that not be the solution to the problem of world hunger?) Why do we not see Christians make the deaf hear? Why do we not see Christians make stutterers stop stuttering? Why do we not see Christians glue back severed limbs? And why do we not see Christians make the dead live, even though Christ said that those who believe in him can do greater works than the ones he did?

Does the dear reader want to have the pleasure of making pastors, gurus, healers, witchdoctors, shamans, etc., feel ashamed? It does not have to be an arm or leg. Take to them someone who has lost a pinky tip and ask them to restore it.

God does not cure because he does not hear supplications. In 1997, the University of New Mexico, United States, conducted an experiment to test the effects of prayer on a group of 40 alcoholics in rehabilitation. The study showed that prayers produced no effect on the participants' alcoholic habits. On the contrary: those for whom no one prayed drank less.

In March 2006, *The New York Times* published the results of a study that cost US$ 2.4 million and was funded by the Templeton Foundation, a Christian philanthropic organization, and led by Harvard University Professor Herbert Benson. It monitored 1,802 people who, in six hospitals, underwent bypass surgery. A third of the patients were informed that prayers would be said on their behalf, a third were told that perhaps someone would pray for them and for a third no one prayed. Members of three different churches made the supplications, mentioning the patients' names. The group with the lowest rate of complications and deaths was that of the operated patients for whom no one prayed, and the worst result had those who knew the faithful were praying for them.

If Christians stopped to reflect on the things they believe, such as prayer, they would have to realize their incoherences. The Bible says that, even though being omniscient, God wants his servants to address supplications to him. Clearly, he likes to see them implore. If each of the 2.4 billion Christians says two prayers a day, every single day the biblical god hears 4.8 billion supplications whose exact content he knows before they are uttered. God knows what a devotee will implore of him fifty years from now. Moreover, God knows what answer he will give even before the believer is born. Is there any profession more tedious than being God?

No matter how ardent the desire of religious people to believe in a Creator who cares about his creatures, listening to their prayers, the truth is that the very attributes of the god of the Bible and the Koran (especially omnipotence, omniscience, omnipresence and perfection) prevent him from existing. If the Universe was created by the deity of these books, who can be limited by nothing, not even by time, he must exist outside space-time. Existing, God is atemporal. Well, in atemporality, that is, where time does not pass, there is no change of any kind. Simply nothing happens. Zero. From this it follows that even thinking is impossible. Creating, however, is an action that results from an impulse generated by a thought. If there was a thought and an impulse, there was change. If there was change, time passed, something that did not exist. How, then, could an atemporal being have had the desire to create the Universe?

By the way, for what? Even if we ignore God's atemporality, a perfect being does not lack for anything, and a being who exists since always has no motive to create anything.

If, by reason of his attributes, the Judeo-Christian-Muslim god cannot be limited by anything, not even by time, for him the future does not exist. Everything happens now, in the present. Therefore, God does not hear prayers, because how could he make happen or not happen what for him is already happening? In consequence, free will, a dogma so essential to the Christian faith, is nothing but an illusion.

Since I am a nice guy, I saved the worst for last: a being that cannot be limited by time cannot exist in a system limited by time. Guess what. The Universe is limited by time! Not being able to be atemporal and temporal at the same time, God has no way to exist in the Universe.

In an attempt to overcome these difficulties, some Christians make use of arguments that end up generating even greater difficulties. They say, for example, that God was atemporal, but that when he created the Universe he became temporal, in order to be able to exist in it. The problem is that that would make God a being limited by time, just like us. Even if he could continue to be eternal, time would take away from him his omniscience and he would no longer know the future, which contradicts the biblical conception of God.

Let us ignore these incongruities and suppose that the god of the book with the black cover intervenes in the lives of his servants. While the great majority of Bible passages referring to prayer assure the faithful that God grants everything they ask of him, in some we read that he gives only when and what he wants. After all, Jesus himself prayed: "Thy will be done". If they ask and receive, believers say: "God answered my supplication". If they do not receive, they say: "God knows what he is doing". Whether or not they receive what they ask for, God's will is always done. That being so, praying is as ridiculous as it is useless, since "in all things God works for the good of those who love him" (Romans 8:28).

Deep inside, the believer knows his prayers will be answered only if he asks for obvious things. If he prays for the cure of a person with advanced cancer, he has consciousness that the chances of his prayers being answered are nil, reason why he ends his prayers with the cliché "You, Lord, know what is best for her". Would a Christian who needs a car, but does not have the money to buy one, ask God for it? Very unlikely. Yet, if he does, what is the probability that he will open his eyes, walk to his front door and find a car parked with a note taped to the window, on which one reads: "To my son Eraldonclóbes. Drive carefully. And don't forget the seat belt. Signed, God"? Now, if he prays saying: "Help me, o Father, to earn money to buy a car", and works hard, saving as much as possible, he may reach his objective. However, if he earns minimum wage, the believer can spend his life praying and hammering away. He will never stop going on foot, bicycle or, when he retires, bus.

What do believers ask for in prayer? Anyone who is or has been a Christian knows: protection, health, wisdom and peace. In essence, that's it. Day after day, year after year, the same petition. After all, what other things would they ask for? "Extinguish, o God, all volcanoes"? "End, o Lord, the earthquakes"? "Do not allow, o Father, black holes to devour stars"? Once in a while, they ask for something a little more specific, like help passing a test. Yet, they study, because they know God will not whisper the answers to them.

How many pieces of evidence are needed to recognize that the Creator of the Universe either does not exist or does not give a damn about his creation? For me, one is sufficient: churches that collapse on believers during worship service.

The discrepancies between what is written in holy books, and preached and sung in temples, and reality are glaring. Even so, billions of people insist on believing in invisible beings who have nothing better to do than listen to messages left on their voicemails and puzzle over whether any petition was sufficiently accompanied by flattery to deserve to be granted. Of these billions, the great majority insists on claiming that religion is good and, therefore, necessary. What, however, does reality say?

The *Global Study on Homicide*, conducted in 2019 by the United Nations Office on Drugs and Crime (UNODC), reveals that the American continent is the most violent region in the world. How, if it is precisely where the countries with the highest concentration of Christians are located? According to a 2020 survey by the Mexican organization Consejo Ciudadano Para la Seguridad Pública y la Justicia Penal, of the 50 cities with the highest murder rates 42 are in Central and South and five in North America (three in South Africa, a nation with almost 80% Christians). In Brazil, the largest Catholic country and the second largest Protestant nation, it is about 50,000 homicides per year (more deaths than in the Syrian Civil War). In contrast, the murder rate in the United States, the country with the largest number of Jesus worshipers, is four times higher than that of the Czech Republic, one of the most atheistic nations on the planet.

In 2020, the Global Business Policy Institute, in New York, asked 370,000 people in 148 countries if they feel religious. More than 98% of the inhabitants of Somalia, Niger, Bangladesh, Ethiopia, Yemen, Malawi, Indonesia, Sri Lanka, Mauritania and Djibouti answered "Yes". Eight of these countries are among the least developed. That's the question: Are they so underdeveloped because they are so religious or are they so religious because they are so underdeveloped? Both options put religion in a bad light. Of the wealthiest nations, the United States is the most religious. In Sweden, Denmark, Norway, Japan, the United Kingdom, Finland, France, Australia, the Netherlands and Belgium, only between 17% and 33% of people feel religious, that is, a clear minority.

And what about dishonesty? In Transparency International's 2019 *Corruption Perceptions Index*, the 20 least corrupt are all countries where most citizens give religion no importance. Notwithstanding being much more religious, the United States is more corrupt: 23rd place. Although it has ever more Evangelical politicians (or is it because of that?), Brazil is among the most dishonest nations, occupying the 106th position. The most corrupt in the world is exactly the most religious: Somalia, an Islamic country.

Those who argue that all this corruption, violence and poverty in the most religious countries has nothing to do with religion will have to explain why it does not prevent all this corruption, violence and poverty. Those who think religion improves the world need to ask themselves why there are still so many ills in it, even though Humanity has always been and continues to be very religious. Those who claim that, in view of so much religiosity, the world is not better because the majority of religious people do not do what God wants will be admitting that religion is useless. It is like an experiment gone wrong. Thousands of years of religious practices of all kinds have not had the desired effect, which is to make our planet a better place to live.

Let us consider topics such as wars, slavery, freedom of conscience, racial, gender and justice equality, social justice, health and education. Is it a coincidence that before the Age of Reason, when the world was dominated by religious thought, in these areas no progress was made, but after it, with the increasing secularization of societies, it was?

If religion is synonymous with morality; secularism, with decadence, should we not expect more justice from the more religious societies and see more injustice in the more secular ones? Since it is the opposite, it is natural to ask whether religions impede the development of Humanity. I have reasons to believe that without them the world would be much more developed.

In their eagerness to stigmatize Atheism as the source of all that is perverse, many believers resort to laughable arguments. The principal one is to claim that Atheism is responsible for the deaths of millions of people, which supposedly proves that without religion the world would be dominated by evil. Names such as Hitler, Stalin, Mao Zedong and Pol Pot are mentioned. To begin with, Adolf Hitler was not an atheist. In the fashion of biblical figures who were called by God to carry out special tasks, Hitler was fully convinced he had been entrusted with a divine mission: "I believe I am acting in the spirit of the almighty Creator: by defending myself against the Jew, I am fighting for the work of the Lord" (*Mein Kampf*, p. 70).

The Catholic Church, which, under the leadership of Pope Pius XII, maintained friendly relations with Nazi Germany, expelled many communists, such as Fidel Castro, but did not excommunicate Hitler. One of the worst genociders in History still today is a member of the Roman church.

Not only were the Nazis Christians but they even considered themselves the true followers of Christ, as an article, written by Karl Holz, a Nazi politician and the editor-in-chief of an anti-Semitic newspaper, shows:

This kind of coward troublemakers [moderate Christians] must be stopped. They are pests of the State and pests of Christianity. They are to blame, if the sane people turn away from Christianity. Because the people understand by religion something different than what these weaklings and hypocritical mamelukes mean and say. These opposition-driven false Christians are the worst weed that can be found among the German people. How to treat it is written in the Gospel: we have to uproot and destroy it.

(*Der Stürmer*, N° 37, September 1934)

In a speech in the city of Passau, in 1928, Hitler made it clear: "In our ranks we do not tolerate anyone who violates the ideals of Christianity [...]. This movement of ours is indeed Christian". As a matter of fact, Hitler had a real dislike for the "godless" and considered the Christian religion indispensable, as his speech in the Berliner Sportpalast, on October 24, 1933, proves: "We have taken up the fight against the corrosion of our religion [...], because we were convinced that the people need and require this faith. Therefore, we have not taken up the fight against the godless movement with a few theoretical explanations: we eradicated it".

Actually, it would not make the slightest difference if Hitler had been an atheist. Christians need to ask themselves why, despite being Christian, the overwhelming majority of the German and Austrian population not only did not oppose Hitler's racist regime but even wholeheartedly supported it. Germans and Austrians continued to go to church as normal, without ever seeing any conflict between Nazism and Christianity.

It is a historical fact that the Catholic Church has never opposed fascist and dictatorial regimes. Most of the time, it supported them. An example of the more than harmonious coexistence between Christianity and despots comes from the Balkans. After the Nazifascist occupation of Yugoslavia, Hitler and Mussolini installed Catholic Ante Pavelić, founder and leader of the ultra-nationalist and terrorist organization Ustaše, whose ideology was a mixture of Catholicism and Fascism, as leader of the Independent State of Croatia.

As soon as he was sworn in, Pavelić began to put into practice his fascist-clerical ideal of ethnic and religious cleansing of Croatia, persecuting gypsies and Jews. Yet, his principal target were the Serbs, who are not Roman Catholics, but members of the Serbian Orthodox Church. Early on, Pavelić commanded the construction of several concentration camps, with the Jasenovac Concentration Camp, also known as the Balkan Auschwitz, being the largest of them all. In it, prisoners, brought in cattle cars, were tortured and murdered by hammering and stabbing. There is no way to pinpoint the exact number of people who lost their lives in Jasenovac. While the government of Croatia claims about 100,000, some historians argue for much higher figures, which may be as high as 700,000 victims.

However, the terror regime instituted by Catholic Pavelić did not express itself only in his concentration camps. Several massacres were perpetrated by his Croatian Revolutionary Movement, the Ustaše, aimed at the almost total extermination of the Serbian Orthodox population. It is estimated that about 400,000 Serbs were murdered during the short existence of the Independent State of Croatia. Only those who converted to Catholicism had any chance of being spared.

In May 1941, a band of Ustaše militiamen detained about 400 Serbs in the small Serbian ethnic majority Croatian town of Glina, forcing them to enter a temple of the Orthodox Church. There, the Ustaše demanded that they present documents proving their conversion to Catholicism. Two, who possessed such documents, were released. The rest was murdered. Following that, the militiamen set fire to the church, but not before positioning themselves in front of the exit to shoot possible survivors who tried to escape the flames.

Is the dear reader's stomach already turned? Not yet? Then, let me tell you just one more episode. Right after that genocide, Ustaše promised freedom to all Serbs who converted to the Catholic Church. In July 1941, about 200 Serbs attended a ceremony of conversion to Catholicism that, it was announced, would take place in an Orthodox church in Glina. To their surprise, they were greeted not by clerics, but by Ustaše militiamen, who locked the doors from the inside and forced them to lie on the floor. Initially, the Orthodox began to be slaughtered with club blows. Soon after, the Catholics proceeded to slit their throats and smash their heads with rifle butt blows. The corpses were then piled on a truck and transported to a ditch. A month later, the church was burned down.

On May 8, 1945, the day of the capitulation of Nazi Germany, Ante Pavelić escaped to Austria, hiding in a small village in the Salzburg region. Almost a year later, using a fake Peruvian passport and disguised as a priest, the Catholic dictator fled to Italy, more specifically to the Vatican, which gave him shelter and protection for more than two years. Krunoslav Draganović, a Croatian Franciscan priest, member of the Ustaše, who in 1943 had assumed the post of secretary of the Confraternity of Saint Jerome, a Croatian organization in Rome, coordinated in detail the escape of thousands of Nazis and Ustaše members to South America, such as that of Klaus Barbie, the Gestapo war criminal known as "The Butcher of Lyon", and that of the genocider Ante Pavelić, who, in November 1948, went to live in Argentina. In 1957, Catholic dictator Francisco Franco granted him asylum in Spain, where Pavelić lived peacefully until he died at the age of 70.

Similar to what happened in Nazi Germany and Austria, it is no secret that Ustaše looted and confiscated the properties of the people it eliminated. There are strong indications that this wealth was converted into gold and deposited in the Vatican Bank and used to finance the ratlines, the evasion of war criminals, organized by Draganović. In 1999, survivors and relatives of Croatian Holocaust victims filed a class-action lawsuit in the United States against the Istituto per le Opere di Religione, aka Vatican Bank, and the Franciscan Order, claiming compensation. However, after several years of legal battle, and based on the American Foreign Sovereign Immunities Act, an appeals court eventually dismissed the case, recognizing immunity for the bank of the Catholic Church.

All conflicts open wounds, but those opened by conflicts with a religious background almost never heal (a "beautiful" example of this is the Middle East). Some 50 years after these unspeakable atrocities, the ground of former Yugoslavia was once again the scene of ethnic cleansing perpetrated by worshipers of one and the same god: Catholics, Orthodox and Muslims.

These people have at least two things in common:

Adolf Hitler, Catholic; Alberto Fujimori, Catholic; Alejandro Agustín Lanusse, Catholic; Anastasio Somoza Debayle, Catholic; Anastasio Somoza García, Catholic; Ante Pavelić, Catholic; António de Oliveira Salazar, Catholic; Augusto Pinochet, Catholic; Chiang Kai-shek, Methodist; Daniel arap Moi, Christian; Ferdinand Marcos, Catholic; Francisco Franco, Catholic; François Duvalier, Catholic; Fulgencio Batista, Catholic; Gabriel París Gordillo, Catholic; Georgios Papadopoulos, Greek Orthodox; Getúlio Vargas, Catholic; Gustavo Rojas Pinilla, Catholic; Humberto de Alencar Castelo Branco, Catholic; Ioannis Metaxas, Greek Orthodox; Ion Antonescu, Romanian Orthodox; Jean-Claude Duvalier, Catholic; Jerry Rawlings, Catholic; Jorge Rafael Videla, Catholic; Jozef Tiso, Catholic; Juan Carlos Onganía, Catholic; Juvénal Habyarimana, Catholic; Leopoldo Galtieri, Catholic; Miklós Horthy, Calvinist; Mobutu Sese Seko, Catholic; Rafael Leónidas Trujillo, Catholic; Reynaldo Bignone, Catholic; Robert Mugabe, Catholic; Roberto Eduardo Viola, Catholic; Teodoro Obiang Nguema Mbasogo, Catholic; Vladimir Putin, Russian Orthodox; Yakubu Gowon, Christian; Yoweri Museveni, Anglican.

This is a roll of dictators and authoritarian (or corrupt, or oppressive, or genocidal) rulers united also by a little thing called religion. All worshipers of Jesus. Not wanting the list to get too long, I left out the Muslim and Buddhist autocrats.

In the largest Christian nation on the planet, the United States, no presidential candidate will be able to get elected if he publicly declares to be an atheist. It will not make the slightest difference if of all the contenders the atheist is the best prepared, the one with the best résumé and of unquestionable integrity. As bizarre as it may seem, the mere fact of not believing in an invisible being is sufficient to be seen as unworthy of leading a country.

Although guided by Christian principles, American presidents have no problem with many of the oppressive regimes. A current example is Saudi Arabia, a theocracy where blaspheming, changing religion or wanting to live without it is punishable with death (any resemblance to biblical laws is not mere coincidence). The United States maintains "special relations" with this Arab monarchy, even though, between 2007 and 2012, it publicly executed 423 people.

It is well known that the largest Christian nation directly supported all Latin American dictatorships, several of which were brutal, such as those in Chile and Argentina. Presbyterian Ronald Reagan, successor of Baptist Jimmy Carter, sent Central Intelligence Agency experts to several countries in Central and South America to give classes on torture to their police. A training manual was elaborated by the CIA to teach the governments' agents to kidnap and murder leftists, blackmail citizens and burn villages. Recently made public, Reagan-era documents attest that, in 1986, the year of the assassination attempt on Catholic dictator Augusto Pinochet, the Presbyterian president planned to travel to Santiago to personally thank the Catholic general for "saving Chile" and offer him the opportunity for an "honorable departure", asking him to go to reside in the United States as a guest of the American government.

At least officially, the United Kingdom was opposed to the Chilean dictatorship, refusing to supply Pinochet with weapons. Yet, one of the first things Margaret Thatcher did when she came to power was to lift the arms embargo against Chile. The friendship between Anglican Thatcher and Catholic Pinochet was so close that he and his family visited the Iron Lady every year. In 1998, Thatcher publicly urged Spain, which was seeking to put Pinochet on trial for crimes of human rights violation, to release him. A year later, she visited "*Mi General*" in his house arrest, near London.

On the occasion of the death of the "Milk Snatcher", the nickname Thatcher received for eliminating free milk for schoolchildren aged 7 to 11, Protestant Barack Obama, in an official statement, declared: "The world has lost one of the great champions of freedom and liberty, and America has lost a true friend. [...] Here in America, many of us will never forget her standing shoulder to shoulder with President Reagan, reminding the world that we are not simply carried along by the currents of History: we can shape them with moral conviction".

Despite their Christian moral convictions, it did not make the slightest difference to Presbyterian Reagan and Anglican Thatcher that Catholic Pinochet personally ordered the creation of the

"Caravana de la Muerte", a squadron of the Chilean Army that, in 1973, toured the country from North to South, perpetrating veritable carnage on political prisoners. Buried in unmarked graves, they were presumed missing. Years later, when asked why the corpses of the executed were not returned to their families former General Joaquín Lagos Osorio replied:

> I was ashamed to look at them. They were torn to pieces. I wanted to put them together, at least in a human form. Their eyes were gouged out with knives and their jaws and legs, broken. At the end, they were given the coup de grâce. It was vicious. They were killed in such a way as to die slowly, that is, sometimes they were shot in parts: first the legs, then the sexual organs, then the heart. The machine guns were fired in that order.

Religion and authoritarianism are not incompatible because they are based on the same principles. Let us see: Do Judaism, Christianity and Islam impose themselves as holders of the absolute truth? Are their leaders endowed with incontestable authority? How did and do these religions treat adherents with divergent ideas? How did and do they treat nonfollowers? Do they tolerate diversity? How is their relationship with the arts?

The very word Islam means "submission", "subjection". Christianity goes even further and commands its followers to submit also to governments and pastors. It orders slaves to submit to their masters even if the latter treat them inhumanely, because "it is an acceptable thing with God, if, from a sense of duty to Him, a man patiently submits to wrong, when treated unjustly" (1 Peter 2:19).

Where submission is demanded, divergence is not tolerated. In fact, the god of the Bible severely punished divergers, and Jesus, the meek version of Yahweh, promised to torture in Hell those who turn their back on him.

Less than 300 years ago, people still were tortured and burned for going against Christian doctrines. Is it thanks to what, then, that Christianity no longer torture and burn anyone? Has it renounced biblical punishments and turned nice? The magic word is secularism. If it were not for the Age of Enlightenment, we would still be living in theocracies and divergers would be being tortured and burned. The Age of Reason made people lose their fear of critically reflecting on the Bible and realize the harmfulness of many of its teachings. The laicization of societies made it possible to create laws prohibiting the execution of heinous biblical orders, such as to murder disbelievers and practitioners of different faiths. To be able to exist, religions need religious freedom, which paradoxically comes from what they most combat: secularity. Only in secular and democratic regimes can there be tolerance.

At a congress of the Assembly of God, wagging his finger and yelling, his trademark, the pugnacious Brazilian pastor Silas Malafaia threatened:

> The pastor is vested with an authority that has been given by God. Who touches an anointed of the Lord and gets away with it? Don't touch God's anointed! This is very serious stuff. Don't take action against a pastor! I have seen people die because of this.

Is forbidding criticisms of authorities not what dictators do and dying for criticizing authorities not what happens in dictatorships? The Bible contains several examples of people who were punished or killed for criticizing "men of God". Even simply laughing at a prophet's baldness was worthy of being torn to pieces by a bear.

Why are divergers executed in Islamic theocracies? Because in theocracies there is no freedom of conscience. Christians cannot be against theocracies. After all, the Bible itself teaches that theocracy is a divine institution. The *Old Testament* is nothing but the story of a theocracy whose people, at the behest of God's representatives, exterminated peoples with different religions and were constantly and severely punished for doubting or turning to other gods. Yahweh never granted Israel such basic rights as these:

> Everyone has the right to freedom of thought, conscience and religion; this right includes freedom to change his religion or belief [...]. Everyone has the right to freedom of opinion and expression [...]. No one may be compelled to belong to an association.
>
> (Articles 18, 19 and 20 of the *Universal Declaration of Human Rights*)

If Heaven exists, I do not want to go there, because I do not want to live in a theocracy. I want to have freedom of thought, conscience, religion, belief, opinion and expression.

In case the dear reader belongs to the group of Christians who spread around that psychopaths like Ioseb Besarionis dze Jughashvili, better known as Stalin, killed in the name of Atheism, I advise you to start spreading also that theistic rulers killed and kill in the name of Theism, unless, of course, you do not mind being a person of illogical reasoning, because if you do not disassociate the actions of a Stalin from his Atheism, why do you separate the actions of a Pinochet from his Theism? If Christian despots are not good examples of Christianity, atheist despots are not good examples of Atheism.

To kill in the name of Atheism is simply impossible. Atheism is not a set of doctrines or principles. Atheism is disbelief in the existence of deities. Disbelief — and nothing more. Does the dear reader believe in the Abominable Snowman? You do not? And in the Centaur? Neither? If those who do not believe in God are atheists, those who do not believe, for example, in Saci Pererê are asacipererereists. Is the dear reader an asacipererereist? I bet you are. The question that every asacipererereist needs to ask himself is: Does Asacipererereism command me to kill? Just like the disbelief in the existence of Saci Pererê, the disbelief in the existence of gods teaches nothing, and what teaches nothing motivates to nothing. Therefore, neither Asacipererereism nor Atheism command anyone to do anything. The inhumanities committed by Stalin, Mao Zedong and Pol Pot have, then, no way to have been motivated by Atheism. What motive would an atheist have, because of his disbelief in God, to blow himself up in a marketplace or fly a plane into a building?

Religions are the ones that are sets of doctrines and principles and codes of ethics that shape thoughts and stimulate to acting. Religious dogmas are the ones that can generate fanaticism and produce intolerance. It is undeniable that the god of the Judeo-Christian and Muslim religions commands to kill. It is written in the Bible and the Koran for any child to read. How, then, could someone be motivated to kill by not believing in the existence of a god who commands to kill?

When they claim that Atheism leads to moral decadence, Christians and Muslims shoot themselves in the foot, because they confirm the total superfluity of Christianity and Islam. For the world to be moral, it would suffice, then, that no one is an atheist, that is, that all people follow any theistic religion, for example Candomblé, an Afro-Brazilian religion.

No matter how old a deity is, there was a time when he did not exist and a day when someone had the idea to create him. One day, someone invented Yahweh, also known as Allah, the god of the Bible and the Koran. Thus, the atheist who is convinced by a Christian or Muslim that Atheism is bad does not need to worship their god, nor those of others. It suffices that he creates his own god.

Let us imagine that I were a heliolater. I believe the Sun is God, but that he does not speak to his creatures. Consequently, he has never asked me to write a book and preach. Question: What harm would my heliolatry do? Other than, because I worship the Sun, me being called a lunatic, none. Now, let us imagine that I not only believe the Sun is God but also that he has desires. The Sun speaks to me and commanded me to preach that all people must worship him. However, not just anyhow. There is only one right way to do it. The Sun gave me a list of the things he requires of everyone. Those who do not worship him or do not worship him the right way are evil, and the evil the Sun tortures in a lake of fire and brimstone. That, dear reader, is not believing in God. That is religion.

Regimes of atheistic dictators have a lot in common with religion. According to several Russian historians, Stalin was a paranoiac who believed in conspiracy theories and did nothing but take advantage of the religious subservience of a gullible and superstitious population, for centuries accustomed to venerating their emperors, who were also the heads of the Church, as saints. Russia's almost miraculous victory over Germany was seen by many Russians as proof that the Soviet leader possessed magical powers.

Speaking to Google employees, in 2007, journalist and author Christopher Hitchens said:

Stalin says all thanks are due, at all times, to the leader and you must praise him at all times for his goodness and kindness. And, incidentally, he always kept the Russian Orthodox Church on his side. It remained part of the regime. Stalin was not so stupid as not to know he had to do that, just as Hitler and Mussolini made an even more aggressive deal with the Roman Catholic Church and with some of the Protestants. And remember: the other great axis of evil person of that time, the Emperor of Japan, was not just a religious person, but actually a god. So Fascism, Communism and Stalinism and Nazism are actually nothing like as secular as some people think, and much more religious than most people know.

I've been to North Korea. I can tell you, North Korea is the most religious State I've ever been to. I used to wonder, when I was a kid, what would it be like praising God and thanking him all day and all night. Well, now I know, because North Korea is a completely worshipful State. It's set up only to do that, for adoration. And it's only one short of a Trinity. They have a Father and the Son, as you know, the Dear Leader and the Great Leader. The Father is still the president of the country. He's been dead for fifteen years, but Kim Jong-il, the little one, is only the head of the Party and the army. His father is still the president, head of the State. So you have in North Korea what you might call a necrocracy. One, just one, short of a Trinity*: Father, Son, maybe no Holy Ghost, but they do say that when the birth of the younger one took place, the birds of Korea sang in Korean to mark the occasion. I suppose I should add they don't threaten to follow you after you're dead. You can leave North Korea. You can get out of their Hell and their Paradise by dying. Out of the Christian and Muslim one, you cannot.

[* In 2011, Kim Jong-un, grandson of the founder of North Korea, became Supreme Leader, thus creating the Trinity]

To associate Socialism and Communism with Atheism is another big simplism typical of religious people. Although socialist governments have been guided principally by the ideas of the antireligious Karl Marx and Friedrich Engels, Socialism was not invented by these two. The communist way of life was practiced long before they were born. There are Christians who argue that Jesus was the originator of Communism. Two of the most central themes of the Nazarene's teachings are simple life, stripped of material riches, and solidarity, so much so that this is exactly how his followers came to live. If the dear reader is a Christian, read carefully:

> All the believers were together and had everything in common. They sold property and possessions to give to anyone who had need.
>
> (Acts 2:44-45)

> All the believers were one in heart and mind. No one claimed that any of their possessions was their own, but they shared everything they had. [...] There were no needy persons among them. For from time to time those who owned land or houses sold them, brought the money from the sales and put it at the apostles' feet, and it was distributed to anyone who had need.
>
> (Acts 4:32,34-35)

Based on these verses, if what the apostles and early Christians practiced was not Communism, then I do not know what it was.

The Bible contains teachings that made, and still make, Christians commit monstrous cruelties. It is true that everything can be twisted, but it is impossible to justify a book being twisted in such a barbaric way by so many people for so long. Is it not incredible that the Creator of the Universe was not able to reveal his will in a way that could not be distorted? In *Godless*, American former pastor Daniel Edwin Barker asks: "Paul wrote that 'God is not the author of confusion', but can you think of a book that has caused more confusion than the Bible?".

On what does the dear reader think did the Dutch Reformed Church in South Africa, whose motto is "One Body and One Spirit", base itself to openly support the policy of racial segregation known as Apartheid? You hit the nail on the head: on a mixture of Calvinist doctrine of predestination with the biblical ideology of chosen people. South African Protestantism followed the line of thought of ultraconservative Calvinist theologian and Dutch Prime Minister Abraham Kuijper, who regarded blacks as descendants of Ham, son of Noah. Genesis 9 relates that Ham saw his father's nakedness, which led Noah to curse his son, Canaan, who would become the servant of his two uncles, Shem and Japheth. According to Kuijper, dark-skinned people are at the lowest level of human evolution and represent a threat to whites, the descendants of Shem and Japheth, reason why the latter have the divine right to subjugate blacks.

The conception that nonwhites are races cursed by God has a long tradition in Christianity. The so-called curse of Ham was repeatedly used by Christians as a justification for slavery especially of blacks, but also of Indians.

In his manuscript *América Abreviada (America Abbreviated)*, from 1693, Portuguese priest João de Sousa Ferreira, missionary of the Order of Saint Peter, states that blacks and Indians are descendants of the cursed Cain and Ham. Both peoples have "the same inclinations, consisting in idleness, sensuality and drunkenness, in catching and eating each other. [...] Indians and blacks are only nations that persevere in these curses and in others, but with a more horrible difference, as people who have been losing faith and completely falling from the grace of God". They are "heirs and imitators of the curse of Ham", which was a "divine disposition" and "is fulfilled to the letter in the Indians as well as in the blacks". The Indians, however, are worse than the blacks, assures the missionary, because "they are barbarians, inconstant and without faith, law and king. [...] Indians are by inclination traitors, fearful, cowardly and superstitious". "There is no divine law that forbids the possession of slaves", says the priest, who also owned some, because nowhere in the Holy Scriptures is slavery reproved. On the contrary: "Our Lord wanted there to be in the world great and small, free and slaves". The catechist reasons that it cannot be injustice to enslave Indians, since, being naturally lost, as servants of Christians they at least have a chance to be saved.

Faithful to the tradition of the belief in cursed people, Marco Feliciano, Brazilian pastor of the Assembly of God Church and congressman, expressed himself, in 2011, through his Twitter account thus:

Possibly the first act of homosexualism in History. The curse that Noah casts upon his grandson, Canaan, spills over the African continent. Hence famine, pestilences, diseases, ethnic wars. Noah's curse on Canaan touches his direct descendants, the Africans. Africans descend from an ancestor cursed by Noah. This is a fact. On the African continent rests the curse of paganism, occultism, miseries, famine, etc. Diseases originating there: Ebola, AIDS.

The account of the more than exaggerated curse that Noah cast upon his grandson Canaan, who, having nothing to do with the story, ended up paying the price for his father having seen his grandfather naked, is not only obscure, and somewhat comical, but also the Bible nowhere makes any reference to black people being damned and, consequently, inferior. As if that were not enough, the justification for white supremacy is based on the naive assumption that this account is a historical fact, and not a legend, which by the very way the event is narrated is evident. And even if it were historical, the curse was not pronounced by God, but by Noah. Add to this several problems of a logical and moral nature. If God really cursed black people to be slaves, the question becomes inevitable: What kind of god is this who brings suffering upon so many generations of innocent people?

Thus it says in the respected *Commentary Critical and Explanatory on the Whole Bible*, written in 1871 by Protestants Robert Jamieson, Andrew Fausset and David Brown and still today published: "Cursed be Canaan — This doom has been fulfilled in the destruction of the Canaanites, in the degradation of Egypt and the slavery of the Africans, the descendants of Ham". On Amazon, readers of this work rate it very good.

The first thing the Spanish conquistadors did when they set foot on the beaches of the American continent was to read to a crowd of curious natives the *Notificación y Requerimiento Que Se Ha Dado de Hacer a los Moradores de las Islas en Tierra Firme del Mar Océano Que Aún No Están Sujetos a Nuestro Señor*, better known as *El Requerimiento (The Requirement)*. The text says the Indians are creatures of the Christian deity, to whom the whole world belongs. He established Saint Peter as Pope, "to be lord and superior of all people of the world and obeyed by all, who was head of every human lineage, wherever men lived, under whatever law, in whatever sect or belief; and gave him all the world for his kingdom and jurisdiction, [...] to rule the world and judge and govern all peoples, Christians, Moors, Jews, gentiles or of whatever other sect or belief they were". One of the successors of this "lord, king and superior of the Universe", a title that, by the way, "will continue until the world ends", "donated these islands and the firm land of the oceanic sea to the said king and queen and their successors in these kingdoms, with everything therein, according to what is contained in certain scriptures [...], which you may see, if you wish". If the natives do not offer resistance and, recognizing "the Church as mistress and superior of the Universe and the world", consent to be evangelized, the conquerors will receive them "with all love and charity". They will not be enslaved or forced to convert. However:

> If you do not do so [...], I assure you that, with God's help, we will enter mightily against you and make war against you in all parts and ways we can and subject you to the yoke and obedience of the Church and Their Majesties and take you and your wives and children and make you slaves, and as such we will sell them and use them as Their Majesties command, and we will take your goods and do you all the harm and damage we can, as to vassals who neither obey nor wish to receive their lord and resist and go against him, and we declare that the deaths and damages that from this will follow will be your fault, and not that of Their Majesties, nor ours.

Grotesque as it may seem, the invaders believed the Holy Spirit made the natives understand Spanish, reason why the conquistadors even gave them time to deliberate. By all appearances, the Holy Spirit did not give a damn about the Indians, because they did not understand a damn word the Spanish said. The rest is History.

In 1401, my ancestor Jean de Béthencourt sold his house in Paris and pawned his castle in Normandy in order to finance an expedition to the Canary Islands. Two Franciscan friars were part of the crew. With the support of Spanish King Henry III of Castile and Antipope Benedict XIII, who promised to forgive the sins of all those who helped Béthencourt in his crusade against the infidels, he forced the natives to convert to Christianity. Many were enslaved and killed and those who were imprisoned died of starvation.

Christians who believe that morality is learned from the Bible either do not read it carefully or ignore everything that causes them discomfort and embarrassment. In fact, it contains innumerable examples of immorality either practiced by God or ordered or endorsed by him. Would the Europeans have committed so many barbarities, if the Book of Books taught that invading nations and enslaving or exterminating their peoples is immoral? It is clear that the invaders were fully convinced they were doing God's will.

When Catholics and Protestants killed each other or executed witches, heretics, followers of other religions and atheists, they were not attacking biblical morality, but doing exactly the opposite: applying it. If killing children, pregnant women, the elderly and the sick were immoral, the god of the Christians would have never given this order:

> You must certainly put to the sword all who live in that town. You must destroy it completely, both its people and its livestock. You are to gather all the plunder of the town into the middle of the public square and completely burn the town and all its plunder as a whole burnt offering to the Lord your God.
>
> (Deuteronomy 13:15-16)

To make matters worse, the killings ordered by the god of the Bible did not even have to make sense. With the death of Solomon, God's chosen people was divided between the Kingdom of Israel, in the North, and the Kingdom of Judah, in the South. Both Jeroboam, the king of Israel, and Abijah, the king of Judah, did "that which was evil in the sight of the Lord", practicing the polytheism of their forefathers. There was even sacred male prostitution. With the objective of reconquering the North, one beautiful day the king of Judah decided to make war against the king of Israel. Although Abijah was wicked, God helped him slaughter half a million of Jeroboam's soldiers — for nothing at all, because the kingdom remained divided and was never reunited. Small detail: years earlier, Abijah's father, Rehoboam, already had made plans to reunite Israel. A prophet, however, forbade Rehoboam to make war and kill his compatriots in the North, since it would be in vain: the division of the kingdom was God's will.

What in the Bible is moral does not justify what in it is immoral. If it is moral for the biblical deity to punish a father, as it did with King David, making his little son die in agony, but it would be immoral for us to do the same, this deity is as much a "Do as I say, not as I do" type of deity as the deities of any other religion. Brandishing a book that they believe to be the foundation of morality, it is with fury that many Christians fight women's right to abortion, despite this morality having been invented by a god who makes use of feticide to punish those who turn their backs on him:

> The people of Samaria must bear their guilt, because they have rebelled against their God. They will fall by the sword; their little ones will be dashed to the ground, their pregnant women ripped open.
>
> (Hosea 13:16)

Is it really necessary to worship such a primitive god, or any other, to distinguish right from wrong? Is there really a need to submit to the irrationalities of a religion to be a good person?

Let us imagine again that I believe the Sun is God. He has revealed himself to me. The Sun asked me to preach that life is a gift of unconditional love. He expects nothing in return. Nothing at all. Zero. The Sun does not reward or punish any person. He asked me to warn people that Paradise and Hell exist. We create them ourselves. Paradise is the automatic result of doing no harm to anyone and being solidary. Acting contrary to this principle results in Hell. All the Sun wants is for us to live life in the best possible way, because it is the only one we have.

There. I have just created a religion far better than all the ones of which I have ever heard. For not following it, no one is discriminated against, nor enslaved, nor persecuted, nor tortured, nor killed, because, unlike the god of the Bible, Koran and others, the god of my religion abhors these things. And as if that were not already sufficient to adore the Sun, on top of that he does not need money. Is it not divine?

What? The dear reader liked my religion, but not the part where the Sun is God? Hmmm... No problem. Take out the Sun and follow the rest.

6

Reason

> "Does the Lord have, to alleviate the suffering,
> someone to implore or fear?
> Because if God has no God, how can he want me
> to be a believer when he is an atheist?"

— Celso Viáfora
(*Deus de Deus*)

ONE OF THE functions of a book's ending is recapitulation. Therefore, do not upset yourself, dear reader, if, between new subjects,
in this last chapter (the next one is an appendix) I make additional
comments on topics already covered. I want, however, to make it
very clear that this in no way constitutes a reason for you to ask
for your money back. If you have any questions, please consult my
team of lawyers in New York, the same that defended O. J. Simp-
son.

Religions exist for the indignant at death. They sell them the
hope of living eternally, which has to be paid for not only with
money but also acceptance of a bunch of doctrines that range
from childish, contradictory, absurd and irrational to wrong.

Conjecturing about life after death is not reprehensible, nor
shameful. It is just a waste of time. So far, so good. The problem
lies in believing that eternal life is a prize and that to be decorated
it is necessary to worship a god, follow a religion, believe everything it teaches and practice its rites. And it is a problem not because it is hogwash, but because it is harmful, since it leads to fanaticism and causes division, disputes and conflicts.

The purpose of life cannot be, as the late Raul Seixas used to
sing, to stay "with a gaping mouth full of teeth waiting for death
to arrive" to go to live in a better world. Possibly, most people
would like death not to be the end. Yet, is living eternally really
good? What do we know about eternity to suppose that it is desirable? It may very well not be. In his novel *A History of the World in
Ten and a Half Chapters*, Julian Barnes tells the story of a man who
dies and goes to Paradise, where all the wishes of all people are

fulfilled. For hundreds of years, the man had three splendid breakfasts a day and sex with countless women, trying out all kinds of possible positions. He got so good at golf that every shot was a hole in one. Notwithstanding, over time everything he did ended up losing its fun. Talking about this with an administration employee, she reveals to him that in Heaven no one is obliged to live eternally: whoever wants can ask to die. Surprised, the man asks: "And how many people ask to die?". The employee answers: "All".

Religious people believe so fervently in eternal life that many of them even think it is a matter of logic. It is supposedly illogical for life to have an end. However, as said by one of the wisest men who ever walked on Earth, whose sneakers' latchet I am not worthy to unloose, "Thou art stardust and to stardust thou shalt return" (1 Bitencourt 24:7). That's it. With the greatest naturalness, believers accept that there was a time when they did not exist, but they do not accept that there will be a time when they will not exist: the same state of nonexistence in which they were before they were born.

Furthermore, life is life. There are not different kinds of life. There are only different kinds of living things, but the life that is in bacteria is the same that is in plants and people. Consequently, life after death should not be an exclusive privilege of human beings. If life does not cease with death, all trees and plants and all vertebrate and invertebrate animals go on living after they die. Why should we continue to live, but not the chimpanzees, with whom we have 99% of DNA in common? As one can see, besides being irrational the religious conception of eternal life is arrogant, since it is anthropocentric.

If the true life is the one that begins after death, the one we now have is false. If this were so, we would have no reasons to seek happiness, nor to prolong life, nor to put children into the world, exposing them to the possibility of perdition. Actually, it would even be logical to kill children, in order to ensure their salvation. Does it sound grotesque? Yes, but that has happened more times than the dear reader imagines. In December 2014, in Texas, the US state with the largest number of churches (precisely 27,848), Lindsey Blansett killed her ten-year-old son Caleb, while he was sleeping. She told police that when she hit Caleb on the head with a rock, he woke up and said: "Mom, stop!". She then stabbed him to death. Following that, she called the police saying she had saved her son "from further suffering in his life". Blansett had decided that "it would be better for Caleb to go to Heaven tonight".

This heinous crime is an excellent example of absurd Christian logic. By it, it is undeniable that this mother did a good deed, because she catapulted her innocent son to Paradise. However, things get even more absurd: if she had consciousness of what she was doing, nothing prevents Blansett from genuinely repenting and going to Heaven to reunite with the son she murdered. Now, if she suffers from mental disturbances, even better: not being responsible for her actions, Blansett already has the keys to her celestial mansion of gold reserved.

If the dear reader is one of those who think that only Pentecostal fanaticism can make a Christian kill relatives, you have not yet heard of John Emil List, from Westfield, United States. As vice-president of a bank, List was a highly respected man. Just like his parents, he belonged to one of the most traditional denominations: the Lutheran Church. In November 1971, List murdered his entire family: mother, wife and three children. The letter he left on his desk was addressed precisely to the pastor of his congregation and reveals that List's greatest concern was the possibility of his loved ones going to Hell, especially because of his daughter's ambition to become an actress. "I was fearful as to what that might do to her continuing to be Christian." If she left the church, List rationalized, this could negatively influence not only her siblings but also her mother, who was not very firm in the faith. The letter further states:

At least I'm certain that all have gone to Heaven now. If things had gone on, who knows if this would be the case? [...] After it was all over I said some prayers for them all. [...] I leave myself in the hand of God's justice and mercy. I don't doubt that He is able to help us, but apparently He saw fit not to answer my prayers the way that I hoped they would be answered. This makes me think that perhaps it was for the best, as far as the children's souls are concerned. I know that many will only look at the additional years that they could have lived, but if finally they were no longer Christians what would be gained? [...] I'm only concerned with making my peace with God, and of this I am assured, because of Christ dying even for me.

Asked why he did not commit suicide, the familicider replied that this would have prevented him from going to Heaven, where he hoped to be reunited with his family.

If the Christian eternal life exists, when List meets his children again they will hug him and say: "Thank you, daddy, for murdering us! You saved us from the lake of fire and brimstone".

On the day I write these lines, Evangelicals Bruce and Deborah Leonard, from Clayville, New York, citizens of a country of enlightened people, beat and flogged their two children for not wanting to go to the worship service. One of them died. Other members of the church, whose name is Word of Life, also participated in this, according to the couple, "counseling session" — which lasted ten hours.

"Millions of Christians do not beat their children to death", a believer will argue. It is true. To the believer I reply like a believer: What does Scripture, which "is given by inspiration of God, and is profitable for doctrine, for reproof, for correction, for instruction in righteousness", teach about this? In Deuteronomy 21:18-21 and 13:6-10, Yahweh-Jesus orders the murder of children for rebellion and family members for turning their backs on him. Therefore, it is for fear of being arrested that millions of Christians do not beat their children to death, or because they feel that this is something that should not be done, and not because it is abominable to the god of the Bible.

In Numbers 31, Moses, the man with whom Yahweh spoke "face to face, as one speaks to a friend", commands the Israelite soldiers to invade a nation and kill all the men, women and boys, but take for themselves the virgin girls. I have never seen a Christian get indignant at this barbaric wickedness.

Christians who, instead of feeling repulse, find justifications for the exterminations perpetrated by Yahweh-Jesus' "chosen people" cannot think it wrong to kill disobedient children, since also that order was given by him. No Christian can say that Bruce and

Deborah are bad examples of Christians. After all, all these parents, with the help of their brothers in Christ, wanted was to prevent their offspring from being thrown into the flames of Hell. To that end, they did precisely what the Christian god commands. Would they have committed that crime, if the book with the black cover condemned the beating and murder of children "who do not obey their father and mother"?

Christians who think the members of the Word of Life Church have committed a terrible sin must stop calling the Bible the Word of God. Orders, commandments and laws given by the inventor of morality cannot be immoral. If it once was moral to stone rebellious children, since it was a divine order, this cannot have become immoral.

A doctorate does not free anyone from having his reasoning deformed by religion. A proof of that is the Christian apologist William Lane Craig, professor at Talbot School of Theology, in California. This is what he thinks about the carnage ordered by the Judeo-Christian god:

> God knew that if these Canaanite children were allowed to live, they would spell the undoing of Israel. [...] Moreover, if we believe, as I do, that God's grace is extended to those who die in infancy or as small children, the death of these children was actually their salvation. We are so wedded to an earthly, naturalistic perspective that we forget that those who die are happy to quit this earth for heaven's incomparable joy. Therefore, God does these children no wrong in taking their lives.

In other words, smiting Canaanite children with the edge of the sword was an act of divine love. Incredible! How did I not think of that before?

Perpetrated by humans, atrocities are atrocities. If that order had been given by a World War II general, Christians would rightly call him a genocidal pedophile monster. Perpetrated or ordered by the biblical deity, these same atrocities are not atrocities, but "God's plan", "God's power" and "divine justice".

However, the most common of the subterfuges used to justify the Bible's barbarities and bizarrenesses is also the most revealing.

When Christians say "Oh, that was the custom of the time", they are admitting and confirming that their religion has nothing divine about it, but is pure reflection of the primitive mentality of the people who conceived it. Yahweh was not only not against but was even in favor of things that in biblical times were customs and, consequently, moral, but that his worshipers today deem immoral, such as incest, polygamy, genocide, slavery and stoning of adulteresses and rebellious children. Special would be the Judeo-Christian god, if, precisely because they were customs, he had condemned all these practices.

The whole of Christendom selects from the book it considers sacred the parts that are convenient for it, deciding what still is valid and practicable. Nonfundamentalist Christians, for example, claim that the horrific accounts in the Bible, such as that of Sodom and Gomorrah, in which Lot, whom apostle Peter calls a "righteous man", offers his own daughters to be raped by a band of wicked men, are not literal, but allegories, from which one should only seek to draw lessons. Well, is that not exactly what we do with any literary work? In this case, there is no reason for the Bible to enjoy a privileged position in relation to other books, including those of other religions.

Religion causes insensitivity. Millions of Jews celebrate on Pesach a liberation in which Yahweh killed, it has been estimated, about 1,000,000 Egyptian children. The religion of the Jews not only seduces them to celebrate an event that, according to archaeologists and historians, never happened but also to have no problem with this liberation having been the work of a god who devastated an entire nation and murdered millions of innocents for the mere pleasure of demonstrating his destructive power: "Pharaoh will refuse to listen to you — so that my wonders may be multiplied in Egypt" (Exodus 11:9). Worse: the deity whom the Jews thank for having delivered them from Pharaoh's hands (not without first letting them suffer as slaves for 400 long years) is the same one that did not lift a single finger to deliver millions of them from Hitler's hands. When God delivers, even by means of genocides, this is cause for celebration. When he does not deliver, "God knows what he is doing".

The bad thing about religions is that they are capable of leading their followers to practice evil convinced they are obeying the orders of the Creator of the Universe. Unable to make their biblical-fundamentalist view prevail in Europe, in the 17th century Puritan Protestants emigrated to North America. However, as everyone knows, the American lands already had owners. The autochthons did not want to sell and the Christians did not want to buy. Solution: usurpation through extermination. When the resistance of the "heathen natives" was great, the invaders thought God was punishing them for their sins and lack of faith. Yet, when they massacred many Indians the Christians thanked God, as evidenced by the document *First Thanksgiving Proclamation*, from June 20, 1676 (any similarity with the genocides ordered and commanded by Yahweh-Jesus will not have been mere coincidence).

In July 1743, Georg Friedrich Händel composed the cantata *Dettingen Te Deum* (of which, by the way, I have sung an aria) to, in London's Chapel Royal, thank the Christian god and praise him for having helped Great Britain to defeat France in the Battle of Dettingen, in Germany. In it, about 8,000 soldiers were killed (plus hundreds of horses, but, when it comes to war, has the dear reader ever seen anyone care about the equines' fate?), most of them French. If the French had won and killed thousands of Britons, they would have been the ones who would have composed a cantata to thank the "Lord of Hosts" and praise him.

Some more than others, but all religions are dictatorships of thought, because they dictate how their adherents must think, what they can accept and what they must reject. If a church labels, for example, the Scientific Theory of Evolution as a satanic teaching, its members will demonize it, even if we show them on their own bodies pieces of evidence that it is factual.

In order to impress the public, inducing it to believe that the number of scientists who disagree with Evolution is significant, the Discovery Institute, a conservative Christian organization from Seattle, United States, published, in 2007, the statement *A Scientific Dissent from Darwinism*. It has been endorsed by about 1,000 scientists, only one-quarter of them biologists. To mock that and demonstrate that the overwhelming majority of scientists defend Evolution, the National Center for Science Education, in Oakland, created the Project Steve, which consists of a list of evolutionary scientists, but only with the given name Steve. Around 1,500 Steves have signed the list.

In fact, scientists who believe in God are a minority. According to The Pew Research Center, in 2009 they made up only 33% of the scientific community in the United States, a number that in Europe is even smaller. Of this minority, only a small part believes in the biblical god, while the majority is deist, that is, does not believe in any specific god. Of all American scientists, 97% defend Evolution, 87% believe it is a purely natural process and only 8% that it is guided by a supreme being.

When flying or when taking medicine, Christians are trusting the advances of Science. Yet, when it comes to Evolution millions of them send this same Science to Hell. According to the biblical literalists, "it takes faith to believe what Science teaches", reason why "it is religion too". That is shooting oneself in the foot, because it is admitting that one should not trust what has to be accepted by faith, something Science, by the way, does not require, since it is based on evidence. Precisely because of this, unlike religion, Science has no problem with correcting itself. It is both hilarious and bizarre that someone ridicules Evolution, but believes in a bunch of things without evidence, like talking snakes and donkeys.

If some denominations have come to accept Evolution, then just because for them it is increasingly difficult to deny the innumerable pieces of evidence that Earth was not created in six days and is not only 6,000 years old. Notwithstanding, they will never acknowledge that the account of the woman who was impregnated by an immaterial being and gave birth to the very being who impregnated her is mythology. For its part, the Catholic Church will never admit that teaching that this mother died a virgin is nonsense.

If it is true that "God's invisible qualities — his eternal power and divine nature — have been clearly seen, being understood from what has been made, so that" no one has any excuse not to believe in the god of the Bible, should the scientists, precisely the people who study Nature in such a meticulous way, not be the first to acknowledge that he exists? Is the scientists' disbelief a plot? Are they deliberately rejecting God, out of malice?

"Forget the scientists!", a Christian will say, "Take the philosophers. The majority of philosophers believe in God". I am sorry to say that nothing could be further from reality. The study *What Do Philosophers Believe?*, conducted by University of Western Ontario and New York University philosophers David Bourget and David Chalmers and published in 2013, revealed that of 931 philosophers, most of them doctors, from 99 Philosophy departments at various universities in and outside the United States, 72.8% are atheists.

Religious people need to ask themselves why the great majority of scientists and philosophers do not believe in God, let alone in the Judeo-Christian god. To say it is because of rebellion is childish. The skepticism of academics demonstrates that inferring from Nature the existence of a Creator is not as natural as apostle Paul would have us believe. The simplism of his reasoning is most evident in the verses after Romans 1:20. Paul states that all those who reject the god of the Bible do so on purpose and automatically become, among other things, arrogant, boastful, cheaters, contentious, deceivers, depraved, disobedient, envy, evil, fools, futile, God-haters, gossips, greedy, haters, idiots, image worshipers, impure, insolent, liars, merciless, murderers, shameful, sinful, slanderers, spiteful, wicked and homosexual. Those who do not worship the biblical deity, the apostle concludes, deserve death. By the beard of the prophet! How not to classify that as delirium?

If the Judeo-Christian god exists, he does not show himself because he does not want to. If the Garden of Eden existed, I was not there to eat from the forbidden fruit. If Jesus existed, I was not there to nail him to the cross. If the Bible is the Word of God, it is not my fault that it is confusing. If I accepted its contradictions and perversities, it was because I was conditioned to do so. The day I reflected on what it teaches, it became evident to me that a book that contains so many absurdities can be anything but divine.

On the internet, contemplate, dear reader, the photograph entitled Hubble eXtreme Deep Field. Try to imagine a universe with two trillion megacolossal galaxies. Supposing they are the work of a supernatural being who wants to reveal himself to Humanity, would you expect the mind that created these fantastillions of stars and planets to choose a collectanea of copies of copies of more copies of rags of fragments of parchments from the Iron Age as a way to communicate? Even if it were by means of a book, would you not expect it to be direct, clear and precise and contain really useful and practical information, especially in the fields of Science and Technology, that would lead to the eradication of hunger and diseases and to a harmonious coexistence among all peoples? Would the author of that book be the same intelligence that gave orders like this one?

> This is what the Lord Almighty says: "[…] Now go, attack the Amalekites and totally destroy all that belongs to them. Do not spare them; put to death men and women, children and infants".
>
> (1 Samuel 15:2-3)

Jesus himself evidenced the superfluity of the nearly 1,200 chapters and 31,000 verses of the Bible, when he said that all of it boils down to just two things: believe in God and do good (Luke 10:27). The fact is that the ethics of reciprocity, or golden rule, that is, the sense that one lives better when one does good, does not even come from the book with the black cover, but was already applied in Ancient Egypt, as attested in the story of *The Eloquent Peasant*, written some 2,000 years before Jesus was born, where one reads: "This is the command: 'Do to the doer to cause that he do [thus to you]'".

If Jesus said: "Look at the birds of the air", I say: "Look at the birds of the air, but also at the galaxies". When we contemplate them, we feel how childish the conceptions that religions have of God are. If he exists, God cannot be so small, capricious, sadistic. This includes liking to be flattered. Yet, flattery is exactly what the biblical deity never tires of demanding. Apostle Paul states that man was made exclusively for the glory of God. It is exactly because of this that the first teaching of the *Westminster Shorter Catechism*, written in 1647 by English and Scottish theologians, is: "Question 1: What is the chief end of man? Answer: Man's chief end is to glorify God, and to enjoy him for ever". If you, like me, are a parent, imagine your children in front of you, kneeling or standing, thanking you, adoring you, exalting you, singing praises to you and shouting "Holy, holy, holy!" and "Glory, glory, hallelujah!". Now, imagine billions of people doing that for infinite centillions of years. My goodness, that is enough to plague a saint!

Faith in him is not the only requirement of the Christian god for one to be decorated with the "crown of life". Jesus also expects the believer to obey a list of regulations, which can range from no smoking, no drinking, no eating this or that, no wearing of pants or jewelry, no nail-painting, no listening to worldly music or reading worldly books and no swearing to no dancing, which reminds me of that joke in which an Evangelical couple decides to change churches. Before joining, the man and the woman want to know from the pastor of the new congregation everything that is forbidden. "In my church", says the man of God, "only dancing is forbidden". The couple looks at each other and asks: "Only dancing?". "Only dancing. Dancing, and nothing else." Husband and wife almost fall backwards with joy. After all, they do not like dancing anyway. Yet, knowing that sex is the thing about which the biblical god is most concerned, they ask: "But what about conjugal life, pastor, any restrictions?" "None. It's really only dancing that's not allowed." Perplexed, the couple inquires if this or that sexual practice is forbidden. "All allowed." Rejoicing, husband and wife joke: "And standing sex? Is it allowed?" To their total surprise, the clergyman replies: "Oh, no standing sex". "Standing sex is not allowed?!?" "No. No standing sex." "But why, pastor?" "Because it incites to dancing."

Besides observing the list of prohibitions of the god of the Bible, making your church grow gives you extra points. However, it really is indispensable to pay tithes, because the Creator of the Universe, the one who said: "Look at the birds of the air; they do not sow or reap or store away in barns, and yet your heavenly Father feeds them. [...] So do not worry, saying, 'What shall we eat?'

or 'What shall we drink?' or 'What shall we wear?' For the pagans run after all these things" (Matthew 6:26,31-32), needs lots of dough to feed and clothe his pastors and maintain his temples.

It is fundamental to participate in its rites, even if knowing what God wants is not as easy as it should be. Does the Holy Communion really have to be with wine or can it be with grape juice? Does the bread really need to be yeastless? And if it has yeast, will God get angry? Will he cry? The other day, I watched a video of a Christian ridiculing a number of churches and accusing their members of being followers of Satan. Reason: to pray standing, instead of kneeling, which, according to him, is what God requires.

While our space probes explore planets, moons and comets, billions of people continue to be guided by the mindset of people who believed Earth is flat and has four corners. Valerie Tarico, Ph.D. in Counseling Psychology from the University of Iowa, USA, published a list of some of the bizarrenesses that, in the 21st century, people in our neighborhood believe. Does the dear reader recognize the religions that teach them? The answers are further down.

- The foreskin of a saint may lie safeguarded in reliquaries made of gold and crystal and inlayed with gems, or it may have ascended into the heavens all by itself. (2)
- A race of giants once roamed the earth, the result of women and demigods interbreeding. They lived at the same time as fire breathing dragons. (1)
- Evil spirits can take control of pigs. (1)
- A talking donkey scolded a prophet. (1, 3)
- A righteous man can control his wife's access to eternal paradise. (6)
- Brown skin is a punishment for disobeying God. (6)
- A prophet once traveled between two cities on a miniature flying horse with the face of a woman and the tail of a peacock. (4)
- God forbids a cat or dog receiving a blood transfusion and forbids blood meal being used as garden fertilizer. (7)

- Sacred underwear protects believers from spiritual contamination and, according to some adherents, from fire and speeding bullets. (6)

- When certain rites are performed beforehand, bread turns into human flesh after it is swallowed. (2)

- Invisible supernatural beings reveal themselves in mundane objects like oozing paint or cooking food. (2)

- In the end times, God's chosen people will be gathered together in Jackson County, Missouri. (6)

- Believers can drink poison or get bit by snakes without being harmed. (1)

- Sprinkling water on a newborn, if done correctly, can keep the baby from eons of suffering, should he or she die prematurely. (2)

- Waving a chicken over your head can take away your sins. (3)

- A saint climbed a mountain and could see the whole earth from the mountain peak. (1, 2)

- Putting a dirty milk glass and a plate from a roast beef sandwich in the same dishwasher can contaminate your soul. (3)

- There will be an afterlife in which exactly 144,000 people get to live eternally in Paradise. (8)

- Each human being contains many alien spirits that were trapped in volcanos by hydrogen bombs. (5)

- A supernatural being cares tremendously what you do with your penis or vagina. (1, 2, 3, 4, 6, 7, 8)

1) Evangelicals; 2) Catholics; 3) Jews; 4) Muslims; 5) Scientologists [Scientology Church]; 6) Mormons; 7) Christian Scientists [Church of Christ, Scientist]; 8) Jehovah's Witnesses.

Nature has equipped human beings with a critical sense, the same that makes believers feel that the invisible beings and places of other people's religions do not exist. If they feel that, then they feel that the invisible beings and places of their own religion do not exist either, believing in them only because of infant conditioning and/or incessant autosuggestion. Those who have learned to fear, for example, the biblical deity dare not doubt his Word.

After all, "Without faith it is impossible to please God" (Hebrews 11:6). It is common for Christians to pray saying "Lord, increase my faith", which evidences the unnaturalness of believing the things the Bible teaches. To believe them, the mind needs to be constrained. If doubting the existence of invisible beings is natural, asking an invisible being, whose existence we naturally doubt, to increase our faith in him is nonsense. Besides, if God increased our faith it would not be genuine, nor would he have any reason to demand faith, because if he can increase it, why not to its fullness, making us never doubt?

If believers had no consciousness that they believe in fantasies, they would not get furious in the face of criticisms of their faith. On YouTube, videos that expose the irrationalities, for example, of the Bible are watched also by Christians, who, unable to contest them with a simple "This is not true", in the comments curse and threaten with infernal torture. It is hilarious, because Hell is one of the things considered grotesque by atheist videomakers, who are as afraid of the Christian Hell as Christians are of the Muslim Hell.

It is immoral for Christianity and Islam to threaten with eternal punishment those who do not accept their nonsense. I try to live a life devoted to good, and that not because I long for a reward, but because it does good to myself. However, I do nothing special, because living a life devoted to good is what the majority of people do. It does not take a genius to know that good generates good and evil generates evil, from which it follows that happiness is possible only where good predominates. There is nothing religious about that. It is a natural consequence. There is no need for God to exist or for a promise of reward and a threat of punishment for people to feel the desire to practice good.

Apropos of that, the threat of eternal punishment goes against the very dogma of free will, so crucial to Christianity. Of what value would a decision be that I made with someone pointing a gun at my head? In Stalin's Soviet Union, between joining the Communist Party and being sent to a labor camp in Siberia I certainly would choose the first option. However, while I pretended to admire Stalin, I still would be able to try to escape. Not so with

Christianity. There is no way to pretend and nowhere to escape. There are only two options: follow Christianity and agree with everything the biblical god did, does and will do or be grilled on Tartarus' braziers for infinite centillions of years.

Free will would be legitimate only if there were no threat of torture and people had not two, but three options to choose from: to live eternally with the biblical god, to live eternally without the biblical god and not to live.

Religion is so deeply rooted in the history of Humanity that the majority of people never ask themselves whether it is necessary. Many people simply assume that without belief in a god one cannot have integrity. If that were true, prisons would be almost empty. Analyzing data on 191,322 inmates, the Federal Bureau of Prisons, in the United States, found that, in 2015, only 197 of them, or 0.1%, were atheists.

Religions are nothing special. Proof of this is that anyone is capable of creating one, including you, dear reader. In Brazil, having your own church takes two days and costs around US$ 100. Amen? And you can even be creative. Any bedtime story can be transformed into a religion. Duly registered, your church will enjoy not only total tax exemption but even the protection of the State: those who ridicule it you can sue for vilification. Want movie stars to be members of your church? Nothing easier: base your dogmas on science fiction books. Many stars are just waiting for someone to launch a competitor to Scientology Church.

To demonstrate how anything can be labeled as sacred and enjoy respect, in 2005 American Bobby Henderson founded the Church of the Flying Spaghetti Monster, whose members are called Pastafarians, alluding to pasta and Rastafarianism, an Abrahamic religion that developed in Jamaica. In the photos of official documents, such as identity cards, it is forbidden to appear covering the head. However, exceptions are made for religious people. Because of this, by law the State has no way to prohibit that also Pastafarians appear covering their heads with the object that distinguishes them from the followers of other religions: a colander.

There was a day when human beings began to ask themselves why they exist. Not knowing how to answer, they invented answers. Religion is the illusion of having answers to questions to which no one has answers. The longing for answers arose before the capacity to scrutinize Nature developed in the human being. It does not take a genius to realize that religions are a reflection of the human mind's state of development at the time they were invented, reason why they are so primitive. If recent religions are no less bizarre, it is because they are reinventions of old ones and were invented for reasons ranging from mental disturbance and charlatanism to manipulation.

Let us imagine that religions had never existed. With the knowledge we have in the most varied scientific fields, especially Anthropology, Astronomy, Biology, Physics, Genetics, Geology, Medicine, Paleontology, Chemistry and Sociology, what is the probability that religions such as Hinduism, Buddhism, Judaism, Christianity and Islam would arise?

"Your imaginary little friend doesn't exist and your little club is fake. My imaginary little friend is the one who exists and my little club is the true one!" Religions, above all else Judaism, Christianity and Islam, have no way to make the world a good place to live because they promote the culture of sectarianism, causing division, the cradle of intolerance. Jesus himself was categorical:

> I have come to bring fire on the earth, and how I wish it were already kindled! [...] Do you think I came to bring peace on earth? No, I tell you, but division. From now on there will be five in one family divided against each other, three against two and two against three. They will be divided, father against son and son against father, mother against daughter and daughter against mother, mother-in-law against daughter-in-law and daughter-in-law against mother-in-law.

> (Luke 12:49,51-53)

If Christianity and Islam were good religions, the more to the letter, that is, fundamentalistically they were practiced the better it would be for the world. Is it not strange that it is precisely the opposite: the more to the letter they are practiced, the worse?

That applies to, probably, any religion, no matter how harmless it may seem.

In Manaus, Brazil, in 2012, thirteen Evangelical high school students refused to do an assignment on Afro-Brazilian culture, claiming that their religion forbids them to promote Satanism. According to their teacher, "They also refused to read works such as *O Guarani*, *Macunaíma* and *Casa-Grande & Senzala* (classics of Brazilian literature), saying that the books talked about homosexualism". Instead, the thirteen lectured on Evangelical missions in Africa.

This Christian smallness of spirit is not exclusive to Pentecostal denominations. The great majority of Evangelical churches regarded as tradicional, those in which no one shouts "Hallelujah! Glory to God" or dance, is equally biblical-fundamentalist and, in consequence, disapprove of almost everything that is not of a religious nature, which includes literature. Such is the degree of narrow-mindedness that Evangelicals repudiate even Catholic works, which are Christian. From Muslim, Hindu and Buddhist books they steer clear.

Beelzebub, the "prince of demons," loves to use the arts to divert God's people from the narrow way to the broad one, "that leads to destruction". If the dear reader is my age or older, you will remember the Evangelical paranoia of the 1980s surrounding rock songs, which, according to fanatical pastors, contained subliminal satanic messages that could be discerned only when the songs were played backwards. What many believers ignored is that, in reverse, even Christian hymns can convey "satanic messages".

Not even disabled children are free from being victims of Christian smallness of spirit. In 2010, Evangelical players of Santos Futebol Clube, among them stars Robinho and Neymar, refused to enter a charity and bring joy to boys and girls with cerebral palsy, when they were informed that it is a Spiritist institution. If these soccer players were not followers of the religion of the "love of Christ", the probability that they would have acted in such a petty way is zero.

The scene I most like in Woody Allen's film *Deconstructing Harry* is the one in which Harry argues with his sister Doris, a devout Jewess:

— Mostly, you caricatured my religious dedication, because it has always enraged you that I returned to my roots.

— What roots? You were a wonderful, sweet kid. You got me through my childhood. Then you go away to Fort Lauderdale and you meet this fanatic, this zealot, and he fills you full of superstition.

— It's tradition.

— Tradition is the illusion of permanence.

— You have no values. Your whole life is nihilism, cynicism, sarcasm and orgasm.

— In France, I could run on that slogan and win.

— I'm a Jew. I was born a Jew. Do you hate me because of that?

— If our parents converted to Catholicism a month before you were born, we'd be Catholics, and that would be the end of it. They're clubs. They're exclusionary, all of them. They foster the concept of the "other", so you know clearly who you should hate.

— That's enough!

— Let me ask you a question: if a Jew gets massacred, does that bother you more than if a gentile gets hurt, or a black or a Bosnian?

— Yes, it does. I can't help it, it's my people.

— They're all your people! Wouldn't it be a better world, if not every group thought they had a direct line to God?

Imagine a world in which, instead of despising each other because of religious convictions, being slaves of fear, superstitions and hopes and believing with all their hearts and souls what is written in sacred books from the Iron and Middle Ages, such as the Bible and the Koran, people lived inspired by the ideas of figures such as Baruch Spinoza, Voltaire, David Hume, Thomas Paine, Mary Wollstonecraft, Lydia Maria Child, John Stuart Mill, Etta Semple, Albert Einstein and Jiddu Krishnamurti. How likely is it that the lessons of teachers like these induce people to discriminate against others, inferiorize women, mutilate the genitals of children, rape and kill for honor, wage war, conquer and enslave other peoples, commit genocides, persecute, torture and perpetrate terrorist attacks?

Christianity and Islam have no way to be beneficial religions because their objective is not to improve the world, but persuade Humanity to see this life as worthless and wait for the true life, which begins after death, in an invisible place called Heaven. What motivation to truly care about the world do people have who hope for it to be destroyed by God as soon as possible?

According to the United Nations World Food Program, 821 million people "do not get enough food to lead a normal, active life". It is 2,5 United States starving. Data from the Stockholm International Peace Research Institute show that all governments together spend close to two trillion dollars on their armed forces. Every single year. Almost double what they spend on research and development — and 6.6 times what it would cost to eradicate hunger. Despite Christianity selling itself as the religion of love, the largest Christian country on the planet, the United States, is also the largest arms exporter and spends about US$ 780 billion (3.7% of its GDP) on its military apparatus. Every single year. Expenditure on research and development: US$ 430 billion. Apparently, this does not bother any Christian. Despite Islam selling itself as the religion of peace, the nation that hosts its holiest cities, Saudi Arabia, spends almost US$ 60 billion (8.4% of its GDP) on its military apparatus. Every single year. Spending on research and development: US$ 1.8 billion. Apparently, this does not bother any Muslim.

It is not necessary to be very intelligent to realize that this is beyond irrational, nor to be smart to perceive that it is useless for country leaders to have religious convictions: they do not lift a single finger to correct this aberrant distortion. The dear reader will see religious people engaged, for example, in combating abortion and gay marriage, calling for the closure of art exhibitions they consider immoral and demanding more rights for churches and the teaching of Creationism in schools, but will not see them demanding from heads of State that all weapons of war be destroyed and the military budget redirected to poverty eradication projects. As naive as it may sound, should that not be the number one objective of the religions that claim to be representatives of the Creator of the Universe?

In Brazil, every year takes place the March for Jesus, in 2009 transformed into federal law by president Lula. It brings together millions of Evangelicals who never take to the streets to march, for example, against social inequalities. Quite the contrary: government social programs are ridiculed and childishly labeled as Communism by the majority of followers of Jesus, a man who, if he existed, dedicated his life almost entirely to the poor. No Christian denomination organizes a March Against Hunger. The ones that occurred were organized by the UN World Food Programme.

One of the principal reasons why religion is indispensable is that religious organizations are the institutions that most help the poor, say believers. To begin with, charitable and philanthropic activities arose as a consequence of the Enlightenment, that is, of society becoming less religious and more secular. In 1739, Englishman Thomas Coram founded the Foundling Hospital, in London, considered the world's first charity institution. At a time when it was extremely unusual and even dangerous to have no religion, it is natural that Coram was a Christian. However, he founded that hospital to treat and help abandoned children precisely because it made him indignant to see that no one cared about them, including the churches.

Among the top ten of a list of the largest charitable entities in the United States by fundraising, made by *Forbes* magazine, in 2015, only one belongs to a religious organization: the Salvation Army, a Christian denomination that, in Australia, was sentenced to pay US$ 12 million to 474 victims of sexual abuse perpetrated by its employees. Besides, almost 10% of the Salvation Army's revenue is government donation.

In the eagerness to extol the Catholic social engagement, an American former governor said, in a TV program, that "In the United States, 50 percent of social services are provided by the Catholic Church". Intrigued, a correspondent of *PolitiFact*, a non-profit organization dedicated to checking the veracity of claims made by politicians, revealed that, in Uncle Sam's land, the Catholic Church is responsible for only 17% of all charitable social service. On the *Forbes* list, Catholic Charities USA comes in 15th place. 65% of its revenue is public money.

Mother Teresa of Calcutta received many millions of dollars in donations to her Missionaries of Charity organization, but many people wonder where these millions ended up (there are strong indications that they flowed to the Vatican), because the patients of Mother Teresa, who, considering suffering a gift from God, was opposed to the use of modern equipment, received precarious and totally inadequate "treatment". Why strive to cure them, if they were close to going to a better world to live the true life? To a cancer patient the nun said: "This suffering is a sign that you have got so close to Jesus on the cross that he can share his passion with you, he can kiss you".

The three greatest philanthropists in the world are, according to *Forbes*, billionaires Warren Buffett, Bill Gates and George Soros. None of them is religious.

As one can see, there is no need to believe in God and follow a religion to feel the desire to be good and solidary. In any case, what is more valuable: doing good for the simple pleasure of doing good or doing good to promote a religion and, from an imaginary friend, receive something in return?

Does the dear reader know the difference between religion and superstition? Let these respected lexicons tell you what superstition is:

Belief in things that are not real or possible, for example magic.

(*Collins Dictionary*)

Belief that is not based on human reason or scientific knowledge, but is connected with old ideas about magic.

(*Cambridge Dictionary*)

A belief or way of behaving that is based on fear of the unknown and faith in magic or luck.

(*Britannica Dictionary*)

The belief that particular events happen in a way that cannot be explained by reason or science.

(*Oxford Learner's Dictionary*)

Belief or practice resulting from ignorance, fear of the unknown, trust in magic or chance, or a false conception of causation.

(*Merriam-Webster Dictionary*)

Belief or feeling without rational foundation, which induces to trust in absurd things, fear innocuous and imaginary things and create false and undue obligations, without any relation between the facts and their causes. Belief in signs and omens, originating in purely fortuitous facts or coincidences, without any proof. A blind and exaggerated belief in some rule, principle or thing, which is worshiped and followed without question.

(Michaelis Dictionary)

What you must have realized is that religion, including the Jewish, the Christian and the Muslim ones, and superstition are one and the same thing. A set of beliefs practiced by a minority is called superstition. A set of beliefs practiced by many people is considered religion.

Idea for a documentary scene. Ask those who believe that Elijah was taken to Heaven in a chariot of fire: "What do you think about Mohammed being taken to Heaven on a winged horse?".

The world has been ruled by religious thought for many thousands of years (and, although perhaps a little less, still is). Religions have had, therefore, more than enough time to prove that they work. If religion were the medicine against evil, it would have to have taken effect already a long time ago, and the results would have to be significant. If hoping that there would be no more violence is too much, at the very least these two things — just two — should no longer exist: hunger and wars. If religion is not capable of preventing at least these two things, it does not work. Guess what? Religion is not capable of preventing these two things. Can there be any greater proof that religion does not work than wars? At the moment I write these lines, Christian Russia is, with the Church's blessing, bombing Christian Ukraine, causing destruction, thousands of deaths (including, of course, of children) and millions of refugees. Amen?

For hundreds of years, many people, even someone like physicist Isaac Newton, believed it was possible to turn lead into gold and discover an elixir of immortality. Since the belief in Alchemy never produced the desired effects, people stopped cultivating it. If we ask Christians and Muslims whether God hears prayers, they will answer "Yes", although evidence shows that addressing supplications to a deity produces as much effect as praying to a stone. If we tell them that, they will accuse us of scorning their religion.

Believing in supernaturalities, worshiping gods and obeying religious precepts do not bring any benefits to Humanity. On the contrary: religions can be, were and are used to promote and justify wrong things, such as backwardness, capital punishment, exploitation, fatalism, homophobia, ignorance, inequality, intolerance, martyrdom, misogyny, mutilation, oppression of minorities, poverty, racism, sexism, slavery, superstition, tribalism, victimization, violence and wars.

While other ideologies also can produce all kinds of evil, only religion bases itself on the supernatural, divine, thus placing itself in a privileged position, exempting itself from criticism and self-correction. When a system of ideas does not work, it either corrects itself or ceases to exist. Although religion does not work, its adherents do not give up on convincing themselves and trying to convince others otherwise. And why is this so? Because of a little magic word: God. Is it divine? Then, it cannot be wrong. And how do they know it is divine? They do not know. They were just induced to think they know. The dear reader wants to teach some things, but does not want these teachings to be verifiable or criticized? Nothing simpler: just say they are of supernatural origin.

Religion is the most dangerous thing because nothing can be superior to that to which a believer attributes divine authority.

"If you have a handle on the ultimate truth and you think that truth comes from God, you are in a very dangerous situation, because then it's perforce your duty to impose that truth on the rest of the world. And that's why religion is bad."

— Jerry Coyne
(Professor of Biology at the University of Chicago, in a debate, in 2011)

Religion is not good either because it cultivates the spirit of subservience, compelling people to consider blind faith a virtue and see doubt as weakness and daring. Billions of parents impose this servilistic mentality on billions of children, conditioning their defenseless minds to find it natural to worship an invisible being who threatens them with punishment and, in a lake of fire, tortures those who did not serve him, or served him, but in the wrong way. What should be considered child abuse is regarded not only as normal but even desirable by a society in which the majority of people have been submitted to this brainwashing.

Christians often say it is because of rebellion that someone does not worship the god of the Bible and does not follow Christianity. Let us imagine a man who led a revolution to liberate his people from the oppression of a dictator, but who, after coming to power, himself became a dictator who orders those who criticize him to be tortured and executed. No matter how many good things he, as a ruler, has done, my admiration he would not have, because I do not admire incoherent people. If I judge leaders by their coherence, why should I exempt gods from being coherent? If a single incoherence is enough to make me not admire a person, how would I be capable of worshiping a deity, for example, who ordered those who gathered firewood on the Sabbath to be stoned? How would I be able to do missionary work for a god who killed children? How could I spend eternity with a deity who tortures people in Hell?

I am not against God existing. I just have no reasons to believe that he exists. Believing is not a virtue. I am not able to accept incoherences, nor do I know why I should. If what is incoherent deserves to be rejected, how much more what is perverse!

There is no need to believe in an invisible being to marvel at the Universe and life. On the contrary: imagining an invisible being behind Nature minimizes the mystery, the awe, the wonder, the fascination, the enchantment. It is easier to understand why the Universe and life are the way they are, with all that is good and bad, beautiful and ugly, without the invisible magician who puts food on the table of believers, but does not give a damn about the hunger of millions of children, who cures a few believers, but is not interested in eradicating the disease.

Those who believe in God do not believe in God, but in a god, and those who follow the true religion do not follow the true religion, but the religion they think is the true one. Believing in God and following a religion is an illusion because there are many possibilities:

- God does not exist.
- God is dead.
- God exists, but does not interact with his creation.
- God is Nature.
- God is evil.
- There is more than one god.
- There is only one god, you believe in Yahweh, the god of the Bible, but Allah, the god of the Koran, is the true god (and vice versa).
- You believe in Yahweh or Allah, but Nhanderuvuçu, the Tupi-Guarani god, is the true god.
- You believe in the true god, but follow the false religion:
    1) Yahweh is the true god, you follow Judaism, but Christianity is the true religion (and vice versa).
    2) Christianity is the true religion, you follow Catholicism, but Protestantism is the true Christianity (and vice versa).
    3) Protestantism is the true Christianity, you are a member of the Lutheran Church, but the Evangelical Church Jesus Is Handsome and Good-Smelling* is the true Protestantism.
    4) You are a member of the Evangelical Church Jesus Is Handsome and Good-Smelling, but the Evangelical Church Jesus Is Handsome and Good-Smelling Reform Movement is the true Evangelical Church Jesus Is Handsome and Good-Smelling.

[* Real name of a church in Brazil]

How could it be wise to have a prefixed, unilateral and inflexible view on the most complex of all things: life? Philosophically speaking, if we know anything about life then that it is a great mystery. If life is a great mystery, there are no predefined answers, capable of satisfying all people. Religions illude their followers with false answers, preventing them from finding the truth, which can be only individual.

If the famous meaning of life exists, it cannot be external, imposed from outside. Each person has, or not, to find the meaning of his own life, that is, give it meaning. For the philosopher Diogenes of Sinope, the meaning of life was to live in a barrel, and for the anchorite Simeon Stylites, on top of a pillar. I confess that this is not quite the meaning I want to give to mine.

I imagine that, like me, what the dear reader wants is to be happy. No feeling is permanent. Consequently, also the feeling of happiness is inconstant. If moments of happiness were not interspersed with moments of sadness or dissatisfaction, we would not even know what happiness is. To be happy is to do what gives pleasure, brings joy, contentment. As I have extensively demonstrated, religions do not have the morals to dictate what is right. If what you do makes you happy and does no harm to anyone, then it is right.

On one of our trips to Rio de Janeiro, my then girlfriend and I decided to hike the trails of the Tijuca Forest. We hired a tour guide, but that turned out to be a not so good idea. Inadvertently, the companion almost ruined our hike. At each step, she pointed to something: "Look!". Not allowing us to stumble on the wonders of that exuberant vegetation, the guide took away from the walk the feeling of surprise, adventure, so essential for most people who seek contact with Nature.

I think life is more or less like a forest and religion more or less like a tour guide who does not stop pointing the finger and talking, not letting us discover things and reflect on them. Only that, for the reasons I have explained, religion is much worse than a chatty tour guide.

By the way, regardless of whether or not one believes in God, where is there more spirituality, that feeling of elevation, sublimity: within the four walls of a building, where someone is constantly talking, shouting or singing, or in the "silence" of a forest, wood, mountain?

Supposing that, by then, the human being has not destroyed it, it is impossible to know what the world will be like in, say, 300 years, but it is likely that there will always be those who prefer to have their minds imprisoned than free. After all, religion is a pleasant prison: its prisoners do not have to think and discover for themselves and the idea of chosen people makes them feel special. In contrast, being a freethinker is difficult: it takes a lot of strength of spirit to bear the reality that, by all appearances, the Universe is not administered by any superman and, consequently, we are left to our own devices. However, the consciousness of being intellectually honest is very gratifying.

Recognizing that "truth is a pathless land, and you cannot approach it by any path whatsoever, by any religion", in 1927 Indian Jiddu Krishnamurti dissolved the Order of the Star, a religious organization whose members had chosen him to be the World Teacher. In two of his many lectures in the United States, Krishnamurti stated:

> Religion is not what you believe. It has nothing to do with whether you are a Christian or a Buddhist, a Mussulman or a Hindu. Those things have no significance. They are a hindrance. The mind that would discover must be totally stripped of them all. [...] A truly religious person is not one who is encrusted with beliefs, dogmas, rituals. He has no beliefs. He is living from moment to moment, never accumulating any experience. [...] The religious man is he who does not belong to any religion, to any nation, to any race, who is inwardly completely alone, in a state of not-knowing.

A freethinker is someone who, in the search for truth, does not trust revelation, tradition and authority, but evidence, logic and reason. To be a freethinker is to combat ignorance by means of opposition to irrationality. How, then, could this not be the right and, therefore, most sensible way to live? If freethinkers were the majority, how could this not be beneficial to the world?

If life can be improved, then not by superstition, that is, religion, but by reason, which the *Houaiss Dictionary* defines as "the capacity to evaluate with correctness; faculty characterized by its power of discernment between true and false; good sense, judgment", the *Aurelio Dictionary* as "the faculty that a human being has to evaluate, judge, know, understand, reason, ponder universal ideas, establish logical relations; intelligence, prudence" and the *Aulete Dictionary* as "the faculty to understand the relations of things and to distinguish true from false, good from evil; the good use of intellectual faculties; uprightness of spirit, prudential judgment, equity, justice; the light, the torch that illuminates the human spirit".

If Humanity can be saved and this Pale Blue Dot transformed into a really good place to live, at least without poverty and wars, then not by people who see life as worthless and spend it dreaming of mansions of gold in an imaginary world, but by people who do not flee from reality and are guided not by primitive mythological beings, but by reason: freethinkers.

Detoxification

"The content is toxic.
Nobody is immune, it's logical.
Programmed only to accept,
directed not to question.
Go in search, to find your place.
Don't be just a cog that turns the gear.
It's not the truth, bro. What they want
is to try to prevent the facts from revealing themselves,
the minds from rebelling,
you from being able to go beyond,
to search for something that does you good."

— Mussoumano
(*Tóxico*)

Help to Leave the Church

What is the probability of a person who has never followed any religion believing in invisible beings and places? That's right. The greatest proof that religion is brainwashing is that it makes you believe in things that do not exist.

Even though they have a common base, obviously religions are not the same. Some are worse than others. When it comes to Christianity, the more biblicistic a denomination, the deeper the brainwashing and, consequently, the more painful the deprogramming, which can take longer if the person was, as they say, raised in the church.

Someone who has never been a member of a church, or left one with ease, cannot imagine that Christianity can cause psychological traumas. Although not believing in it (anymore), they see the religion of Jesus as harmless. This is due to the fact that Christianity is old. It was brought to the Americas 500 years ago by Europeans, who had been practicing it already for centuries. In consequence, it is rooted in our culture. Accustomed to it, the majority of people think only of its cute doctrines, such as forgiveness and charity. The truth is that the *New Testament* teaches also things with the potential to generate emotional disturbances and that can continue to haunt people who have already left the church, for example:

- Absurd and dangerous promises (It is not necessary to seek medical help and take medicines, because the sick can be cured by the power of prayer).

- Alienation from reality (The world is under dominion of the Devil and is evil. Almost everything is worldly, that is, sin. Your world is Heaven).

- Aversion to erudition (Intelligence and wisdom are foolishnesses. The Kingdom of Heaven belongs to the poor in spirit).

- Cruelty (Eternal torture in a lake of fire and brimstone, even for simply doubting).

- Fanaticism (Demons exist, enter people, cause illnesses and have to be cast out through exorcism).

- Human sacrifice (The crucifixion of Jesus to placate the wrath of God and the glorification of Abraham and Jephthah, who were willing to immolate their children for God).

- Humiliation (You are bad by birth, insignificant, unworthy, deserving of punishment and in need of salvation).

- Imposition of guilt and shame (You too are responsible for the torture and death of Jesus).

- Impossible and bad teachings (Love your enemies, do not worry about tomorrow and be perfect like God. With faith, everything is possible. Do not defend yourself against physical aggressions, never deny loans to people, sell everything to follow Jesus and for his sake hate your own family and your own life).

- Inferiorization of women (Women must be submissive to men because the woman was created after the man and for him. That in the world there are disasters and suffering, which are consequences of sin, is the woman's fault).

- Injustice (Because Eve and Adam disobeyed God, you too deserve to suffer).

- Sadism (To test your faith, God makes, or lets, you suffer. If you are persecuted and suffer because of Jesus, you must rejoice).

- Sexual repression (Feeling sexual attraction to a person without being married to that person is a sin. Homosexuality is bad and homosexuals deserve to die).

- Terrorization (Sin against the Holy Spirit, prophecies about the end of the world and the Last Judgment frighten people and inflict fear of being lost).

- Total control (God is watching you day and night and noting down in a book all your actions and thoughts).

- Unconditional submission (All rulers are instituted by God. Consequently, also the bad ones).

Breaking oneself free from the church is relatively easy, compared to liberating oneself from the psychological structure of the Christian religion. Examples of mental patterns reinforced by Christianity:

- All-or-nothing thinking (There are no sinlets. Jesus said that a person can be thrown into the lake of fire and brimstone just for cursing. Jesus told people to be perfect. Peter tells them to be holy. Moderate Christians are disparaged as lukewarm, for which reason they are vomited out of God's mouth. You are either saved or lost. Sport? Enjoying is not enough. You need to immerse yourself body and soul ["No pain, no gain"]. Work? You are a real worker only if you return to the computer after dinner. The right to brag start at 60 hours a week. Politics? The more absolutist your statements, the more you will gain followers).

- Apocalyptic rupture (Ex-Christians no longer expect the rapture, the mark of the Beast, or Jesus riding on a white horse. Nevertheless, the idea of the end of the world, now in the form, for example, of nuclear holocaust, pandemic or overpopulation, still haunts many of them and affects their world view).

- Good guys and bad guys (Jesus said: "Whoever is not with me is against me, and whoever does not gather with me scatters". In the black and white thinking, people are either one of us or one of them, either patriots or communists, either anti-racists or racists. Disagreement is synonymous with heresy and separation. When Christians discover the faults of public figures, like Bill Gates, they move them from the good guys box to the bad guys box. Christianity does not offer a mental model in which people are complicated and nevertheless decent. We are all fallen [according to John Calvin, totally depraved] and either washed in the blood of Jesus or tools of Satan).

• Hyperactive guilt detection (Do you know any other religion that blames people even for crimes they did not commit [the disobedience of Adam and Eve and the crucifixion of Jesus]? James 5:16 tells Christians to confess their sins to one another, converting them into true weightlifters of the guilt muscle. We live in a world full of things we should and should not do. Since biblicistic Christianity gives everything an enormous weight, day-to-day failures [things we left undone and goals we did not achieve] are seen as moral failures).

• Idealizing leaders (Living in a cloud of anxiety makes us more susceptible to demagogues and authoritarians, people who exude the self-confidence we lack, convey to know what is true and right and how to solve problems, feed on our fears and on our desire to be and do good. Taking advantage of our sense of ourselves as sinners, they tell us how we can redeem ourselves. They exploit our dichotomous thinking, reinforcing our sense that people who do not share our world view are bad and should be silenced or defeated).

• Living for tomorrow (People who consecrate their lives to God focus more on the future than on the present. For those who have their eye on the heavenly prize, the small day-to-day wonders, which constitute the center of the joy of a conscious life, are mere distractions. An American Christian song about Paradise says: "It's such a joy to know that I am only passing through". The habit of focusing on the future can make it difficult to concentrate on the present, see and enjoy the beauties of the moment).

• Never feeling sufficiently good (Since they are aware of their faults, many Christians find it difficult to stay themselves out of the bad guys box. Some alternate between "I am wonderful" and "I am rubbish". Others have an irritating internal critic who tells them that nothing they do is good enough. After all, the biblical standard is perfection).

• Sexual problems (For many ex-Christians, it is impossible to talk about guilt without talking about sex. In the Bible, sex is such a grave thing that committing adultery and coveting the neighbor's wife even share the list of the ten worst sins with killing and stealing. The virginity and purity of Mary [only an unused woman could be good enough to give birth to a perfect child] is given tremendous value. The book with the black cover conveys the idea that sex is a filthy thing. Proof of that is that, after intercourse, men and women had to ceremonially purify themselves — even though they were married. Most churches, if not all, consider masturbation a sin. Some even swear that it is bad for health. Confirming the *Old Testament*, the *New* one throws all homosexuals in the same pot and accuses them of choosing to be homosexuals, on top of that for the mere pleasure of practicing evil).

Some time ago, you realized that the Bible contains absurds. This generates internal conflict: you were induced to consider Christianity good, but you now perceive that the book on which it is based teaches also evils. For some reason, the religious brainwashing is no longer being able to force you to justify the perverse doctrines of the Word of God. Furthermore, you realize that between much of what the Bible says and reality there is a huge discrepancy.

You want to liberate yourself from this ideological prison, but this is one of those cases in which saying is easy, doing is difficult. After all, the religious brainwashing has spent perhaps decades threatening you with torture in a lake of fire and brimstone for doubting. In you, it instilled that hesitation is bad and your fault: you are being weak and listening to the enemy. Moreover, most probably all your family and all your friends are Evangelicals. Maybe you even work for a church member. Because of this, you feel lonely, are afraid and do not know how to proceed. I am sure these reflections will help you:

Become conscious that the fear you may still have of definitely breaking with religion has been embedded into you by religion itself. It does not take a genius to realize that the threat of hellish punishment is a weapon to keep you from fleeing the religious prison. It is God pointing a revolver at your head and saying: "Believe in me, obey me, love me and adore me, otherwise…". Well, any system of ideas that coerces you to accept and intimidates you not to question is perverse and deserves to be thrown in the trash.

Be honest with yourself. Religion is no longer making sense to you. So, stop forcing it to make sense. Just like in an abusive relationship, religion blames you and tells you to try harder. Get real. You have already realized that religion is a parallel universe. Stop, therefore, trying to live in the parallel universe of religion. If, out of fear of hurting or angering them, you are keeping up appearances, pretending that you still believe, one day you will have to tell the truth to your family and friends. It is not easy, but necessary, in order to have personal integrity and mental health. Do not spare people from having negative feelings about your loss of faith. You are not committing any evil. Your relationships will go through some challenging adjustments, but it will be worth it. If you are a teenager and your parents threaten you with physical punishment, report them. No one has the right to force you to go to church.

Calm down. By calming down, you will retake control of your mind. Religion has spent years intoxicating you. Thus, detoxifying from it takes time. You will have to deal with different emotions and feelings, such as anxiety, anger and loneliness. However, little by little you will regain confidence in your ability to think for yourself, express your own points of view and make decisions. Eventually, your wounds will heal. You will feel stronger and able to love and take care of yourself. Even if you feel alone, you are not. A lot of people have gone through what you are going through. Read deconversion stories. If it is difficult to leave Christianity, think about how much more difficult it is to leave Islam. Yet, every year thousands of people abandon Islam and become atheists, or irreligious. Some share their experience in books or on the internet.

Religion intoxicates not only intellectually but also psychologically, especially if you have been indoctrinated, that is, intoxicated since childhood. Some people can free themselves from religion and nevertheless continue to be affected by it. Doctrines like Hell and the End Times can still make them have nightmares. Do the work of curing the wounds of religious abuse. Get support and help in every way you can, in online and local groups, but, if necessary, also from a therapist.

Religions have a lot in common with dictatorships. They do not want you to know too much, discover their rottenness. You have spent years hearing that the Bible is divine and that your church was instituted by none other than the Creator of the Universe himself. Learning about how this pile of copies of copies of more copies of rags of fragments of parchments from the Iron Age with tales also from the Bronze Age was compiled will confirm to you that the Bible has nothing divine about it, and researching the history of the churches will put an end to the last shred of enchantment you still may feel for yours. All denominations spring from discords and rifts. The book with the black cover itself tells that the early Christians fought among themselves over who knew what God really wants. Not long after, the worshipers of Jesus would spend centuries mutually massacring each other because of the Word of God. There are, therefore, no reasons for you to feel bad for rejecting the Bible. A book that generates so much arrogance, confusion, division, hostility and violence deserves to be rejected. Religion is no longer controlling your mind. You are now free to acquire knowledge, for example, in History, Philosophy and Science. Enjoy this freedom.

Christianity infantilizes people. Good things come from Saint Nicholas, aka Santa Claus, (God) and bad things come from Krampus (the Devil). You are a little robot controlled by either Jesus or Satan. The Christian religion makes people also dependent. As a famous gospel song says, you are weak, but God is strong, reason why you do not leave home without begging for divine protection, and it is only with the help of God that you achieve something. Freed from this childishness, you will need to rethink who you are and what life is. You will have to learn to have trust in yourself and take responsibility for your choices. Create a life around new values and that works for you. Life is an adventure. So, venture out. Open up to new experiences and friends.

Evangelicals are conditioned to see their church as their family and trained to repeat "God is in charge". With its doctrine of reward after death, Christianity makes you deny reality, alienating you from the world. Well, perfection does not exist anywhere in the Universe. Therefore, not on this planet either. It, however, is our world. So, face reality. Facing it will help you get your life back on track. Accept the idea that your home is Earth and your family, Humanity. Any child realizes that no god is in charge. Improving the world depends on us. You can contribute to the solution of some problems. We are all interconnected. Join with others to make our home a more pleasant place.

As you acknowledge that you are part not of an invisible, imaginary world, but of this, the real one, you realize that, contrary to what religion has instilled in you, you are valuable and do not need to deserve to exist. Embrace this life, without worrying about a next one. Enjoy being alive. You have the right to enjoy life without the feeling of guilt. Your life now is not governed by a bunch of rules, many of them ridiculous, but by only one: do no harm. Instead of judging people, try to appreciate them. Regain your creativity and express yourself any way you want, and no longer to glorify an invisible being. Love yourself and be proud of yourself. Considering that religion still imprisons the minds of billions of people, feel privileged and enjoy the inestimable pleasure of being a freethinker.

[I wrote this text inspired by ideas of two great psychologists, Drs. Marlene Winell and Valerie Tarico, who specialize in deprogramming from religious brainwashing.]

Propagate Freethought

If the dear reader did not like my book, tell me. Fear not: I will not send you to Hell. If you liked it, tell your relatives and friends, but also the world, writing a review on Amazon.

Read also my other book *Wasting Time on God*.

I offer all my e-books for free (their printed versions, as cheap as possible). I dedicate my life to, by any possible means, helping people liberate themselves from the religious prison — and I do not earn a penny for it.

> "I want to congratulate and thank you for your hard work in trying to enlighten the pigheaded. You are right about everything! I am 67 years old, was an Evangelical all my life, a pastor for 20 years. Today, I am free of deception."
>
> — Joaquim Luiz de Godoi

If you value the propagation of Freethought, please visit:
sites.google.com/view/freethinking

Made in the USA
Monee, IL
26 September 2022

14693596R00125